STONEHENGE

AND ITS
MYSTERIES

'God knows what their use was!
They are hard to tell, but yet may be told.'

Samuel Pepys, 11 June 1668

STONEHENGE

AND ITS MYSTERIES

MICHAEL BALFOUR

CHARLES SCRIBNER'S SONS · NEW YORK

Acknowledgements

ILLUSTRATION CREDITS: Source photography by Sara Ellis. Aerofilms, Plates 76, 85, 127; Ashmolean Museum, Plate 12; Professor Richard Atkinson (Malcolm Murray), Plates 63, 66, 67, 72, 73, 79, 80, 82, 83, 84, 86, 87, 89, 90, 94, 95, 101, 103, 104; Michael Balfour, Plates 32, 81, 96, 97, 98, 99, 100, 105, 122, 133, 134, 135, 136, Figures (maps and diagrams by Ken Smith), 5, 7, 9, 11, 12, 13, 14, 16, 17, 20, 22, 24, 25, 27, 28, 29, 30, 31, 34, 36, 37, 38, 39, 40, 41, 42; B. T. Batsford Ltd., Plates 68, 74, 88; Bodleian Library, Figure 2; British Library, Plates 2, 3, 15, 16, 20, 36, 37, 46, 75; British Tourist Authority, Plate 120; Cambridge University Aerial Photographic Unit, Plate 117; Controller of Her Majesty's Stationery Office, Crown Copyright/Department Of The Environment, Plates 21, 39, 41, 42, 43, 44, 45, 47, 56, 59, 64, 69, 108, 119, 121, 129, 130, 132; Figures 6, 23; Corpus Christi College, Cambridge, Figure 21; Courtauld Institute of Art, Plate 52; Crown Copyright and Avebury Museum, Plate 110; Devizes Museum, Plates 33, 140; Sara Ellis, Plates 123, 128; Robert Estall, Plate 71; Institute of Historical Research, Figure 21; Knight Frank and Rutley, Plate 144; Trustees of David Low and Evening Standard, Plate 147; Maryhill Museum of Art, U.S.A., Plate 34; National Geographic Society, Smithsonian Astrophysical Observatory and Hunting Surveys Ltd., Figure 19; National Museum of Wales, Plate 51; Executors of R. S. Newall, Plate 101; Mrs O'Neil, Plates 60, 93; Radio Times Hulton Picture Library, Plate 27; Salisbury Museum, Plates 40, 57, 111, 112, 142, 145, 149; Society of Antiquaries, Plates 62, 70, 91, 92, 143; St. John's College, Cambridge, Plate 30; Sir Dennis Stucley, Plate 17; Syndication International Ltd., Plate 139; Tate Gallery, Plate 58; Times Newspapers Ltd., Plate 148; Executors of Guy Underwood, Figure 15; John Edwin Wood, Figure 10; *Yorkshire Post*, Plate 29

TEXT REPRODUCTION CREDITS: The Estate of Lewis Thorpe (Penguin Books Ltd), Professor Stuart Piggott (Clarendon Press), Evan Hadingham (William Heinemann Ltd), Professor Richard Atkinson (*Journal For The History of Astronomy*), Geoffrey Grigson (*Country Life*), Henry Moore, O.M. (Marlborough Art Gallery), Stephen Spender (Marlborough Art Gallery), Erich von Daniken (Souvenir Press Ltd), Aubrey Burl (Yale University Press Ltd), J. R. L. Anderson and Fay Godwin (Wildwood House Ltd), Michael Dames (Thames and Hudson Ltd), The Executors of Guy Underwood (Museum Press Ltd), John Michell (Garnstone Press Ltd), Sid Rawle (Times Newspapers Ltd).

Reprinted 1981

First U.S. edition published 1980

Copyright © 1979 Michael Balfour

Library of Congress Cataloging in Publication Data

Balfour, Michael David, 1939–
   Stonehenge and its mysteries.

   Bibliography: p.
   Includes index.
   1. Stonehenge. I. Title.
DA142.B32   1980   942.3'19   79-64916
ISBN 0-684-16406-X (Cloth)
ISBN 0-684-17272-0 (Paper)

3 5 7 9 11 13 15 17 19 Q/C 20 18 16 14 12 10 8 6 4 2
1 3 5 7 9 11 13 15 17 19 Q/P 20 18 16 14 12 10 8 6 4 2

Printed in the United States of America

Contents

Preface

Stonehenge is a mystery that may never be solved. Still it stands on its remote Plain as an object of wonder and almost natural beauty, melancholy, suffering the rigours of time and immense popularity. But, as we shall see in both words and pictures, Stonehenge is slowly yielding enthralling clues to some of the secrets which crowd its past.

By now, for instance, it is accepted that Stonehenge was not developed, consciously or otherwise, through all its six stages of construction, as a work of art to brighten up the landscape. Yet Stone 56 (see Plate 71), for instance, is a mason's work of art almost unrivalled in prehistoric Europe – for Stonehenge *is* very beautiful. We can also agree that the monument was probably not a job creation scheme to keep prehistoric minds and bodies occupied; a remarkable feat of communal construction when we consider the extraordinary fact that the estimated population in Britain at the end of the Neolithic Age was around 20,000 people (Hoskins 1969).*

The Druids, or rather those we know from our newspapers today, have nothing to do with the place; the recent history of the summer solstice ceremonies is a sad affair, which badly serves the most commonly asked question – what was it for? Alleged Druidic traditions apart, the monument could have been used as a sort of temple of worship, although it probably ceased to function as such long, long ago.

What is more certain is that Stonehenge, in spite of its constant depiction by eighteenth and nineteenth century artists and engravers with contented sheep grazing among the fallen stones, was not developed as a sheep pen, farmer's grange, or even as the finest market place in the world, magnificently thatched over giant wooden rafters. Nor was it a cemetery, as excavation so far has proved, in spite of the presence of

This refers to the dated reference source in the Bibliography at the end of the book.

at least 460 barrows in the immediate area. Nor has Stonehenge yet been proved to have been a king's palace, a battle ring or a place for sport and pleasure. Some researchers' wild imaginings that Stonehenge held, in the arrangement of its stones, a core of knowledge that sustained the lost Kingdom of Atlantis (and where was that anyway?) is a theory best unheeded just as that of others who happily believe that Stonehenge was a UFO base. I think not – the facts are more surprising than such exotic suggestions.

The finished instrument, a calculator or computer, for that is what it probably became, was in use for less than 1,500 years. Then it fell into ruin, and became a dead thing. No Roman historian mentions Stonehenge, though their legions laid straight roads nearby. William the Conqueror's *Domesday Book* makes no note of it. Stonehenge had descended into oblivion, a relic of a long-forgotten knowledge of the heavens and earth never before attained (and, some would say since). The last heirs of the oral traditions of the old astronomer-priest had gone.

It was not until the beginning of this century – or rather the very last night of the last one – that the secrets of Stonehenge captured the general public imagination. A few years after it was sold for £6600 . . . and had the owner's son and heir not been killed in 1915, one of the greatest prehistoric wonders of the world might still be privately owned.

After the fall of the stones on 31 December 1900, the self-styled Vicar of Stonehenge wrote to *The Times* to recommend that a leaning sarsen should not be set upright; that would, he said, be 'spoiling Stonehenge'. Thus the Rev Arthur Phelps of Amesbury neatly encapsulated both the fascination and the problems of Stonehenge, which attract more than 800,000 visitors a year.

When I started writing this book, I was

surprised at some of the facts of ancient Wessex history and seemingly unanswerable questions which confront the enquiring visitor. Stonehenge itself, which pre-dates the Great Pyramid, is not only one of the biggest of over 900 stone circles in Britain but is also the largest and most complete megalithic monument in Europe. But why, I wondered (and how for that matter), were the bluestones brought from so far away? The Cursus is the second largest of only twenty in the British Isles – was it really only a race-track? Wiltshire has 148 out of the known 260 long barrows in Britain – but why, at West Kennett, that long limb of earth beyond the chambers of the largest barrow? Silbury Hill is the most immense man-made mound in western Europe and its three successive cone centres coincide with each other to within 1 m (39·37 ins): all just for an observation platform? Hundreds of Bronze Age barrows cluster in groups around Stonehenge – but why almost always containing skeletons carefully laid in a crouching position, with their heads facing north, and the grave goods shattered?

In December 1978, Professor R. J. C. Atkinson announced Stonehenge IV, a sixth construction phase, dated at c. 1100 BC; this exciting extension to our knowledge of the monument is outlined in Part 4. *Stonehenge and Its Mysteries* is deliberately cast into parts and not chapters, because it is intended to present a series of profiles in words and pictures of Stonehenge, from a variety of angles: historical, artistic, petrological, and so on. Part 6 displays personal prejudice, and I make no apology for this! For Stonehenge is a monument to the genius of its builders; it is a part of our national heritage, and seems to demand positive responses from its commentators as well as visitors.

My grateful thanks are due to Professor R. J. C. Atkinson, of University College, Cardiff, for his kindness and detailed comments on parts of this book in its draft form; I am greatly indebted, as all students of the monument should be, to his classic work *Stonehenge* (1956), its subsequent editions and to his articles in learned journals, which are constantly and elegantly refining Stonehenge scholarship. Any errors in fact and interpretation in this book are nevertheless solely my responsibility. I thank Sara Ellis for her help in selecting some of the many illustrations my publishers have kindly allowed me to include, and for her assistance in other ways as well. Thanks also to Nigel Henbest for the benefit of his knowledge of astronomy, to Dr D. F. Williams, of Southampton University, for advice on petrology, and to Ken Smith for the maps and diagrams. I am grateful to Anjou Merchant for turning my manuscript into typescript so cheerfully, and to Lance Vatcher, Peter Saunders and Sir Philip Antrobus for their generous help. Lastly, I express my gratitude to my wife who has constantly and in so many ways supported this attempt to display Stonehenge in all its majesty.

Michael Balfour

Thou noblest monument of Albion's isle,
  Whether by Merlin's aid, from Scythia's shore
To Amber's fatal plain, Pendragon bore,
Huge frame of giant hands the mighty pile,
T'entomb his Britons, slain by Hengist's guile:
Or Druid priests, sprinkled with human gore,
Taught 'mid thy massy maze their mystic lore:
Or Danish chiefs, enrich'd with savage spoil,
To Victory's idol vast, an unhewn shrine
Rear'd the rude heap; or, in thy hallow'd round
Repose the kings of Brutus' genuine line;
Or here those kings in solemn state were crown'd:
Studious to trace thy pon'drous origin,
We muse on many an ancient tale renown'd.

Thomas Warton, 1802

For My Parents

who took me to live by the
Stones of Stennes
at the right time,
and then introduced me to
Stonehenge

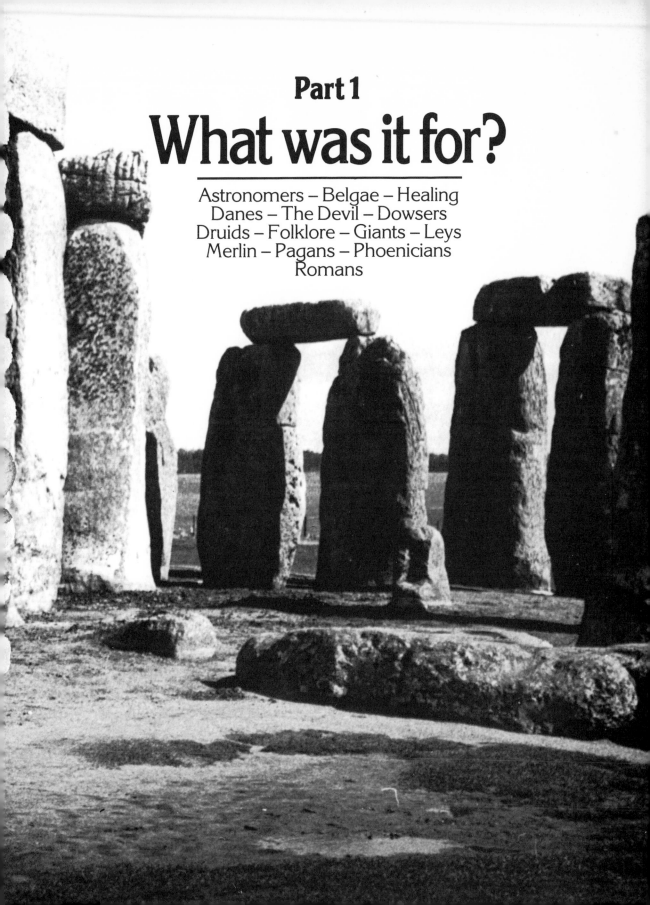

Part 1
What was it for?

Astronomers – Belgae – Healing
Danes – The Devil – Dowsers
Druids – Folklore – Giants – Leys
Merlin – Pagans – Phoenicians
Romans

Henry of Huntingdon, who died in 1155, gives Stonehenge what is sometimes referred to as its first mention in English literature; he makes it the second of his four wonders of Britain in *Historia Anglorum* (Henry of Huntingdon 1154), and writes of where 'stones of an amazing size are set up in the manner of doorways ... nor can anyone guess by what means so many stones were raised so high, or why they were built there!' The next known commentator goes into these matters in some (not very reliable) detail. The earliest extensive written account of Stonehenge (from which Henry borrowed his account) was to be found in Geoffrey of Monmouth's (1100?–1154) famous lost *Historia Regum Britanniae : The History of the Kings of Britain* (Geoffrey of Monmouth 1135, viii, 10–14) which was abridged and edited by Alfred of Beverley and published as *Historia de Gestis Regum Britanniae*. In this invaluable yet puzzling work, the origins of which are as shadowy as some of its contents, Geoffrey proposed that Stonehenge was erected at the command of the British King Vortigern, as a memorial to 460 British chiefs massacred by the Saxon Hengist in AD 490. The King, records Geoffrey, visited the dead laid out in 'the monastery near Kaercaradduc which is now called Salisbury', and was wondering how to commemorate them, Tremorinus, Archbishop of the City of the Legions, said: 'If there is anyone anywhere who has the ability to execute your plan, then Merlin, prophet of Vortigern, is the man to do it. In my opinion, there is no one else in your kingdom who has greater skill, either in the foretelling of the future or in mechanical contrivances.' It is hard to believe that, in Lewis Thorpe's famous translation, this mention of the role of prophecy at Stonehenge in the twelfth century exists to come ringing down the years to the astro-archaeologists of today.

Merlin was brought to the King who listened to his idea for a suitable monument, having refused a prophecy of the future in its connection: 'Send for the Giants' Ring which is on Naas (Kildare) in Ireland. In that place there is a stone construction which no man of this period could ever erect, unless he combined great skill and artistry. The stones are enormous and there is no one alive strong enough to move them. If they are placed in position round this site, in the way in which they are erected over there, they will stand for ever.'

Several things here should interest us. They are discussing the adornment of an existing place (a monastery) which is 'round': this could be a reference to the bank and ditch of Stonehenge I (the construction phases are set out in detail in Part 3, and the stones and transportation in Part 4); though some presume it to mean Amesbury Abbey, which (according to William Probert's translations of Triad 84, Probert 1823), was one of Britain's three perpetual choirs (the other two being at Llan Iltud Vawr in Glamorgan and at Glastonbury). No mention is made of burial; no extensive tombs have ever been found in the henge except a few graves and cremation sites. Merlin mentions the 'Chorea Gigantum', the Giant's Dance or 'the Giants' Ring'; there are many Giants' Rings in Britain, some in Wiltshire, and giants loom large in British legend and folklore (often in a destructive capacity or as naughty creatures caught in a naughty act and 'frozen' for all time). Merlin's words probably refer to the bluestones of Stonehenge II (again, see Part 3), and Geoffrey's faulty account of their origin in Killaraus (Kildare?) no doubt reflects the common usage of the Irish–Wessex trading route since the times of the Late Neolithic Beaker people. That the bluestones came from the Prescelly Mountains along the route in South Wales was not confirmed until 1923.

The seer confirms to the King that it is an existing 'stone construction', as if to imply that it is already proved to be in working order, and he insists that it must be 'placed in position' in the same way at the new site. So we sense that Merlin understands the crucial importance of the arrangement of these stones – so vast and permanent to the King for his memorial, and yet so subtle and carefully tuned as an instrument of power and influence to the King's wizardlike adviser.

PLATE 1

He then goes on to confide to the doubtful King that the stones have special medicinal properties, and that they had been brought by Giants all the way from Africa at a time when Ireland was inhabited by them. Under the direction of Uther (or Utherpendragon as he was known later), who was the King's father, and Merlin, with the help of 15,000 men, the stones were brought to Britain (in a whirlwind, according to Thomas Heywood in 1641) and then re-erected 'in a circle round the sepulchre, in exactly the same way as they had been arranged on Mount Killaraus.' Geoffrey later tells us that Aurelius Ambrosius, Utherpendragon and Constantine II were buried in the circle, but this may have been at Amesbury Abbey, a few miles to the east. Michael Dames (Dames 1977) links the Giant name with tombs all over north-west Europe.

Whatever the clues it holds to the truth, this account of Merlin's involvement with Stonehenge is important because it became the accepted one for long afterwards, in spite of the fact Geoffrey of Monmouth might have been as Professor Stuart Piggott declares: 'The least reliable and most suspect chronicler of the Middle Ages' (Piggott 1941, p. 305).

Latin writers, such as Giraldus Cambrensis (1146–1223) in his *Topographica Hibernica*, embroidered somewhat upon the story, in versions which again gained the stature of fact through repetition (Cambrensis 1187). However Sir Richard Colt-Hoare (of whom more later) was impressed by the part of Giraldus'

PLATE 1   An imaginative reconstruction drawing of Stonehenge, as it could possibly have appeared if all the phases in the construction of Stonehenge (see Part 4) had remained complete until Stonehenge IIIc (about 1550 BC) was finished.

△ PLATE 2

PLATE 3 ▽

story which concerns us; he wrote:

'In following the Iter of Giraldus through Wales, I never had reason to complain of his want of accuracy in the description of places, however he might have staggered my faith in some of his marvellous stories. He appears to have seen with his own eyes, during his tour of Ireland, about 1186, an immense pile of stones on the plains of Kildare, consisting of upright stones, with their imposts, and corresponding exactly with those at Stonehenge' (Colt-Hoare 1812)

Colt-Hoare interested himself very much in the subtler tones of the picture Geoffrey of Monmouth painted:

'I never saw a more likely spot, or one better situated for a Stonehenge, than the Curragh of Kildare, and I regret very much that, when in Ireland, I did not examine this verdant and extensive plain more attentively. I observed earthen works and barrows, the indicia of ancient population, and if ever a temple existed on this spot I have no doubt its site, even at this remote period, might be discovered.' (Colt-Hoare 1812)

But Colt-Hoare would have been as aware as we are that Geoffrey of Monmouth appears to merge the Stonehenge site with those of Amesbury Abbey and Avebury, neither of which is far away.

John Leland (1506–52) maintained the wizard Merlin's interests. He had been appointed the 'King's antiquary' in 1533 by Henry VIII, and during 1534–43 he travelled the country collecting books and manuscripts from religious and secular buildings and colleges. He also studied antiquities extensively, and the redoubtable Merlin keeps his role in the Stonehenge story as it is related by Leland in his *Commentarii de Scriptoribus Britannicis* (Leland 1707); but he has the wizard ordering the assembly of stones from all over Salisbury

PLATE 2   Merlin comforts Uther Pendragon, on a page of one of the earliest manuscripts to give a representation of Stonehenge (MS., BM. Egerton 3028).

PLATE 3   A folio in a 12th century manuscript (MS., BM., PS 6/13981), which shows the end of Geoffrey of Monmouth's *History* (c. 1135) and the beginning of Robert Wace's verse *Brut or Geste des Bretons* (1155).

Plain. Were the bluestones (Stonehenge II construction phase) therefore recognized by Leland as being distinct from the sarsen stones (Stonehenge III a)?

There were other early Latin chroniclers who were clearly indebted to Geoffrey of Monmouth's confusing yet exhilarating book. Layamon, whose *Brut* or *Chronicle of England* was a poetic work (c. 1200) of some 32,250 lines based partly on Wace's French version of Geoffrey's *History*; in 1235, two years before his death, Roger of Wendover wrote *Flores Historiarum*, a history of the world from the Creation to his own times. Matthew Paris produced *Chronica Majora*, another world history but which concentrated on events in England in his lifetime which ended in 1259. Writers in English were also keeping Geoffrey's book open in front of them. They included Alfred of Beverley (c. 1150) and Robert Wace of Jersey (c. 1100–1175) whose Anglo-Norman 15,300 line *Roman de Brut* or *Geste des Bretons* is dated at 1155 and is a broad translation of the *History*. Alexander Neckham (1157–1217) reflected knowledge of the Merlin story in verse in his *De Laudibus Divinae Sapieniae*, c. 1200.

In 1325, Ranulf Higden finished *Polychronicon*, his Latin prose history of the world from the Creation to 1327; it was later continued by others on to 1357, and he died in 1363. In 1387 (the year in which Chaucer commenced *The Canterbury Tales*) John de Trevisa translated Higden's work into English. Almost a century later, in 1482, William Caxton brought the chronicle up to date, and printed an edition of it. Thus it was that an account of Stonehenge first reached a printed page, and that a wider circulation of its mysteries became possible for the first time. Caxton was later to print a version of Sir Thomas Malory's *Morte d'Arthur* (1469); if one of Geoffrey of Monmouth's greatest bequests to our heritage was his interest in Stonehenge, another was certainly his stories of Arthur.

Polydore Vergil (c. 1470–1555), the Italian who became Archdeacon of Wells, held a jaundiced view of Geoffrey of Monmouth's *History*, and in his own, commissioned by

THE ATHENIAN MERCURY III, no.19. 1691.

Quest. What reason can you assert why the Miracled Stones on Salisbury Plain *can't be number'd? I design to go that way speedily, if you will give me your opinion what method I should use, I'll spare no costs to accomplish my design in numbering 'em?*

Ans. Numbring is the *prerogative* and right of Rational Beings, that we may number, and number perfectly is *certain to a demonstration*, unless hindered by some Superior Agent, we are forbidden numbring in two cases (unless superstitiously) by Heaven, nor can I ever believe that our *free will* is restrained in it. I'm sure Angels and Spirits act not without *particular Commission* in any thing we do, and sure I am, whatever power good Angels may have over us by Commission, the Devil and his Angels can't hinder us, unless *we are become so little as to be his Servants,* by false perswasion and a blinded Faith, I mean as to any operations they can have over us, by the means of *Number, Charms, Characters,* &c. So that our advice is either to *let 'em alone,* which would shew a great command over your self at such an opportunity, and also a *slighting the Devil,* by not honouring him so far as to doubt of his power by a tryal, but if you are resolv'd to try, because you think it a *Fable:* use your own reason in *marking a place* to begin at, as you would in other things, if there be really any thing in it, as to an impossibility of Numbring 'em, pray give us a particular *Account of your Tryal,* at your return, and you shall have our further thoughts upon the whole.

PLATE 4

Henry VII, he said as much and attracted abuse for disparaging British antiquities in general. The inscription below an engraving of Stonehenge in *The Theatre of The Empire of Great Britain* (1627) by John Speed (Speed 1627) (c. 1555–1629) however maintained the common genuflection to Geoffrey's accounts, and even before him so had John Stow (c. 1525–1605)

PLATE 4 A correspondent of *The Athenian Mercury* in 1691 wrote to ask 'What reason can you assert why the Miracled Stones on Salisbury Plain can't be numbered?' The editor's reply advises him 'either to let 'em alone . . . slighting the Devil . . . or use your own reason in marking a place to begin at, as you would in other things.' Legends of the impossibility of accurately counting stones are common.

THE

moſt notable

ANTIQUITY

OF

GREAT BRITAIN,

vulgarly called

STONE-HENG

ON

SALISBURY PLAIN.

RESTORED

By INIGO JONES Eſquire,

Architect Generall to the late

KING.

LONDON,

Printed by James Fleſher for Daniel Pakeman at the ſign of the Rainbow in Fleetſtreet, and Laurence Chapman next door to the Fountain Tavern in the Strand. 1655.

PLATE 5

quoting William of Malmesbury in his famous *Chronicles of England* or *Annals* (1580–92) as they were called in later editions (Stow 1580).

Fresh royal interest in the monument was initiated in rather poignant circumstances by Charles II. On 3 September 1651 he lost the Battle of Worcester; on 7 October he spent the day at Stonehenge, just ten days before he fled to France. He must have been a rather abject figure 'reckoning and re-reckoning its stones, in order to beguile the time', as his companion recorded. Incidentally, counting stones making up circles is apparently an old problem; stories of its impossibility are attached to the Rollright Stones, Oxfordshire, Long Meg and Her Daughters, Cumbria, and of course The Countless Stones (Lower Kits Coty House), Kent. John Wood wrote of the circles at Stanton Drew (Wood 1750, vol 1): 'No one, Say the Country People about Stantondrue, was ever able to reckon the Number of these metamorphosed Stones, or to take a Draught of them, tho' several have attempted to do both, and proceeded until they were either struck dead upon the Spot, or with such an illness as soon carried them off.' The use of loaves of bread for marking a stone once counted recurs in several such stories; Daniel Defoe records one in 1724 in his *Tour Through England and Wales* (Defoe 1724): 'A baker carry'd a basket of bread, and laid a loaf upon every stone, and yet could never make out the same number twice.' As for the fact at that time we are offered John Evelyn's count of 95 stones in 1654 and John Ray's count of 94 stones on 14 July 1662 (Ray 258).)

So the old legends still lingered on – but not for much longer in the academic world. A new chapter in the Stonehenge story was to begin, and in it some *facts* were to inform the speculations of some outstanding men. The Devil had had his fling. Merlin's reign was over.

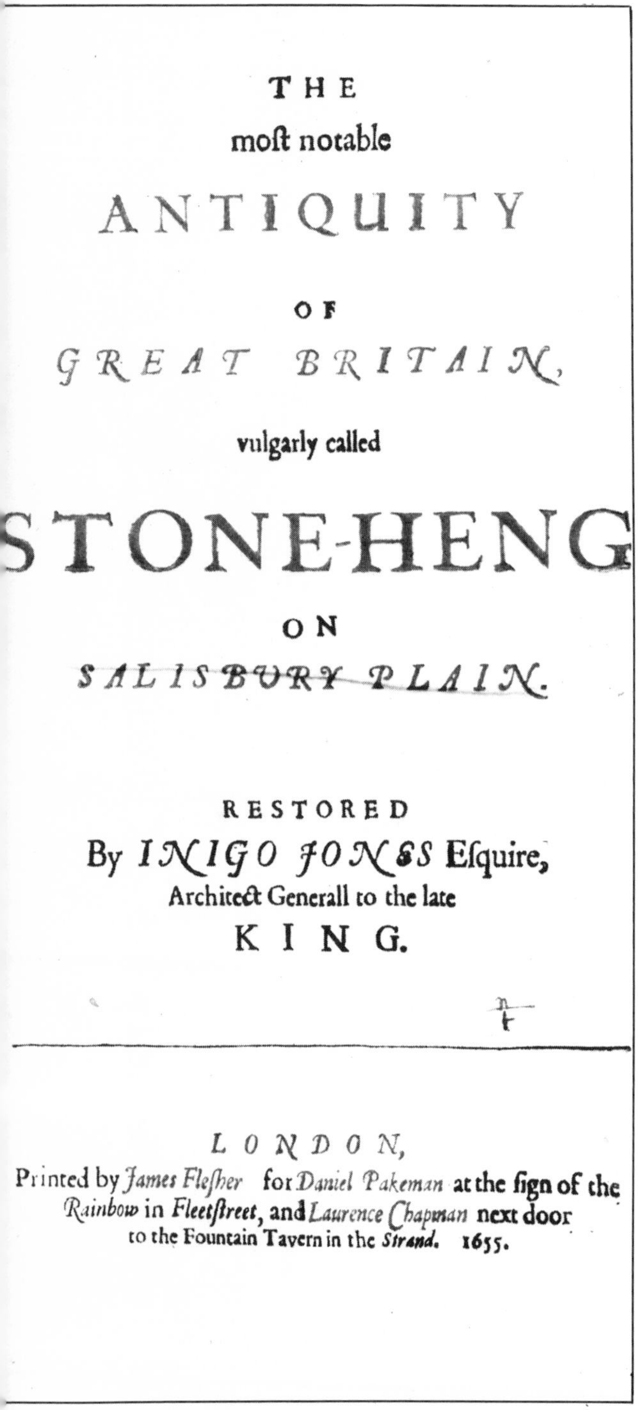

PLATE 5 The title page of *The Most Notable Antiquity of Great Britain, Vulgarly called Stone-Heng on Salisbury Plain* by Inigo Jones (1573–1651), Architect-General to James I. It was first published in 1655.

Serious Research Begins

Who built Stonehenge? Long before our time this question was asked of an architect by a King, and it introduced fierce, even acrimonious debates about the connections between the mysterious stones standing and lying dishevelled on the vast Plain, and the Druids, Phoenicians, Belgae, Danes, Romans and other more exotic contenders for a role in the final solution. The architect was Inigo Jones (1573–1652), whose important illustrated book *Stone-heng Restored* (Jones 1655), after being edited from his 'few indigested notes' by his former assistant and son-in-law John Webb was posthumously published in 1655. Inigo Jones was born in London, studied architecture in Italy and became much influenced by the work of Palladio. James I employed him to design scenery for Ben Jonson's masques, and he designed the famous Banqueting House in Whitehall, The Queen's Chapel in St James's Palace, St Paul's Church, Covent Garden, and the Queen's House, Greenwich. James I was staying (probably in 1620) with the Earl of Pembroke at Wilton House, and wanted to know more about nearby Stonehenge. And when his favourite, the Earl of Buckingham, did a little digging for the Altar Stone, it was for Inigo Jones, his Architect-General, that the King sent. Thus began what might be called the second stage of Stonehenge scholarship. Jones studied the stones at length, took extensive notes and was the first person to measure them.

His close observations resulted in the first serious attempt to get at the mysteries of Stonehenge (and the first book to be published solely about Stonehenge) – and he found himself opposing the legends and theories of that first stage in Stonehenge research and record, initiated by Geoffrey of Monmouth. For Inigo Jones rejected the idea of the Druids and their rites: 'The truth is,' he wrote, 'those ancient Times had no knowledge of publick Works, either sacred or secular, for their own use, or Honour of their Deities.' The architect's fine mind was inclined by education and what

IGNATII IONES MAG: BRIT: ARCHITECTI GE-
NERALIS,   VERA EFFIGIES,

Anth: van Dycke Eques pinxit.   *W: Hollar fecit aqua forti.*

PLATE 6

he had experienced in his travels to the classical order in things created. He saw Stonehenge, with its Vitruvian geometry, as a temple in ruins. 'The form of the temple,' wrote Vitruvius, 'should be analogous to the character of the divinity.' Inigo Jones found it so – and Roman at that, built after 79 AD and dedicated to Cœlus, 'proved from authentic authors and the rules of art.' He carefully pointed out that Romans did not destroy stone edifices which were sacred to the people of the day, but did cut down 'the Britains' [sic] woods and groves, amongst them reckoned holy, and consecrated

PLATE 6   The frontispiece portrait of Inigo Jones (drawn by Anthony Van Dyck and engraved by Wenceslas Hollar) for his book on Stonehenge.

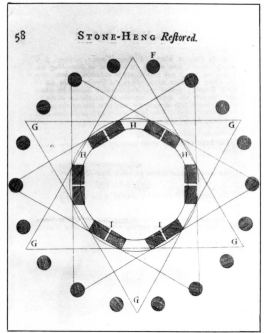

58   STONE-HENG *Reſtored.*

FIGURE 1

to their execrable superstition.' He also questions lightly why there was no Merlin at hand to help transport the stones from Africa to Ireland! So neither Merlin the Magician nor the Druids were, he believed, involved in the construction of Stonehenge. The Ancient Britons get short shrift as well: 'As for their manner of living, the Britains were then a savage and barbarous People, knowing no use at all of garments. ... Now, if destitute of the knowledge, even to clothe themselves, much less any

FIGURE 1   Page 58 in *Stone-Heng* by Inigo Jones. The perfect Vitruvian geometry which he wrongly perceived in the 'temple' (as he called it) is well displayed.

PLATE 7   Plate 42 in Inigo Jones's *Stone-Heng,* 1655

PLATE 8   The title page of the second edition of *Chorea Gigantum: or The Most Famous Antiquity of Great Britain, Vulgarly called Stone-Heng, Standing on Salisbury-Plain, Restored to the Danes* by Dr Walter Charleton, first published in 1663.

knowledge had they to erect stately structures, or such remarkable Works as Stone-heng.'

Inigo Jones's sense of order (which was to produce the three entrances and the erroneous symmetry found in his drawings) was soon disturbed by a situation which even today aggravates researchers. He lamented:

'Those of the inner Circle, the lesser Hexagon, not only exposed to the fury of all-devouring age, but to the rage of men likewise, have been more subject to ruin. For, being of no more extraordinary proportions, they might easily be beaten down, or digged up, and, at pleasure, made use of for other occasions. Which I am the rather induced to believe, because since my first measuring the Work, not one fragment of some then standing are now to be found.'

A year later, in 1656, Dr Thomas Fuller (died 1661) published his *Church History of Britain* and he was quite clear in his mind about the old Stonehenge story: 'As for the tale of Merlin's conjuring them by magic out of Ireland, and bringing them aloft in the skies (what, in Charles's Wain?) it is too ridiculous to be confuted.' (Vol 1, ch. 26). But the doctor of divinity pronounced a very shaky diagnosis on the question of the origin of the stones (he doesn't say which group): 'It seems equally impossible that they were bred here, or brought hither; seeing (no navigable water near) such voluminous bulks are unmanageable in cart or waggon. ... This hath put learned men on necessity to conceive them artificial stones, consolidated sand ... now they are protected by their own weight and worthlessness.'

Dr Walter Charleton (1619–1707), who was Physician-In-Ordinary to Charles I and then Charles II, didn't like Inigo Jones's Roman temple theory at all; and he had a better one. In 1663 he published *Chorea Gigantum,* and his sub-title grandly indicates it: *The Most Famous Antiquity of Great Britain, Vulgarly Called Stone-Heng, Standing On Salisbury-Plain, Restored To The Danes.* The good doctor, a constant correspondent with the Danish antiquary Ole Worm had this to say: 'Having diligently compared Stone-heng with other

P. 7

S S
Nu: 5.

PLATE 7

antiquities of the same kind, at this day standing
in Denmark, and finding a perfect resemblance
in most, if not all particulars, observable on
both sides . . . I now at length conceive it to have
been erected by the Danes, when they had this
nation in subjection; and principally, if not
wholly, designed to be a Court Royal, or Place
for the Election and Inauguration of their
Kings.' Dr Charleton also pointed out the
errors in Inigo Jones's Vitruvian geometry and
Roman theories in a manner so vigorous that
John Webb was bound to reply. Sir William
Dugdale, the leading antiquarian of the time,
was convinced by Charleton's theory, which
concluded by supposing that Alfred the Great
(c. 848–c. 900) was able to defeat the Danes
because they were so exhausted after celebrat-
ing the completion of Stonehenge!

In 1665 Webb's reply came, and it was called
A Vindication of Stone-Heng Restored. He
made good use of his title page, for the sub-title
was *In Which the Orders and Rules of Architecture Observed by the Ancient Romans, are
discussed. Together with the Customs and
Manners of Several Nations of the World in*

PLATE 8

CHOREA GIGANTUM:

Or, The Most Famous

ANTIQUITY

OF

Great Britain,

Vulgarly called

STONE-HENG,

Standing on SALISBURY-PLAIN,

Reſtored to the DANES.

By *WALTER CHARLETON,* M.D.
and Phyſician in Ordinary to His Majeſty.

*Quæ per conſtructionem lapidum, & marmoreas moles, aut terrenos tumulos in magnam
eductos altitudinem, conſtant; non propagabunt longam diem: quippe & ipſa intereunt.*
Seneca, de Conſolat. ad Polyb.

The SECOND EDITION.

LONDON:

Printed for D. BROWNE *Junior,* at the *Black-Swan* without *Temple-Bar,*
and J. WOODMAN and D. LYON, in *Ruſſel-Street, Covent-Garden.*

A
VINDICATION
OF
Stone-Heng Restored:
In which the ORDERS and RULES of
ARCHITECTURE
Observed by the Ancient
ROMANS,
ARE DISCUSSED.

Together with the Customs and Manners of several
Nations of the World in matters of

BUILDING
Of Greatest ANTIQUITY.

As also an Historical Narration of the most memorable
Actions of the DANES in ENGLAND.

By JOHN WEBB of Butleigh in the County of
Somerset Esquire.

1693

LONDON,
Printed by R. Davenport for Tho. Bassett, and are to
be sold at his Shop under S. Dunstan's Church in
Fleet-street. MDCLXV.

PLATE 9

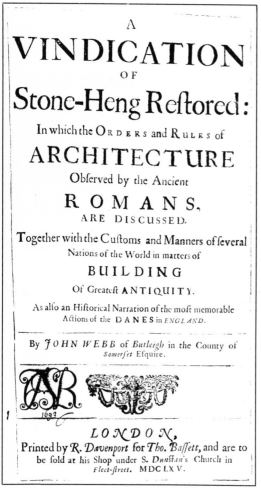

14   STONE-HENG,

" A, Stones called Corseftones, weighing twelve Tun, carrying
" in Height twenty four Foot, in Breadth seven Foot, in Compass
" sixteen.
" B, Stones named Cronets, of six, or seven Tun Weight.
C, Two of the Stones of the outward Circle.
D, One of the Stones of the inner Circle.
E, Two Stones of the greater Hexagon.
F, One of the Stones of the inner Hexagon.
G, One of the Stones of the inner Circle, as it lies along on
the Ground.
H, The Architraves (or Stones) which Mr. Camden calls over-
thwart Pieces, lying upon the erected Stones twenty eight Foot high.
I, The two Stones of the Entrance from the North-East, stand-
ing on the inside of the Trench.
K, The Stone omitted by Dr. Charleton.
But to proceed, he tells us,
2. " The former saith, all those three Courses are circular: The
" latter saith, of his four, two only are circular, the other two
" hexagonal.
This, I conceive, makes them both accord, more rather than dif-
agree, in their Descriptions; for, first, Mr. Camden (borrowing the
Expression from Polydore Virgil) delivers, that the general Aspect
of our Antiquity bears the Form of a Crown; and Mr. Jones saith,
the whole Work in general is of a circular Figure; and who knows
not

PLATE 10

matters of *Building of Greatest Antiquity. As also an Historical Narration of the most Memorable Actions of the Danes in England.* John Webb's defence of his father-in-law's 'temple of the Tuscan order' theories was a little muted, but he roundly discredited Dr Charleton's *Chorea Gigantum*; it was, he wrote, a 'capricious conceit'. In 1725 a publisher, D. Browne Junior, enterprisingly re-issued Jones, Charleton and Webb in one volume, with added illustrations and pictures – a sure indication of the growing popularity of Stonehenge. Bishop

PLATE 9   The title page of *A Vindication of Stone-Heng Restored* by John Webb, 1665, in which the author defended the ideas of his late father-in-law, Inigo Jones, whose controversial book on the monument had been edited by Webb for posthumous publication in 1655.

PLATE 10   Page 14 in *A Vindication of Stone-Heng Restored* by John Webb, 1655.

PLATE 11   The title page of D. Browne's omnibus volume on Stonehenge, published in 1725; it contained the books by Inigo Jones, Walter Charleton and John Webb, new plates and an index.

Gibson's edition (1695) of Camden's *Britannia* was already on its subscribers' shelves and in the shops, and he steered clear of both Romans and Danes: 'I should think one need make no scruple to affirm that it is a British monument.'

This great antiquarian squabble had not escaped the notice of the great diarists of that (and indeed any) age. John Evelyn (1620–1706) visited Salisbury Plain on 22 July 1654 and, after a good lunch at his uncle's farm nearby, 'we were arrived at Stonehenge, indeed a stupendous monument, appearing at a distance like a castle; how so many and huge pillars of stone should have been brought together, some erect, others transverse on the tops of them, in a circular area as rudely representing a cloister or heathen and more natural temple, is wonderful. The stone is so exceedingly hard, that all my strength with a hammer could not break a fragment, which hardness I impute to their so long exposure. To number them is very difficult . . .' He was unknowingly sharing in a common experience by attempting to chip off for himself a souvenir, and in not finding a stone count easy.

Samuel Pepys (1633–1703) was there on 11 June 1668. 'So the three women behind W. Hewer, Murford, and our guide, and I single to Stonehenge, over the Plain and some great hills, even to fright us. Come thither, and find them as prodigious as any tales I ever heard of them, and worthy this journey to see. God knows what their use was! they are hard to tell, but yet may be told. Gave the shepherd-women, for leading our horses, 4d.'

The other constant and learned traveller of the time was the Wiltshire born antiquary John Aubrey (1626–97). After studying law, he journeyed widely in Britain, recording an enormous breadth of local knowledge, folklore and legend, quite apart from details of antiquities. He had a number of patrons such as Ashmole and Hobbes, and his table-talk must have been brilliant. Outside the antiquarian field he is famous for his *Brief Lives* (first published in 1813). Within his field he holds a pivotal position, in which he was later joined by Dr William Stukeley: both were Freemasons,

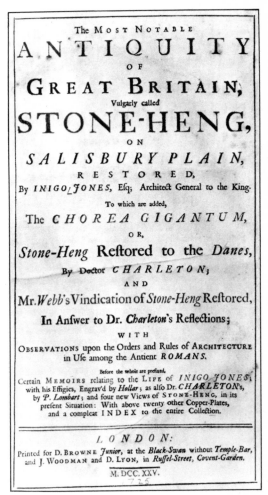

The Most Notable
ANTIQUITY
OF
GREAT BRITAIN,
Vulgarly called
STONE-HENG,
ON
SALISBURY PLAIN,
RESTORED,
By *INIGO JONES*, Esq; Architect General to the King.

To which are added,
The *CHOREA GIGANTUM*,
OR,
Stone-Heng Reſtored to the *Danes*,
By Doctor *CHARLETON*;
AND

Mr. *Webb's* Vindication of *Stone-Heng* Reſtored,

In Anſwer to Dr. *Charleton's* Reflections;
WITH
OBSERVATIONS upon the Orders and Rules of ARCHITECTURE
in Uſe among the Antient *ROMANS*.

Before the whole are prefixed,
Certain MEMOIRS relating to the LIFE of *INIGO JONES*,
with his Effigies, Engrav'd by *Hollar*; as alſo Dr. *CHARLETON's*,
by *P. Lombart*; and four new Views of STONE-HENG, in its
preſent Situation: With above twenty other Copper-Plates,
and a compleat INDEX to the entire Collection.

LONDON:
Printed for D. BROWNE Junior, at the *Black-Swan* without *Temple-Bar*,
and J. WOODMAN and D. LYON, in *Ruſſel-Street, Covent-Garden*.
M. DCC. XXV.

PLATE 11

and both believed that Druids were connected with the origins and purpose of Stonehenge. As far as we are concerned his most important work was *Monumenta Britannica: A Miscellanie of British Antiquities* (Aubrey c. 1666). Part 1 of this unpublished manuscript is called *Templa Druidum,* which was originally the title of a book Aubrey planned, and is now in the Bodleian Library. The second part is lost. Professor Atkinson has expressed a hope to publish a critical edition of the *Templa Druidum* one day, and all students of Stonehenge must hope he will. Parts of it were published in the 1695 edition of Camden's *Britannia* by William Long in 1876.

John Aubrey's association with Stonehenge will in any event always be remembered, because the Aubrey Holes which were named after him by R. S. Newall, who had noticed Aubrey's reference to some 'cavities' in his manuscript. When he was 22, Aubrey had discovered the Great Circle at Avebury, whilst out foxhunting; it does, he recorded, 'much exceed in greatness the so renowned Stoneheng as a Cathedral doeth a parish Church.' This comment may yet turn out to be true; research into the stone circles in and around the village of Avebury is in its earliest stages compared with the work proceeding a few miles away on the Plain.

John Aubrey was fascinated by everything he found at Stonehenge, and had obviously 'read up' his subject. In his manuscript he notes the story of Merlin's great feats with the stones from Ireland, and includes the legend of the stone with which the Devil hit him on the heel on his way over, and that the imprint is still visible. This is in fact on Stone 14 in the outer circle according to Professor Richard Atkinson – 'and not on the Heel Stone, which has a similar mark, but gained its name in another way (see Part 3). Aubrey notes that 'grey weathers' (a common old name for sarsen stones) are on the downs within fourteen miles around, unaware that they were different from the bluestones in the legend. During his visits he came across Mrs Mary Trotman, who clearly told tales as fanciful as some of his own. She is responsible for the repetition in print of many unreliable stories about the monument (partly because Stukeley, after him, was the more purposefully gullible). He also has some sound thoughts of

PLATE 12

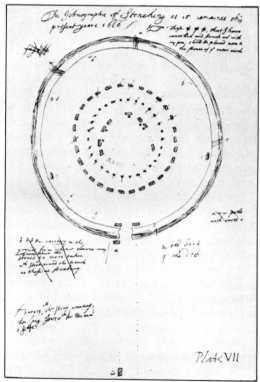

FIGURE 2

PLATE 12 John Aubrey, drawn by William Fairthorne.

FIGURE 2 The projected Plate VII for Part I of *Monumenta Britannica* in John Aubrey's manuscript, which has never been published. It is in the Bodleian Library, Oxford.

his own: 'Had not this Antiquity of Stonehenge consisted of such an extreme hard and ill coloured stone, that it is hardly fit for any use, without much trouble, this venerable Temple had long since been erased and forgotten' (Aubrey c. 1666). This Temple, we should note, he thought to be Druidic – and so he had the title for the first part of his manuscript.

Into the Age of Enlightenment

In Aubrey's fortieth year, fire gutted London. But the disaster seemed to ignite an explosion of achievement throughout the arts and sciences that was to last almost a century, and initiate intellectual chain reactions which continue to this day.

Within view of the rising new city, Greenwich Observatory was founded in 1675, with John Flamsteed as the first Astronomer-Royal (to a family that was actually interested); in the same year the Philosophical Transactions of the Royal Society of London were initiated. In 1718 the Society of Antiquaries was re-founded (becoming 'Royal' in 1751), with Dr William Stukeley as its first Secretary. The first circulating library was founded in 1726, and the first real daily newspaper (as we would recognize it, its survival dependent on its advertising revenue) came in 1730: the percentage of the population in Great Britain and Ireland of seven and a half million able to derive benefit was very small, but 'the market was there'. Literacy spread; more books were 'done into English' than ever before.

'Of the thirty or forty books,' Professor Piggott has written, 'published between 1670 and 1740 concerned with British or Romano-British antiquities, about half appeared around 1710–30' (Piggott 1950, p. 6). This was, as he points out in his elegant and invaluable account of William Stukeley's life, perhaps as a result of the publication of Edmund Gibson's translated, edited and expanded edition (1695) of William Camden's (1551–1623) *Britannia*, which, among much else, reprinted large parts of Aubrey's *Templa Druidum* and contained

PLATE 13

Robert Morden's fine county maps. The horizons of the British landscape, and the relics concealed in its folds, were dramatically revealed for enquiring minds who found history and topography excitingly combined in the ensuing intellectual debate; it was to bring forth some strange ideas indeed in the name of Stonehenge.

As travel grew fashionable, it became safer, especially if one followed the new road maps. John Ogilby's ingenious and detailed strip road maps had been published in 1675 (and were,

PLATE 13   William Camden (1551–1623). An antiquary and historian, who first published his *Britannia Descriptio* in 1586; he became headmaster of Westminster School in 1593. Bishop Edmund Gibson published his translated, edited and expanded edition of Camden's *Britannia* in 1695, and it influenced the course of Stonehenge scholarship.

incidentally the first to adopt the Standard Mile), and no doubt the antiquarians of the age indicated their own discoveries with the same excitement that John Aubrey noted his. Imagine discovering the stone circles at Avebury whilst out fox-hunting, far from the new turnpikes and neighbouring 'beaten tracks'!

The brilliant and maddening Irishman John Toland (1670–1722) met Aubrey, and formed an impression of him which passed indirectly to William Stukeley, a key figure in the Stonehenge story. The opinions gained and expressed by Toland contained a word which is now (to the everlasting regret of all archaeologists) inextricably connected with Stonehenge: 'Druid'.

Aubrey was, wrote Toland in 1726, 'the only person I ever met, who had a right notion of the temples of the Druids, or indeed any notion that the circles so often mentioned were such temples at all'. This baiter of the rigidly orthodox Church of England read widely – and he would have eagerly devoured this passage about the circles of stones at Stenness and Brodgar in the Orkney Islands: they 'are believed to have been Places design'd to offer Sacrifice in time of Pagan Idolatry; and for this reason the People called them the Ancient Temples of the Gods. ... Several of the Inhabitants have a Tradition, that the Sun was worshipped in the larger, and the Moon in the lesser Circle' (Martin, *The Western Islands of Scotland* 1703, p. 365).

PLATE 14   Page 101 in Aylett Sammes' *Britannia Antiqua Illustrata* (1676). The page starts: 'The next Order of People in Britain were the Druids, who did not totally abolish all the Customs and Opinions of the Bards, but retained the most useful parts of them, such as the Immortality of the Soul, to which they added the Transmigration of it, according to the opinion of Pythagoras, about whose time, or a little after, I believe the Greeks entered this island. Moreover they continued the customes of rehearsing things in Verse, which they either brought out of Greece, or continued it as they found it established here?' Sammes was the first English writer to propose that the Phoenicians constructed Stonehenge.

PLATE 14

The author was the Reverend Martin Martin, and Toland the deist was most excited, because he knew that the same story was told of the stones at Callanish on the Isle of Lewis, in the Hebrides. Was the Anglican hierarchy ignoring (or, worse, hiding) something? This matter is of the greatest interest (and I am indebted to Professor Stuart Piggott's scholarly account of these chains of influences) because the renowned William Stukeley was to depict the inner circles at Avebury in his 1721 plans as Lunar and Solar. It is certain that he had known Toland, and by then was certainly alerted to the possible Druidic origins of stone circles.

William Stukeley and Druidism

Dr William Stukeley (1687–1765), Lincolnshire doctor, surgeon, artist, archaeologist and friend of many of the great minds of his day, first visited Stonehenge on 18/19 May 1719; thereafter he was there and at Avebury frequently, undertaking extensive fieldwork, of which he was, with Aubrey, a pioneer in Britain. He discovered and named The Cursus in August 1723, and also the Stonehenge Avenue (see Part 5). In 1740, Stukeley published *Stonehenge: A Temple Restor'd To The Druids*, and three years later *Abury, A Temple Of The British Druids*. Stukeley followed Aubrey in believing that Stonehenge was not Roman or Danish, not a magically conveyed ring of Irish petrified giants, not a defensive construction, not a place of continuous habitation, and not a cemetery.

We know that before he arrived at Stonehenge Stukeley was well familiar with most of the books, both in Latin and English and some of their authors, which discussed the possible origins and purpose of the monument and with some of their authors. His friend Roger Gale had transcribed parts of *Monumenta Britannica*, and Stukeley will have read this firm opinion: 'Now my presumption is, that the Druids being the most eminent order of priests among the Britaines, 'tis odds, but that these

monuments [Stonehenge and Avebury] were temples of the priests of the most eminent order, viz., Druids, and it is strongly to be presumed that they are as ancient as those days' (Aubrey c. 1666). Jones' and Webb's Romans and Charleton's Danes, as the original builders of the monument were considered and rejected. The ideas of Aylett Sammes had more appeal: his *Britannia Antiqua Illustrata*, 1676, proposed that Aubrey was right about the Druids, but that they had arrived in Britain with the Phoenicians under the leadership of Hercules, the King of Tyra. Sammes was taking further the ideas of Samuel Bochart (1599–1667), a French scholar whose books greatly impressed Stukeley, who had found in them the proof that Gaul was repopulated by the Phoenicians after the Flood, and that the classical myths with which he was so familiar were derived from the Old Testament of the Bible. (Bochart also thought Welsh was really Hebrew and something like Man's language before Babel.)

In his wide reading on the subject of monuments, temples, or whatever they were, in north western Europe, Stukeley certainly knew of the work of the sixteenth century Danish scholar Worm as well as the works of his own near contemporary Keysler. Despite this, Stukeley was convinced that the circular British structures could not be simply tombs or sepulchres. But wouldn't the immensity and precision of the structures be more appropriate if they had been the altars of those Druids who arrived with that oriental colony of Phoenicians? They were, Stukeley came to believe in the years after he studied Stonehenge, the last inheritors of the knowledge and traditions of the great patriarchs of the Old Testament, and they were able to preserve these in their new country because they were 'left in the extremest west to the improvement of their thoughts'.

Stukeley's ideas were given further impetus towards the state of mind which has bred the confusion in which Druidic champions now find themselves, by what he found in a book published in 1723 by the Rev. Henry Rowlands called *Mona Antiqua Restaurata*. His parish was in Anglesey, an island rich in neolithic

ANTIQUITATES SELECTÆ CELTICÆ
ET
SEPTENTRIONALES.

ANTIQVITATES
SELECTAE
SEPTENTRIONALES
ET
CELTICAE
QVIBVS
PLVRIMA LOCA CONCILIORVM ET
CAPITVLARIVM EXPLANANTVR, DO-
GMATA THEOLOGIAE ETHNICAE CELTARVM
GENTIVMQVE SEPTENTRIONALIVM CVM
MORIBVS ET INSTITVTIS MAIORVM NO-
STRORVM CIRCA IDOLA, ARAS, ORACVLA,
TEMPLA, LVCOS, SACERDOTES, REGVM
ELECTIONES, COMITIA ET MONV-
MENTA SEPVLCHRALIA
VNA
CVM RELIQVIIS GENTILISMI IN
COETIBVS CHRISTIANORVM
EX MONVMENTIS POTISSIMVM
HACTENVS INEDITIS FVSE
PERQVIRVNTVR.
CVM FIGVRIS AERI INCISIS.
AVTORE
IOH. GEORGIO KEYSLER
SOCIETATIS REGIAE LONDINENSIS
SOCIO.
HANNOVERAE
SVMTIBVS NICOLAI FOERSTERI
BIBLIOPOLAE AVLICI SACRAE REGIAE
MAIESTATIS BRITANNICAE
MDCCXX.

PLATE 16 ▽

standing stones and tombs, and Rowlands proposed that they were adapted by the Druids for their ceremonies. The next step on the ladder of thinking was short – and false. Stukeley read the following, and found that the idea fitted neatly into his growing patriarchal vision: 'Might not Stonehenge and Roll-rick Coronets be very well the Relicks of antient Druidism?' (Rowlands 281).

From now on William Stukeley's beliefs careered ever further away and the Sublime gave way to the ridiculous. From his wide reading he was aware that no classical writer associated Druids with stone monuments (only with sacred groves), but that the Old Testament certainly mentions stone altars ... and so we see how he came to find Tacitus wanting in his Druidical accounts, and to date the construction of Stonehenge at 460 BC, 'not long after Cambyses' invasion of Egypt ... this was at a time when the Phoenician trade was at its height, the readier a conveyance to Britain' (Stukeley 1740). The frontispiece to his book depicts 'A British Druid' standing under an oak tree, a reminder of the old groves, with Wessex barrows in the distance behind him. They were the graves of the Druid constructors of the great sanctuary, the last depository of knowledge of the patriarchal religion he had fervently espoused with his ordination into the Church of England in 1729.

Causes, resistance and liberty were in the air in any case, and so Rev. Stukeley and Dr Stukeley were at one. The Druidic tradition survived the coming and going of the Roman oppressors; it represented free thinking yet,

PLATE 17

like the Church itself, was subject to its inherited purity and achievements (such as Stonehenge, Avebury, etc.). Stukeley prefaced his book on Stonehenge as follows:

'My intent (besides preserving the memory of these extraordinary monuments, so much to the honour of our country, now in great danger of ruin) to promote, as much as I am able, the knowledge and practice of ancient and true Religion; to revive in the minds of the learned the spirit of Christianity ... to warm our hearts into that true sense of Religion, which keeps the medium between ignorant superstition and learned free-thinking, between enthusiasm and the rational worship of God, which is no where upon earth done, in my judgement, better than in the Church of England.'

Most would agree today to a calmer interpretation of the Druids and their role in the Stonehenge saga – that they were ancient Celtic priests in both Gaul and Britain, that they only have a recorded place in history

PLATE 15 The splendid frontispiece and title page of *Antiquitates Selectae Septentrionales Et Celticae* by Johann G. Keysler; it was published in Hanover, Germany, in 1720, and William Stukeley was familiar with Keysler's work.

PLATE 16 The first illustration in Keysler's 1720 book was of Stonehenge.

PLATE 17 Dr (and from 1729 The Rev) William Stukeley (1687–1765), who is a key figure in the story of Stonehenge.

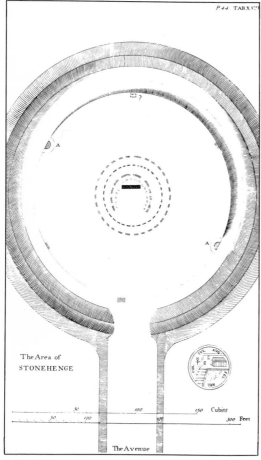

P 44 TAB XXth

The Area of
STONEHENGE

The Avenue

△ FIGURE 3

because of the passage of civilized Romans and Greeks (and thus the books of Caesar, Mela, Pliny, Tacitus, etc.), and that they have little or no association with the construction of our stone circles, beyond bequeathing a few such shrines for adaptation by priests who came after them.

The influence of theories about Druidic origins of Stonehenge and other monuments spread far beyond the notebooks of antiquaries and gentlemen of the shires. In 1725 John Wood the Elder (1704–54) designed the Cursus in Bath – and he had a known interest in Druids which surely guided his mind's eye In 1747 he published in *Choir Gaure* his own account about the stones; it was, he wrote: 'a temple erected by the British Druids, about a hundred years before the commencement of the Christian era'. Merlin is there, but the Devil himself is employed to collect the stones from Ireland, and of course he dropped one of them near the end of the journey. This is a repetition of an oft-repeated legend. The three huge Devil's Arrows, near Boroughbridge, Yorkshire, were fired from the top of a nearby hill, but missed the town of Aldborough; the mighty monolith in Rudston churchyard, again in Yorkshire, fell short of the door at which the Devil aimed it: were all such stones folk-memory of the transportation of stones through the air, a theory via which modern research techniques might one day prove amazing powers of sound and harmony? (A perpetual choir sang near Stonehenge.) Modes of transportation are mentioned in Part 3.

Down in the south-west William Borlase (1695–1772) was prey to the neo-Druidism, as he confirmed in his classic *Antiquities of Cornwall* in 1754; 'There is such a wildness in this grand structure, that to imagine it is

---

PLATE 18 ▽

FIGURE 3   Table 23 in William Stukeley's book on Stonehenge. The stone he suspected to be opposite the causeway entrance to the Avenue is indicated, beside a question mark.

PLATE 18   'A peep into the Sanctum Sanctorum', drawn by William Stukeley, and dated 6 June 1724.

Roman erection After Julius Caesar's time is too groundless a supposition to be worth confuting'.

The visionary work of William Blake (1757–1827) magnificently proclaims the peak of Druidic invention, and Stonehenge has its central place in his plates: influenced artistic achievements are discussed and illustrated in Part 2.

One of the many reasons why William Stukeley remains such an attractive and entertaining source of information about Stonehenge is that he somehow kept his religious fervour reasonably distanced from his antiquarian interests (until about 1733 that is). He made more than two thousand measurements at Stonehenge, and concluded that the unit of measurement used was pre-Roman, and it was the 'Druid's Cubit', 20·8 inches, and its multiples. (Flinders Petrie was to show in 1880 that in fact it was the Roman unit of 11.64 inches. Nevertheless Stukeley's interpretations of Stonehenge and Avebury have been very influential, and some of his observations were not confirmed until Colonel Hawley's excavations in 1920. He also made an interesting attempt to date the monument in a severely practical (for him) way, by analysing magnetic variations, because he thought that the main axis had been set out with the aid of a magnetic needle, the proportions of which were, he was certain, known to the Phoenicians.

Stukeley's 1740 comment on that axis, from the foot of the Great Trilithon, through the centre to the Heel Stone and beyond, reverberates through all subsequent speculation: '. . . whereabouts the Sun rises, when the days are longest'. He was indicating that Stonehenge was an astronomical observatory – and so it has proved.

△ PLATE 19   PLATE 20 ▽

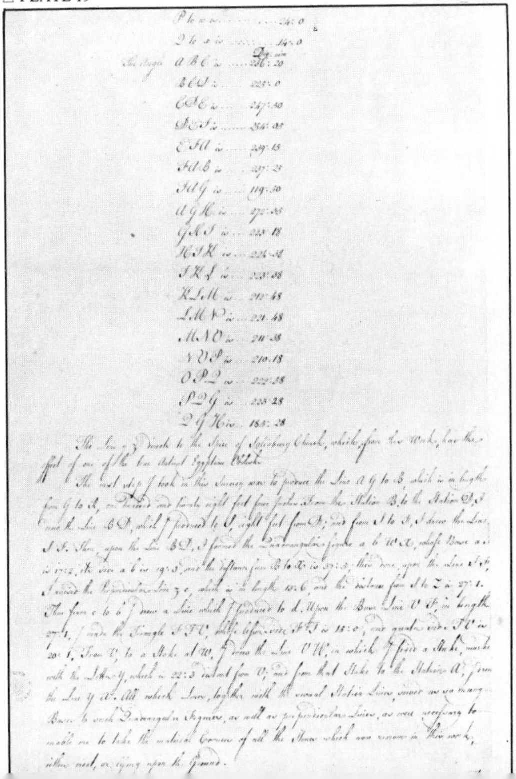

PLATE 19   Dr William Stukeley, in a plate from his classic book *Stonehenge, A Temple Restor'd To The British Druids* (1740), no doubt pointing out the wonders of the monument to his companions.

PLATE 20   An elegant page of John Wood's manuscript *Choir Gaure*, 1747.

PLATE 21 Not a midsummer solstice sunrise ceremony, but a 'Druid's Day' celebration on 24th August 1905.

Delving into the Mystery

The heavens above the migrating Phoenicians and the Druidic works within or without sacred groves, were not ignored. Dr John Smith, practising medicine in the nearby village of Boscombe, took up some of Stukeley's ideas in 1771, in his book *Choir Gaur: The Grand Orrery Of The Ancient Druids, Commonly Called Stonehenge*. He emphasized that the alignment with the midsummer sunrise was deliberate, and that 'the Arch-Druid standing against his stall, and looking down the right line of the temple . . . sees the Sun rise from behind that hill.' Smith also regarded the sarsen circle as a calendar, a suggestion ahead of its time; 'I conceived it to be an Astronomical Temple.'

One of the most interesting accounts of the astronomical uses of Stonehenge is found in *The Celtic Druids* by Godfrey Higgins, to which I shall refer again. He mentions a natural philosopher and astronomer named Waltire who evidently worked there in about 1792 (nobody knows his first name!), and quotes from notes now lost:

'Mr Waltire thought this temple had been constructed for several uses; that it was peculiarly well contrived for the performance of secret rites which were practised in early times – as, if a person stood without he could not see any thing that was done in the centre, provided the entrance were closed, as it might be very effectually, by three persons standing before it. If a person stood on the large stone or altar, within the inner curve, which is a parabola and not an ellipse, he might be heard, when speaking, by all within the temple. Another use for which he thought this structure had been erected, was that of making

---

PLATE 22   The title page of *Choir Gaure, The Grand Orrery Of The Ancient Druids, Commonly Called Stonehenge* by Dr John Smith, 1771. The continuation of the title indicates the book's pioneering importance; *Astronomically explained, and Mathematically proved to be a Temple erected in the earliest Ages, for observing the Motions of the Heavenly Bodies.*

PLATE 23   The first plate in *The Celtic Druids* by Godfrey Higgins, 1829.

CHOIR GAUR;
The Grand ORRERY of
THE ANCIENT DRUIDS,
Commonly called
STONEHENGE,
ON
SALISBURY PLAIN,
Aſtronomically explained, and Mathematically proved to be a TEMPLE erected in the earlieſt Ages, for obſerving the Motions of the HEAVENLY BODIES.
Illuſtrated with Three COPPER PLATES.

By Dr. **JOHN SMITH,**
INOCULATOR of the SMALL-POX.

Felix, qui potuit rerum cognoſcere cauſas.
VIRG.

SALISBURY:
Printed for the AUTHOR,
And Sold by E. EASTON:
Sold alſo by R. HORSFIELD, No. 22, Ludgate-Street;
And J. WHITE, Lincoln's-Inn-Fields, LONDON.
M DCC LXXI.

PLATE 22

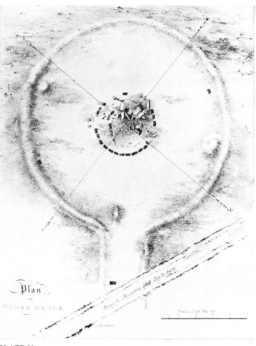

PLATE 23

astronomical observations on the heavenly bodies. By careful observations made on the spot, Mr W. found, that the barrows or tumuli surrounding this temple accurately represented the situation and magnitude of the fixed stars, forming a correct and complete planisphere. Eight hundred only can be seen by the unassisted eye, but he thought he traced fifteen hundred, the smaller representing stars too minute to be observed without some instrument similar to a telescope; and that there are other proofs of the occupiers of this structure having possessed something answering to our reflecting telescope. He thought he could prove that other barrows registered all the eclipses which had taken place within a certain number of years; that the trilithons are registers of the transits of Mercury and Venus; the meridian line had then been even with avenue or approach and the grand entrance and the altar-stone within the innermost curve, but which is now removed seventy-five degrees from it.' (Higgins 1829, p. xviii)

Mr Waltire touches upon a mysterious fact – that some ancient constructions in the British landscape are best seen and thus intended to be seen from the air. They include hill figures and zodiacs constructed many centuries before the first balloon ascended; and so we must hope that Mr W.'s reported theory will be explored.

If ever it is, the Wiltshire volumes of the wealthy land owner and antiquary Sir Richard Colt-Hoare of Stourhead will once again demonstrate their unique value. The magnificent volume on south Wiltshire, with Philip Crocker's illustrations, was published by him in 1812, and in it he was complimentary about Dr John Smith's book; in his own views he is very conservative: 'The Revolution of ages frequently elucidates history, and brings many important facts to light; but here all is darkness, and uncertainty; we may admire; we may conjecture; but we are doomed to remain in ignorance and obscurity.'

PLATE 24 Six interpretations over two centuries, of the ground plan of Stonehenge.

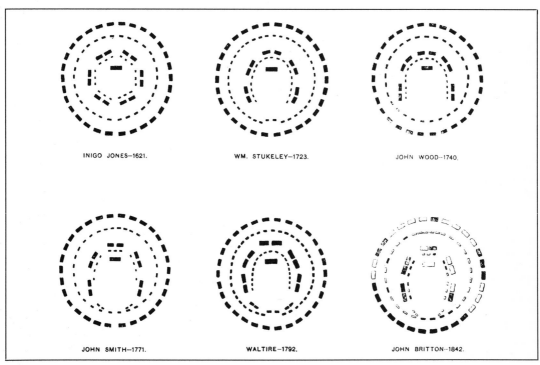

INIGO JONES—1621.

WM. STUKELEY—1723.

JOHN WOOD—1740.

JOHN SMITH—1771.

WALTIRE—1792.

JOHN BRITTON—1842.

PLATE 24

Edward A. Downman certainly expressed a wish in writing in 1908, that the banking heir *had* remained in obscurity. He put it like this in his manuscript on the 'Earthworks in Wiltshire', which he surveyed between 1889 and 1908; although he thought everything in the Stonehenge area was Norman and only interesting if it was a fortification, his central point is still shared by some zealots:

'Tumuli and Beacon Mounds were once the unique glory of Wiltshire, no other part of England being able to boast of so many: these had been respected for long ages both by the owners of the land, the farming classes, and the wise country folk, till in an evil day curious men and idle, such as R. C. Hoare (may his coffin be split into firewood and his monument be broken up into paving stones), with no reverence for the resting places of the dead, or consideration for people yet to come, under the pretence of science and historical research, set to work to destroy these ancient tombs, or what they thought were ancient tombs; hence the ruin and wreck which meets the eye of the true antiquary. Where is the Norman Castle mound of Marden, the destruction of which Hoare commenced in AD 1809, mistaking in his ignorance a castle mound for one of the graves of the ancient folk, the contents of which he desired to ravish? Where – ? But enough, my choler rises and my hand quivers as I write of these vandals who have disgraced the name of antiquary.'

The widely read John Britton was more confident than Colt-Hoare of when this temple of the stars was erected. In *The Beauties of Wiltshire* he said: 'Stonehenge was the work of the Romanized Britons, about the latter end of the fifth century.' And he meant AD (Britton 1801, Vol. ii, pp. 129–180). Only Sir William Flinders Petrie has ever dated it more recently (Sarsens: 730 ± 200 AD), 'owing to an error in his application of the change of obliquity' (Lockyer 1906, p. 62).

Godfrey Higgins produced for himself in 1829 a large and elegant volume of essays, to which I have referred, called *The Celtic Druids*; this passage in his Preface to the Second Edition is clear, and much to the point he had set out to make in the First: 'It is gratifying to the Author ... that no error of any importance has been

PLATE 25

pointed out, nor have any of the great principles laid down in his argument, or casually introduced in the progress of the work, been attacked with the slightest success.' We should note that on page 158 he indicates that Stonehenge was built in 4,000 BC, 'which will astonish most persons who have not been accustomed to examine subjects of this kind.'

Higgins's new Preface continues:

'Such attacks as are deserving notice, the Author flatters himself will be fully refuted in a work which he is now preparing for press; in which the extraordinary race, the Buddhists of Upper India (of whom the Phoenician Canaanite, Melchizedek, was a priest) who built the Pyramids, Stonehenge, Carnac, etc., will be shewn to have founded all the ancient Mythologies of the world, which, however varied and corrupted in recent times, were originally ONE, and that ONE founded on principles sublime, beautiful, and true.'

The Beginnings of Astro-archaeology

Whatever their provenance, the Reverend E. Duke, who lived near Stonehenge, had some exciting ideas in *The Druidical Temples Of The County Of Wilts,* published in 1846: '. . . our ingenious ancestors portrayed on the Wiltshire Downs a Planetarium or stationary Orrery, located on a meridianal line, extending north and south the length of sixteen miles; that the planetary temples thus located, seven in number, will, if put in motion, be supposed to revolve around Silbury Hill as centre.'

After Dr Thurnam (see 'The Barrow Groups', Part 5), Sir Norman Lockyer (1836–1920) was the next important figure to arrive at Stonehenge with map and compass. He was the author of a number of distinguished books (and co-author of *The Rules Of Golf*), a member of learned societies all over the world, explorer into the orientation of Egyptian pyramids, Editor of *Nature* for many years, and, whilst Director of The Solar Physics Laboratory in London, also, in 1906, the author of *Stonehenge And Other British Stone Monuments, Astronomically Considered.* It attracted much attention when it appeared, for not only did it confirm to many that Stonehenge (which he thought was erected about 1860 BC, plus or minus 200 years) was a 'sun temple' partly erected for the purpose of making observations of the May-year sunrise, but he opened up intelligent speculation about the purpose of many other 'temples' as he called them. He not only explored their orientations, with due regard for local folk-lore and rural traditions, but he also, as Stukeley had before him, proposed that some astronomical sight lines extended over a considerable distance. (John Michell has found that many of Lockyer's alignments can be ruled on maps still further, and that they are what have become known as leys.) Lockyer had respect for the Druids; he believed he had found among his stones and their traditions a more exactly termed prehistoric leader: the astronomer-priest. He wrote:

'In a colony of the astronomer-priests who built and used the ancient temples we had of necessity (1) Observations, i.e.; circles in the first place; next something to mark the sight-lines to the clock-star for night work, to the rising or setting of the warning stars, and to the places of sunrise and sunset at the chief festivals. This something, we have learned, might be another circle, a standing stone, a dolmen, a cove, or a holed stone . . . (2) Dwellings which would be many chambered barrows, according to the number of astronomer-priests at the station . . . (3) A water supply for drinking and bathing.' (Lockyer 1906)

Without knowing it, Lockyer was indicating the astronomer-priests' knowledge and use of *earth,* as well as heavenly phenomena which now occupy so much research.

The rows of standing stones at Callanish on the Island of Lewis, in the Outer Hebrides, have had a curiously important place in the fast developing history of megalithic astronomy. John Toland knew of them, and was probably responsible, as we have seen, for alerting William Stukeley to what he had read in Martin's *Description Of The Western Islands Of Scotland* about lunar and solar circles. In 1908, Rear-Admiral Boyle T. Somerville found himself, with spare time because of bad weather, on the bleak head of Loch Roag. Being a very fine surveyor he would have known of Lockyer's work, and he addressed himself to these impressive stone rows. He wrote a paper in 1912 based on what he found and recorded; it was an astronomical observatory. In 1934, bad weather, more common than the other in those parts, caused another fortuitous visit, and it is interesting to read of the very moment where astro-archaeology left its infancy and began to grow into the lusty science it is today. It is

PLATE 25   Sir William Flinders Petrie (1853–1942), author of *Stonehenge: Plans, Description, and Theories* (1880), photographed about 1894. The numbers he ascribed to the stones are used.

PLATE 26   (*next page*)   A reconstruction drawing by W. B. Robinson for *Illustrated London News* (13 May 1922) showing J. E. Gurdon's theories. 'A prehistoric Westminster Abbey, Exchange and Epsom', ran the title, indicating Stonehenge for worship, The Cursus for chariot races (see Part 5), and the branch of the Avenue to the River Avon.

THE CURSUS

Tumuli

Slope for Spectators

Tumulus

Earthwork

The Avenue

"Hele Stone

Earthwork

"Slaughter Stone

Solstice Stone (N.W.)

Solstice Stone (S.E.)

STONEHENGE

Earthwork Surrounding the Stone Circle

Tumuli

Tumulus

Village

Ford

Tumulus

Slope for Spectators

Tumuli

Avenue to R. Avon

Tumuli

Tumulus

THE POOL

PLATE 27

recalled by Evan Hadingham (1975). A Scottish engineer named Alexander Thom sheltered his boat in Lock Roag, just as the moon was rising among the stones above him – and he recalled reading Somerville's paper all those years ago:

'We had a meal and then went ashore to visit the stones. I stood on the rock outcrop to the south and looked along the line of stones over the top of the great menhir. The pole star was shining directly over this line, and so Somerville (*sic*) was right that this line accurately defined a meridian or north line – in fact to within 0·1 of a degree. This was an extraordinary thing, because I knew that four thousand years ago there was no pole star there to help them set out this line . . .'

Since his retirement Professor Thom has written many articles for learned journals, had his causes championed by controversial writers such as John Michell (who did much to make his work known to the general reading public), and he has published three important books: *Megalithic Sites in Britain,* 1967, *Megalithic Lunar Observatories,* 1971 and *Megalithic Remains in Britain and Brittany*, 1979.

The English-born Gerald Hawkins caused storms quite unlike those at Callanish with the publication of the results of his computerised investigation into the meaning of Stonehenge; first in papers, and then in two books: *Stonehenge Decoded,* 1966, and *Beyond Stonehenge,* 1973.

Among the attacking reviewers, the toughest was perhaps Professor Richard Atkinson who had provided so much new data from his excavations between 1950 and 1964. His own book *Stonehenge,* 1956, has become the classic account of the monument, and he remains our foremost authority on its archaeology. Let us look at the astronomy with which he has since become so much involved.

PLATE 27   Professor Alexander Thom, one of the leading figures in the field of what has become known as astro-archaeology. Apart from publishing many influential articles in learned journals, often with his son and grandson, he is the author of three important books.

Astronomy and Stonehenge

The sun appears to rise at different points on the horizon during the year because the Earth's axis is not at right angles to its orbit around the sun. The effect is that the sun rises due east (and sets due west) only at the equinoxes, March 21 and September 23. After the spring equinox, the sun rises progressively north of east, reaching its most northerly rising on midsummer day (June 21). After this, its rising point moves south again, passing due east at the autumn equinox, and reaching its furthest south point (roughly south-east) on midwinter day (December 22).

The builders of Stonehenge could have fixed the date of midsummer each year by watching successive sunrises until one occurred along the already aligned axis. Latter-day Druids still flock to Stonehenge at midsummer (warned of the date by modern almanacs!) to watch the spectacle of a midsummer sunrise framed by the ancient impassive stones. As the red disc of the sun rises slantingly from the distant horizon, its

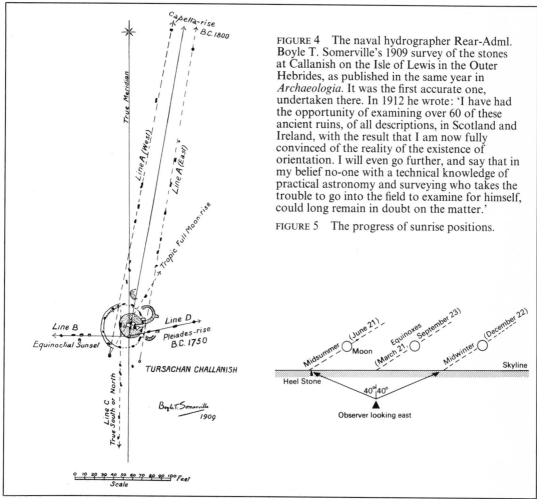

FIGURE 4   The naval hydrographer Rear-Adml. Boyle T. Somerville's 1909 survey of the stones at Callanish on the Isle of Lewis in the Outer Hebrides, as published in the same year in *Archaeologia*. It was the first accurate one, undertaken there. In 1912 he wrote: 'I have had the opportunity of examining over 60 of these ancient ruins, of all descriptions, in Scotland and Ireland, with the result that I am now fully convinced of the reality of the existence of orientation. I will even go further, and say that in my belief no-one with a technical knowledge of practical astronomy and surveying who takes the trouble to go into the field to examine for himself, could long remain in doubt on the matter.'

FIGURE 5   The progress of sunrise positions.

FIGURE 4

FIGURE 5

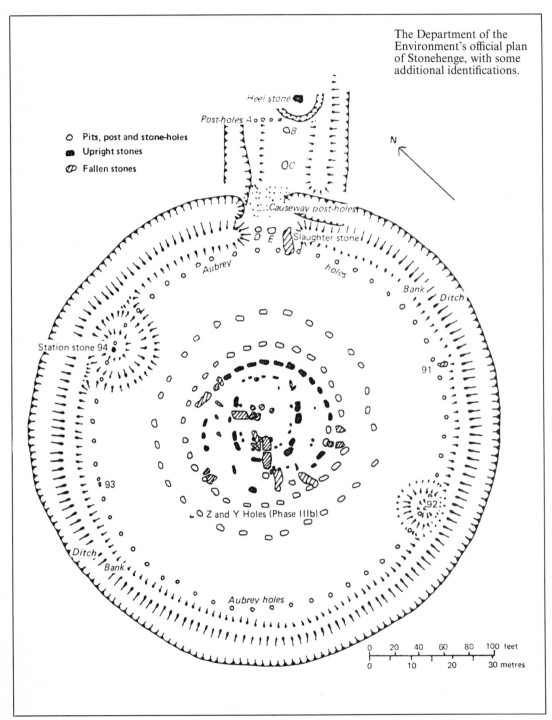

The Department of the Environment's official plan of Stonehenge, with some additional identifications.

FIGURE 6

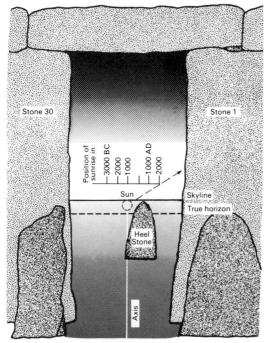

FIGURE 7

full disc skims the tip of the Heel Stone, appearing briefly as a golden globe atop a dark pillar.

Despite this impressive spectacle, the Heel Stone itself cannot have been the original midsummer sunrise marker. The sun approaches its extreme position gradually. The difference in rising point between the day before and midsummer day itself is only 1/70 the Sun's diameter (Thom 1967, p. 117), and such a movement cannot be noticed with the unaided eye unless a very distant horizon is used for the sighting. The Heel Stone is too close to give anything but a very rough indication of midsummer.

But even more to the point is the fact that the inclination of the Earth's axis is changing, albeit extremely slowly. When Stonehenge I was built, the midsummer sun rose slightly further north (to the left), and it would have sailed clear over the top of the Heel Stone. The Heel Stone was probably a moonrise indicator, unconnected with the summer sunrise, as there is good evidence that Stonehenge I was a lunar observatory.

The central line of the Avenue, dating from the Stonehenge II period, is however undoubtedly a summer sunrise alignment. Sir

FIGURE 6   The stones of Stonehenge, as they are today, in the central area. A more detailed and numbered plan is given in Part 4.

PLATE 28   Sir Norman Lockyer (1836–1920), author of *Stonehenge and Other British Stone Monuments* (1906), photographed about 1904. He is regarded by some researchers as the father of British astro-archaeology.

FIGURE 7   A view of the axis that Sir Norman Lockyer established, from the centre of the sarsen circle, between Stones 30 and 1, past the Heel Stone and down the centre of the Avenue as he calculated it. Today we know that the Avenue belongs to the Stonehenge II construction phase, but the sarsen circle is in Stonehenge IIIa; nevertheless Lockyer established a date of 1680 BC for the sarasens, which, after corrections (as we now have a more accurate rate of change of the obliquity (would be 1840 ± 200 BC. This compares well, though fortuitously, with the latest estimated date for Stonehenge IIIa, which is 2000 BC (Atkinson 1978b).

Norman Lockyer made an accurate survey of Stonehenge in 1901. By combining his astronomical knowledge with the evidence of the stones, he effectively founded the science of astro-archaeology decades before it became an acknowledged discipline. Lockyer realized that the direction of the Stonehenge axis can be used to date its construction. The gradually changing rising point of the midsummer sun means that a sunrise alignment would only be accurate for the date at which it was set up, and it is relatively simple to calculate the date appropriate to any alignment set up at Stonehenge.

Lockyer determined the centre of the Avenue at several points along its length, and concluded that it lies 40° 24′ 9″ north of the east point (although he used slightly inaccurate tables in his calculations). This is the direction of the first twinkle of the rising midsummer sun around 1680 BC; and allowing for various uncertainties he deduced that Stonehenge was built about the era 1900 to 1500 BC (Lockyer and Penrose, 1901). These dates were rather optimistic in their precision, for if an observer used his left eye rather than his right (or vice versa), they would change by 500 years (Atkinson 1956, pp. 88–89). Later more accurate measurements (Atkinson, 1978) have shown reasonable agreement with this date and the archaeologically derived date for Stonehenge though by different method. Lockyer's was an important and bold pioneering step.

Professor Richard Atkinson, of University College, Cardiff, re-surveyed the Avenue in 1978 with higher precision. He found its direction to be 40° 5′ 48″ north of east, differing from Lockyer's by 2/3 of the sun's diameter. The Avenue has now been dated by the radiocarbon analysis of two deer antler picks to 2165 ± 80 BC. At this date the first gleam of sunrise ocurred almost a sun's diameter to the left of the Avenue alignment – unless there were trees on the horizon. Over tree-tops 10 metres (10·9 yards) high, the first twinkle of the sun would in fact have occurred almost exactly along the line of the Avenue (Atkinson 1978).

Lockyer also noted that the lines of the Station Stones (91 to 92, and 93 to 94) are

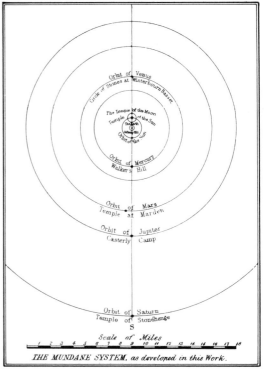

FIGURE 8

parallel to the midsummer sunrise axis. This fact had previously been noted by the Rev. Edward Duke in the 1840s, although it was only part of his conception that most of Wiltshire was a huge model of the solar system. As seen from the centre of Stonehenge, Station Stone 93 marks the sunset on about May 6 and August 8, while Stone 91 shows sunrise around February 5 and November 8. Midsummer sunrise is well indicated by the Stonehenge axis, and by the Station Stones; taking this line in reverse gives approximately the position of

FIGURE 8   An illustration of Rev. Edward Duke's hypothesis that Stonehenge, Silbury Hill and other prehistoric sites in the area were part of a huge planetarium – as shown in this plate from his book *The Druidical Temples of the County of Wiltshire* (1846).

midwinter sunset. Hence Stonehenge defines a calendar of 8 'months', each of roughly 45 days. Only the equinox lines are missing, and C. A. Newham discovered in 1963 that a line from Station Stone 94 to stone-hole C in the Avenue does run exactly along the expected east-west line.

The association of Stonehenge with the sun has been refined in recent years. As well as Atkinson's new survey of the Avenue, Professor Gerald Hawkins claims to have found alignments from Station Stones to empty stone-holes, indicating midsummer sunset and midwinter sunrise – although these are still in some dispute (Hawkins 1963). Astronomer Sir Fred Hoyle has suggested that slight discrepancies in some sightlines may have allowed observations a few days before and after midsummer, which would have led to an accurate date by taking the average (Hoyle 1966). And a precise survey of the Trilithons by Professor Alexander Thom has revealed that the axis of the Trilithons, a Stonehenge III structure, points to midsummer sunrise around 1600 BC (Thom, Thom and Thom, 1974) – but only if sunrise is defined as the moment when *half* the sun shows above the horizon. Atkinson squares this survey with the more usually accepted first-gleam sunrise by showing that the axis should be rotated slightly to allow for the tilt of one of the Trilithons. The axis then points close to the first twinkle of the midsummer sun in 2045 BC, the best radiocarbon date for the construction of Stonehenge III.

By the early 1960's, Stonehenge's role as a 'Sun Temple' or solar observatory was undoubted. Subsequent research now concerns exact details, such as whether sunrise was the first gleam of sunlight, or the half-disc or whole disc on the horizon; and by how much the height of the horizon was raised by trees (in fact there were probably none there 4000 years ago).

But 1963 saw the appearance of a new hypothesis which rocked the archaeological establishment: Stonehenge may have been a *lunar* observatory. The moon's motions are far more complex than those of the sun. They do

---

THE YORKSHIRE POST SATURDAY MARCH 16 1963

The Mystery of Hole G

BY DOUGLAS EMMOTT

Attention this week has once again been focused on Stonehenge, where one of the uprights was blown down in a gale. In this article, The Yorkshire Post Science Correspondent discusses an amateur astronomer's intriguing theories which may add a new chapter to the story of Stonehenge.

Mr Peter Newham: A new theory about Stonehenge

STONEHENGE, that mysterious monument which rises above Salisbury Plain, may be a little less inscrutable than had been supposed. An amateur astronomer, Mr Peter Newham, 63, of Tadcaster, has formulated an intriguing hypothesis which, if proven, might open up whole new fields of inquiry in a subject which has yielded very little significant new information since the last major excavation nearly 40 years ago.

If Mr Newham's line of reasoning is sound, the positions of certain hitherto inexplicable features of Stonehenge would be explained. For the purposes of this inquiry the plan of Stonehenge given here is reduced to the elements bearing upon the new theory.

In 1846, the Rev. E. Duke discovered that the North mound 94 lined up with a stone numbered 93 at the last light of the setting sun on the shortest day of the year. Conversely, a line drawn from the South mound 92 to stone 91 aligned with the rising sun on the longest day of the year.

It was discovered, too, that the axis of the Sarsen stone circle was similarly aligned. In fact, the positions of sunrise and sunset are slightly different today owing to the progressive shift of the earth's axis.

So much, then, is established. What follows is speculation. On several occasions in the past few years Mr Newham has visited the site and made careful observations of his own.

The first remarkable discovery he made was that a line drawn from mound 94 to G would appear to coincide with the point on the horizon where the moon rises at its most northerly point during its 19-year cycle. Conversely, the line from 92 to 93 marks the moonset at its most Northerly setting point. The sun section line, these two alignments are of significance in that the moon Sarsen circle stones is about a yard off-centre with the outer Aubrey circle of holes.

Had it been quite concentric, the 92/93 sighting would have

been obscured. Is this the reason for the off-centredness which has puzzled generations of archaeologists?

It must be remembered that the layout of Stonehenge has been drawn up generally with remarkable precision. The ancient architects were evidently knowledgeable geometricians; indeed, the feat of measurement would tax a modern surveyor with the most up-to-date instruments and techniques.

Unusual feature

From this point, attention is turned to another unusual feature. This is catalogued as "hole G, the middle of three equally spaced "holes" lying to the East and just beyond the Aubrey circle, and for which there is no convincing explanation.

Most Stonehenge authorities have dismissed these disturbances as natural or "shrub-holes." Their disconcerting symmetry and the absence of similar features within the whole of the area that has been uncovered have prompted doubts in more cautious minds.

Mr Newham has noted that a line drawn from 94 to G appears to mark the rising sun on the shortest day of the year. Mound 92 to G marks the moonrise at its most Northerly point.

Thus, six of the eight major solar lunar events of the year are apparently accounted for within the theory. To complete the octet, Mr Newham has postulated the existence of a further marker hole in the unexcavated part of the site, about 16 yards South of 93. This he has provisionally designated G2.

Now, a line drawn from 92 to

G2 would mark the setting sun on the longest day. 94 to G2 would mark the moon set on its most Southerly point. Thus the hypothesis has the added merit of inviting confirmation. If the hypothetical G2 should, in fact, be discovered the possibility of coincidence could be virtually eliminated. The key which now seems to fit the lock would surely turn.

Advanced culture

It would seem, therefore, that Stonehenge might be a far more comprehensive calendar in stone than has been supposed. This, in turn, would suggest that the builders of the later portions of the monument were of a more advanced culture than the native inhabitants of Britain at that time says Mr Newham. There is supporting archaeological evidence for this view.

A few years ago, there would have been no difficulty in obtaining permission to excavate in search of positive confirmation of the existence of G2. One would simply have dug about the point indicated and sought the necessary proof.

Today, however, archaeologists tread with infinite care. In the past, crude pickaxe excavating has destroyed a wealth of detailed information which modern science would have been capable of deciphering. Such brutal methods have wrought such havoc with the "shrub-holes," for example, that it is now almost impossible to determine their real significance even with advanced techniques.

Reluctant to dig

Conscious of this fact and realising that future generations of investigators will read much greater meaning into Stonehenge than we might hope to do, the custodians of Stonehenge are reluctant to dig. Nearly one half of the remains is virtually unexplored below ground and only in exceptional circumstances will the Ministry of Works sanction further excavation.

It is, conceivable, however, that archaeological adviser will recommend a search for Mr Newham's ghost-hole, G2 by preliminary above-ground detection methods. Encouraging soundings would indicate a call for spade and trowel—and, perhaps, the opening of a new chapter in the story of Stonehenge.

PLATE 29

PLATE 29 Reference is often made to a letter from C. A. 'Peter' Newham in *The Yorkshire Post* of 16 March 1963. His ideas were in fact the subject of an article that day by Douglas Emmott, the paper's Science Correspondent. 'Peter's Mound, a possible midsummer sunrise marker (according to Professor Alexander Thom) about 2736 m (3000 yds) northeast of Stonehenge, is named after Newham (1899–1974).

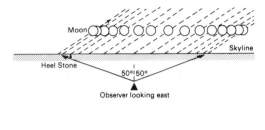

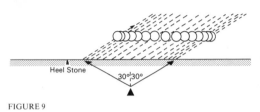

FIGURE 9

not recur exactly year after year, and observations have to be made – and recorded – for around nineteen years before any pattern can be derived from them. And this implies a level of organization and intellectual sophistication far higher than some people had then previously credited to the builders of Stonehenge.

To interpret the relation between the complex movements of the moon and the alignment of stones on the ground requires that new type of specialist, the astro-archaeologist, versed in both astronomy and archaeology. Despite Lockyer's work early this century, astro-archaeology was until recently a subject with no professional standing, and those who worked in it had widely different backgrounds.

The first connection between Stonehenge and the moon was drawn by C. A. ('Peter') Newham, formerly Group General Manager of the North Eastern Gas Board. His letter to the *Yorkshire Post* in March 1963 was not widely read, and the Stonehenge Bookshop would not stock his privately printed book *The Enigma of Stonehenge*; it is a sign of the changing academic climate towards astro-archaeology

that it does now sell his later book *The Astronomical Significance of Stonehenge* (Newham 1972). At the same time, Professor Gerald Hawkins of the University of Boston, Massachusetts, brought in the calculating abilities of a computer to investigate the astronomical significance of the lines from virtually every stone in Stonehenge to every other. He found strong evidence that important lunar lines are marked, and he published his work in an influential scientific journal (Hawkins 1963). Indirectly supporting Newham's and Hawkins's evidence for a prehistoric lunar observatory at Stonehenge, are Alexander Thom's analyses of Scottish megalithic sites. Thom has produced impressive evidence that the moon was very carefully observed from several sites in Scotland (Thom 1971). In recent years, many archaeologists, including Professor Atkinson, have admitted it is difficult to avoid the conclusion that megalithic man was indeed capable of accurate and long-sustained astronomical observations. (Atkinson, 1975, contained the lines: 'I am prepared, in other words, to believe that my model of European prehistory is wrong, rather than that the results presented by Thom are due to nothing but chance ... Thom's astonishing contribution will find its rightful place').

The moon moves around the sky in 27·3 days, roughly following the sun's yearly path. In the space of a month, then, the moon's rising point moves from east up to north-east, back through east to south-east, and returning to east. Neglecting the phases of the moon, caused by the differing angle of illumination by the sun, the moon's motion would be easy to follow if it took exactly the same path as the sun. But it does not. Suppose we drew the Earth's orbit around the sun on a flat sheet of paper; the moon's orbit about the Earth is then drawn on another (much smaller) sheet angled at about 5° to the first. And to add to the complication, the line where the two sheets meet (the 'line of nodes') is gradually swinging round, turning once in about 19 years

The practical effect is that moonrise positions go through a long cycle, repeating exactly only after 18·61 years. During each month, as we have seen, the moon will rise at points lying between (roughly) north-east and south-east. Let us concentrate on the northernmost rising of the moon each month. Suppose that this year the northernmost rising point just happens to coincide with the sun's midsummer rising position, marked by the Stonehenge axis about 40° north of east. Each successive month, we would find the northernmost rising point slightly further north, until after 4·65 years the moon's northernmost rising would be 50° north of east. (Its southernmost rising changes similarly, to 50° south of east, so during each month the moon rises at different points along a 100° arc of horizon.) It has now reached what Alexander Thom calls 'major standstill' – although the moon rises at different points during the month, its northernmost limit stays almost constant. For the next 9·3 years the northernmost rising point retreats again until it is only 30° north of east, at 'minor standstill'. Over another 4·65 years it returns to its original position, having completed a swing in northernmost rising position of 18·6 years duration.

There should thus be eight important directions indicated at a lunar observatory, lying at angles of 50° and 30° north and south of the east point, and at the same angles relative to the west point to mark moonset. Newham pointed out that the other two sides of the Station Stone rectangle (92 to 93, and 94 to 91) mark moonrise and moonset at times of major standstill. Hawkins found other lines, using a diagonal (91 to 93), the centre of the rectangle, and alignments with empty stone-holes. These alignments have provoked much discussion. Purely by chance, we would expect some lines at Stonehenge to point in astronomically important directions, but there seems little doubt that more than coincidence is involved. Hawkins estimates there is less than one chance in a million of his alignments being accidental, Professor Hoyle estimates the odds as 160:1 against. Either way, the evidence is convincing, and it is supported by Alexander Thom's measurements at megalithic observatories in Scotland.

'Peter' Newham showed that another set of holes (in *fact* now roughly dated at 4700 BC) also provide accurate sun and moon lines as seen from the Station Stones and the Heel Stone. To be visible from the higher level of the centre of Stonehenge, these posts in the vicinity of the present-day car park must have been at least ten metres (11 yards) high, and excavations show their bases were suitably massive, some three quarters of a metre (30 inches) in diameter (Newham 1972, pp. 23–5).

Even more unexpectedly, Newham found strong evidence that the earliest phase, Stonehenge I, was a lunar rather than a solar observatory. The entrance causeway to Stonehenge I (which consisted of the bank, ditch, Heel Stone and Aubrey Holes) was not centred on midsummer sunrise like the later Avenue, but was slightly further to the north (to the left, as seen from within the bank). From the centre of Stonehenge I, the gap spans just that part of the sky from the moon's rising at major standstill (furthest north) to its halfway rising position. In the gap, moreover, there are small post-holes in a rough grid, in just the positions expected if a post had been set up each midwinter to mark the rising of the full moon. The six lines of holes seem to show that the observations were carried on for six 18·6 year cycles, or some 110 years (Newham 1972, pp. 15–16). These post-holes may well be the remains of the 'instrument' with which our ancestors discovered the lunar cycle.

As seen from the centre of Stonehenge, the right-hand causeway posts might have stood in front of the Heel Stone; and it is unlikely that the latter was erected after the observations were concluded, to record permanently the moon's northernmost rising point halfway between major and minor standstills (Wood 1978, p. 163).

To the left of the Heel Stone are four large holes which once held wooden posts, known as the A posts. The gaps between these may have been semi-permanent markers for following the moon's northernmost rising points as it gradually progressed northwards to major standstill (Brinckerhoff 1976). R. F. Brinckerhoff has also discovered extraordinary evidence linking

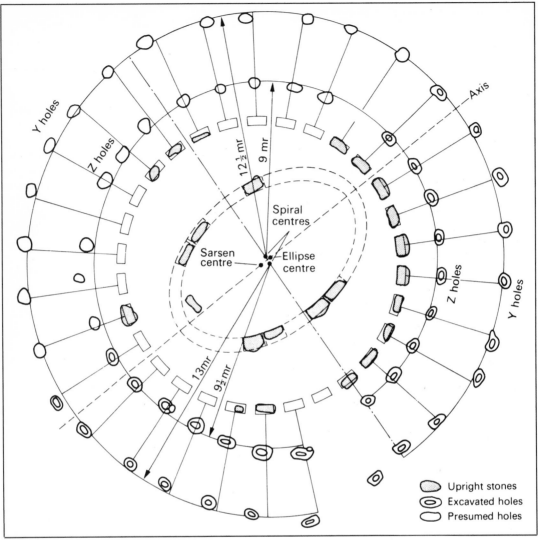

FIGURE 10

the massive sarsen circle of Stonehenge III with lunar observations. He had done what few have considered – climbed up on to the lintels of the circle, on the side nearest the Avenue – and on the top surfaces he found some small holes, from 4 to 25 cm (1½ to 10 inches) in diameter. Although these may be natural Brinckerhoff has been able to show that wooden 'wands' (as he called them) placed in these holes would have lined up with the A posts and the moon's northernmost rising limit when seen from the opposite side of the lintel ring. In each case there is an offset of 0·2°, as one would expect from the changing angle of the Earth's axis between the times of Stonehenge I and Stone-

FIGURE 10 'Stonehenge IIIa. Thom's geometrical constructions for the Sarsen Circle, the Trilithons, and the Y and the Z holes are superimposed. Based on diagrams in the *Journal for the History of Astronomy 5*, by kind permission of Dr M. A. Hoskin'. This concise diagram and caption appear in *Sun, Moon and Standing Stones* (1978) by John Edwin Wood. 1 mr (megalithic rod) = 2·40 m. Professor Alexander Thom's surveys indicate that the megalithic yard and rod (two and a half times the my) and their multiples in whole numbers, were used in Stonehenge IIIa (c. 2000 BC) and *perhaps* in Stonehenge I (c. 2800 BC)! It can be seen that the geometry of the Y and Z holes created spirals.

FIGURE 11 Six important astronomical alignments found by Professor Alexander Thom to centre on Stonehenge.

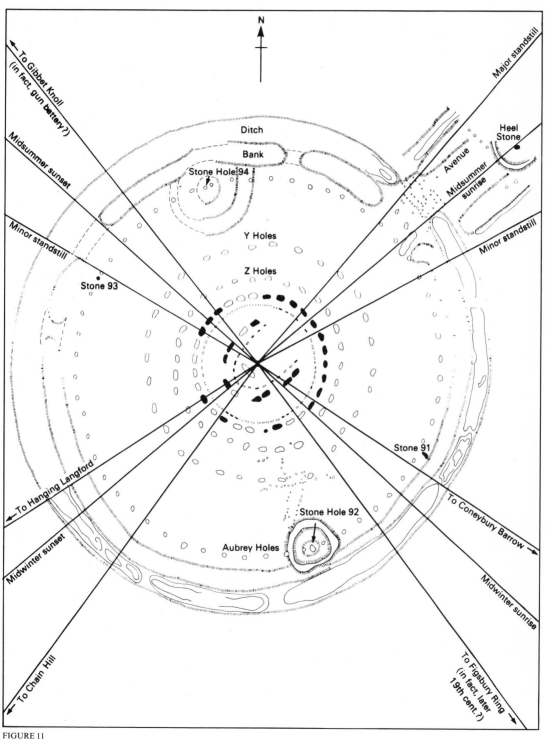

N

To Gibbet Knoll
(in fact, gun battery?)

Midsummer sunset

Minor standstill

Stone 93

To Hanging Langford

Midwinter sunset

To Chain Hill

Major standstill

Heel Stone

Ditch

Bank

Stone Hole 94

Y Holes

Z Holes

Avenue

Midsummer sunrise

Minor standstill

Stone 91

To Coneybury Barrow

Stone Hole 92

Aubrey Holes

Midwinter sunrise

To Figsbury Ring
(in fact, later 19th cent.?)

FIGURE 11

henge III. Brinckerhoff's suggested sightlines would have been blocked by the Great Trilithon, however, so his hypothesis is only sound if this Trilithon was erected after the surrounding sarsen circle which it was not.

Professor Thom and his family of colleagues have searched for distant horizon markers along the important lunar directions. They have proposed that some prehistoric mounds may have been the bases for large wooden horizon foresights (as Waltire and others have before them), but excavation is needed to discover whether some barrows are as early as Stonehenge (Thom, Thom and Thom 1975). The Barrow Groups are discussed in Part 5.

The Thoms have suggested that the siting of Stonehenge was to provide good, not too distant horizons in the important solar and lunar directions. But Newham has pointed out a (possibly) more important consideration, and it relates to one of the oddest of the many coincidences among the mysteries of Stonehenge: the Station Stones form an accurate rectangle, with two parallel sides indicating the midsummer sunrise, while the other two show the moonrise and moonset at major standstill . . . and it is *only* at the latitude of Stonehenge that these directions are perpendicular; elsewhere the Station Stones would have formed a parallelogram rather than a rectangle. Fifteen years later, in his 1978 survey, Atkinson discovered the hole for Stone 94, and found that the angles at the corners of the rectangle deviate almost insignificantly from right angles, the largest discrepancy being only 1° 2′ (Atkinson 1978). If Stonehenge were situated only 50 miles (80 km) north or south of its present position, these angles would be fully 2° off a right angle (Hoyle 1977, p. 36). As Stonehenge I appears to have been purely a lunar observatory, it seems unlikely it was constructed here just because of the coincidences of those important sun and moon directions. What is much more likely is that Stonehenge I was chosen from amongst several other similar observatories in England for further development after the unique property of its latitude was discovered.

PLATE 30

The later (bluestone) Stonehenge II phase and the (sarsen) Stonehenge III phase seem to have less astronomical significance, apart from the midsummer sunrise alignment, and just possibly the holes on top of the lintels. Hawkins has discovered that the view from the narrow Trilithon arches through the gaps between the stones of the sarsen circle show important sun and moon rising and setting points, but these

PLATE 30 Sir Fred Hoyle (drawn by Richard Tollast in 1972 for St John's College, Cambridge).

FIGURE 12 The alignments found by Gerald Hawkins and included in his controversial book *Stonehenge Decoded*, 1966. (After John Edwin Wood.)

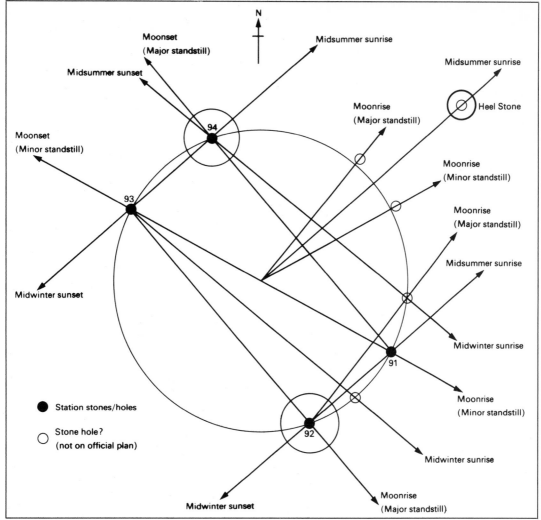

FIGURE 12

gaps are surely too wide for accurate observations. Professor Owen Gingerich, of Harvard
University, has suggested that Stonehenge III is
a splendid, but non-functional monument to
the earlier important observatory of Stonehenge I (and possibly II, depending on the date
of the Station Stones). He draws a parallel with
the five impressive stone observatories of Jai
Singh, erected in eighteenth-century India long
after the telescope had made such observatories
obsolete (Gingerich 1957).

Today, the most controversial topic in the
discussion of the astronomy of Stonehenge is
no longer whether it was an observatory, but
whether it was also a computer – a calculator
specifically designed to predict eclipses of the
sun and moon. Gerald Hawkins published a
second paper in *Nature* in June 1964, showing
how the solar and lunar observations might
have been supplemented by the movement of
six markers around the 56 Aubrey Holes,
advancing them one hole each year. The
presence of a marker in a particular hole
indicated the approach of an eclipse near
midsummer or midwinter. The simplicity of
Hawkin's computer arrangement is connected
with regularities in the occurrence of eclipses.
But it is too simple: Fred Hoyle and others have
pointed out that many of the predicted eclipses
would not be visible from Stonehenge (which
admittedly might not be relevant – why should
they have been, there?); a few do not occur at

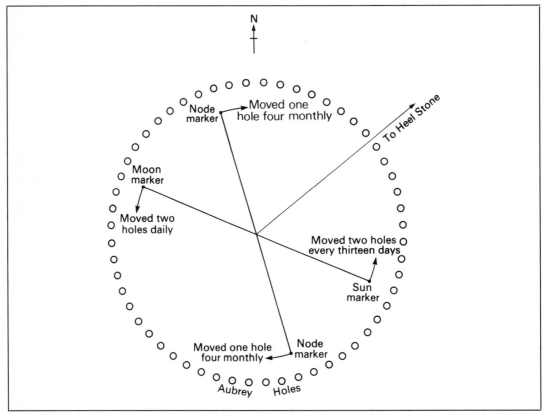

FIGURE 13

all; and, lastly, Hawkins's system predicts only a small fraction of all the eclipses which *are* visible from Stonehenge (Hoyle 1972).

There are other ways of predicting eclipses. Professor Thom has evidence that Scottish megalithic astronomers used very distant sky-lines to investigate small wobbles in the moon's motion which are related to eclipses. If his putative horizon markers on Salisbury Plain are of the Stonehenge era, perhaps the method was first perfected in Southern England. An even simpler method, at a site with a flat horizon, is to measure the rising point of the moon relative to the sun; during an eclipse danger period, it rises exactly 180° away from sunset direction. The Aubrey Holes, on this

hypothesis, were intended as a large protractor with the observer at the centre (Colton 1969).

Professor Hoyle countered Hawkins's 'computer' role for the Aubrey Holes with another suggestion. The Aubrey Hole circle could be a model of the sky: by moving a stone marker for the sun two holes every thirteen days it would make one circuit each year, and similarly a moon marker would be moved two holes each day to take it round a full cycle in a month. Another pair of stone markers always opposite each other, and moved three holes per year complete the primitive 'computer'. (Astronomically, these represent the nodes of the moon's orbit.) An eclipse will occur when a node marker lies in, or immediately next to, a hole containing one of the other markers, if 'sun' and 'moon' are either opposite (lunar eclipse) or in the same hole (solar eclipse).

Hoyle's is an exact eclipse predictor – except in so far as the 'sun' and 'moon' markers need fine adjustment. The 'sun' moves round in 364 instead of $365\frac{1}{4}$ days, and the 'moon' in 28 rather than 27·3 days. More serious, however, is the criticism that it would be extremely difficult to set up. The nodes are invisible points in the sky: their motion is only obvious when the theory of the moon's motion is understood. It is difficult to understand how megalithic man could have deduced the positions and motions of the nodes – and to reposition the node markers as they gradually drifted away from the correct positions.

Yet all too often, even in the recent past, archaeologists have underestimated the capabilities of ancient man. The intellectual heights of these people are difficult to gauge – some would say without the evidence of writing . . . and yet is it not all about us, but on such a huge scale that we (literally) cannot believe it? The thousands of stones on the hills and plains of Britain, the impressive pile of Stonehenge, they *are* the written proof that megalithic man was capable of observing the rising and setting of sun and moon extremely accurately. We must therefore believe he could interpret his results (possibly in ways we have not yet divined) so as to predict the terrifying disappearance of sun or moon in an eclipse. He must have experienced it often (*per se*) – so why *did* he have to know *precisely* when one would occur? What effects do an eclipse have? When we know the answer to this question, perhaps we will be at the heart of the matter of Stonehenge.

FIGURE 13   Professor Sir Fred Hoyle proposed in his book *On Stonehenge* (1977) that the 56 Aubrey Holes could have been a model of the sky, used for calculating the occurrence of eclipses.

PLATE 31   An engraving (by W. Bidgood) of the thin patterned plate of gold found in Barrow 158 (Bush Barrow), near Wilsford, on the breast of a skeleton. It is 18 cm (7 ins) long.

PLATE 31

Other theories

One modern researcher who has done much to 'open up' discussion of the mysteries of Stonehenge is John Michell. Chapter five in his *The View Over Atlantis* (Michell 1966) sets out the view that it was designed according to the geometry and the numbers of the square of the sun's dimensions, and that the tetractys (diamond) of equilateral triangles contained within the mystical 'vesica piscis' formed its basis. I am reminded of the patterns on the plate of gold, found upon the breast of a skeleton in barrow 158 (see Plate 31). Michell thinks of Stonehenge as a monument to a former cosmology, to which the Great Pyramid also stands as testimony, enshrining a very ancient concept of universal law. Modern surveying techniques tell us all, and the process of interpreting facts is under way. But not without controversy. The whole subject of 'earth mysteries' vexes many

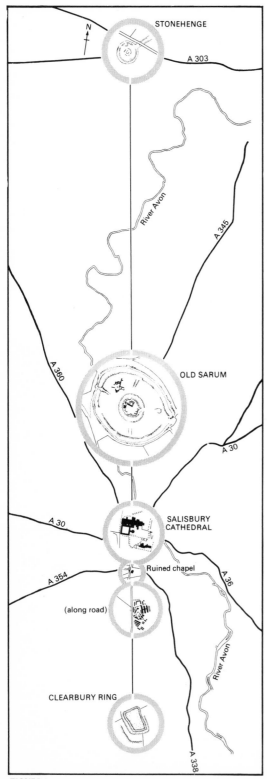

FIGURE 14

commentators; thus Geoffrey Grigson concludes a book review in *Country Life* on 18th May 1978:

'I cannot myself see all that difference between the late Dr Otto Muck on Atlantis and some modern pseudo- or semi-archaeologists – or archaeologists – on Stonehenge and Avebury. Dottiness is endemic, especially dottiness about the past; it is too strong, I suppose, to be more or less wiped out like the smallpox in our time.

For myself I would as soon believe in Atlantis and the asteroid as in earth circles and stone circles mathematically devised by our neolithic ancestors to give them advanced news of the heavens.'

John Michell also points out in his book that the axis of Glastonbury Abbey points directly to Stonehenge. He has been responsible for the growth in recent years of research into what is now known as the ley system. The word 'ley' was coined by Alfred Watkins at the beginning of this century, and it has cropped up in many 'earth mystery' books; a ley is an invisible straight line on the landscape, along which will be found precisely placed sites, constructions, and deliberate alterations, all of pre-Christian antiquity, which may also be a sighted trackway, the purpose of which has yet to be conclusively confirmed. In fact Watkins's rediscovery of the existence of such alignments was pre-dated by Colonel Johnston, Director-General of the Ordnance Survey in the 1890s, who pointed out to Lockyer and Penrose the odd fact that a straight line can be drawn on the

---

FIGURE 14   The so-called 'Stonehenge ley'. It runs from the centre of the monument exactly 6 miles (9·7 km) to the well in the centre of Old Sarum, a further 2 miles (3·2 km) to the Chapter House of Salisbury Cathedral, a quarter of a mile (0·4 m) to an old ruined chapel, and a final 3 miles (4·8 km) to the edge of Clearbury Ring (or Camp). The extent of the alignment can be expressed exactly as 90 furlongs.

PLATE 32 (*right*)   Looking along an alignment (or ley) which can be tracked from Stonehenge, to Old Sarum (from where this view is taken), to Salisbury Cathedral, and on to Clearbury Ring (or Camp) on the horizon.

map between Stonehenge, Old Sarum, Salisbury Cathedral, and Clearbury Ring (see Figure 14). Avebury Church and Silbury Hill are also on an alignment (see Part 5). Major C. F. Tyler developed Alfred Watkins's ideas in his 1939 booklet *The Geometrical Arrangement of Ancient Sites*, and offers a curious diagram on page 36, depicting 'circular leys', concentric circles radiating from Stonehenge (or rather the west side of its bank) in multiples of 950·4 feet (288 m), upon which occur earthworks, bar-

rows, and churches. Grigson's strictures would have applied to such visions. Nevertheless map work around Stonehenge certainly reveals a great number of alignments passing through the monument and further sound research is needed before final comment can be made.

The interesting question of whether any of the stones have medicinal properties was recently brought up again by another protagonist in 'earth mysteries' literature. The dowser, Guy Underwood, suggests in his fas-

cinating book *The Patterns of the Past* (1968) one of the stones *always* holds water because it is located above a blind spring. Now the church font holds water which is sanctified or made holy for christenings – does this connect up with Geoffrey of Monmouth's comment that 'there is not a stone without healing virtue'? In Anglo-Saxon., the words 'holy' and 'healing' are cognate. Underwood's book explores in great detail the blind springs, geodetic lines, aquastats and so on at the site, and proposes that they dictated the location of Stonehenge. And so the theories multiply.

FIGURE 15   A drawing by Guy Underwood, made in 1956, for his book *The Patterns Of The Past* (1969). It shows, he wrote, 'the network of aquastats within the Great Circle, and the manner in which they form small enclosures into one of which every stone, recumbent or otherwise, fits without overlapping. This argues that recumbent stones could not be fallen stones, but were shaped and precisely placed within the enclosures and for some good reason – possibly as mark stones or occasionally as altars.' In a footnote to this provoking passage, Underwood adds the speculation that if Stonehenge did have a main altar, 'the most likely stone for this purpose would seem to be No. 160a.'

PLATE 33   The mysteries of Stonehenge have always inspired . . . fresh ideas. The Scotsman Hamish MacHuisdean sent his to the Wiltshire Archaeological and Natural History Society on 1 October 1932, with a confident letter attached.

PLATE 34   One man's dream. A replica of Stonehenge, beside the Columbia River, Washington, U.S.A.; it is part of a trust left to Maryhill Museum of Art by its founder Samuel Hill.

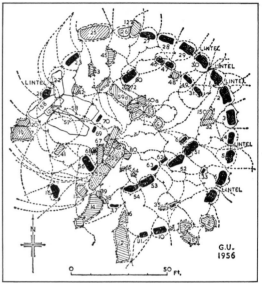

FIGURE 15

TELEPHONE:
DOUGLAS 531.

CODEX:
A.B.C. 5TH EDITION.
BENTLEY'S PRIVATE.

141 BATH STREET,
GLASGOW. C.2.
1st October 1932.

The Secretary,
Wiltshire Arch. & Natural History Socy,
Clyffe Vicarage,
SWINDON. Wilts.

STONEHENGE.

Dear Sir,

    I noted that some scientists are at a loss to understand why STONEHENGE was placed exactly where it is rather than at the south pole or Timbuctoo.

    The enclosed blue print showing some geodetic points that are linked up with STONEHENGE will be of interest to your members, and it is sent to the Society with my compliments.

        I am,

        Yours faithfully,

        Hamish MacHuisdean.

1 Encl.

PLATE 33

PLATE 34 △

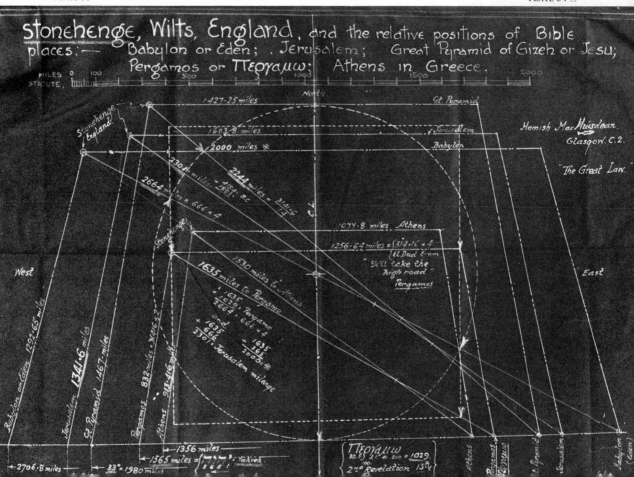

Huius tẽpe p. iiii. mẽses
constantinopoli circuitonis
locis terra fluctuauit quã
orã oĩbs scelatis ? iacẽ
dina iuitate ? admonĩte
ut sic clamantes os ca
nerent: sc̃s deus. sc̃s
fortis. sc̃s ? immor
talis miserere nobis
nil aliud
annunciãte. Quo facto cessauit tremor.

Hoc tẽpe sc̃s Paulinus
romane ciui
tatis epc̃, p cuiusdam filio
uidue se tradidit ? i affricam
deductus fuit. de quo scribit bs
gregorius i dialogo suo.

Zenon

Iste zenõ
imperauit ã
nis. xvii.

Huius tẽpe iussa ? sc̃s Theodo ric[us] r. G.

Aurelius ambrosius

Stonhenges iuxta Ambesburi in anglia sit

Hoc anno chorea gigantum
De hybernia uĩ: arte in
lim deuecta apud stonhenges.

Iste au
relius ambro
sius filius con
stantini ã
nis. xx.
.iiii. B.

Eyse

Anastasius

Iste anastasius
imperauit ãnis. xxvii.

Tẽpe gelasii pape inuenitur
corpus bĩ barnabe apli ? eu
uangelium qd ppria manu
scripserat [illegible] mathei.

Huius ? tẽpe
sc̃a ? iuentio
corporis sci mi
chaelis i mon
te tumba.

Huius tẽpe floruerunt isti sci

Depositio sci
remigii archiepi

Remigius. Arnulphus. Maxencius. Leodegarius.

Sc̃us Dubricius.

Huius tẽpe fl...
in britannia
dubricius ur
gionẽ archie...

Sc̃s Daniel epc̃

Vortigern

Iste in
tẽpe

Hoc tẽ...
antiho...
? lup' ...
laud' ...
brannu...
larũ

Iste
filius h...
ti annis
regnauit
...cauga.

Part 2

In Art and Imagination

Painted – Recorded – Interpreted Invoked

'The mysterious monument of Stonehenge, standing remote on a bare and boundless heath, as much unconnected with the events of past ages as it is with the uses of the present, carries you back beyond all historical record into the obscurity of a totally unknown period . . . still the thing was ingenious.'

– John Constable's own caption to his watercolour when it was exhibited at the Royal Academy in 1836.

The artists who have given us their impressions of Stonehenge have traditionally taken liberties with their subject; but the earliest, working one supposes from the description of travellers, owe almost everything to their imaginations. The first recorded likeness, in a fourteenth-century manuscript of the 'Scala Mundi' in Corpus Christi College, Cambridge (Plate 35), appears to be a cross between a child's playpen and a backgammon board. The next, a fourteenth-century Romance, shows Merlin, the supposed builder of the monument, so large that any sense of its size is lost; the Trilithon could be any doorpost (Plate 36). The earliest recognizable view of the entire monument is the engraving of 1571 in the British Museum by 'R. F.' which was used with slight variations by the Dutch author 'L. D.' in his

Short Account of English Events, 1574 (Plate 37), and reproduced by William Camden in the later edition of his *Britannia* in 1660 (Plate 38). All the subsequent uses of this engraving show even further fanciful additions of undulating uprights, sausage-shaped imposts, concentric walls, and fairy castles in the background, until the site becomes scarcely recognizable.

That there was however a degree of familiarity with the general appearance of Stonehenge at this period is shown by the proliferation of county maps, such as that of John Speed in 1610, showing the site in the cartouche. Earlier map makers, such as Christopher Saxon in 1579, show a Trilithon for Stonehenge, but none so charmingly as Michael Drayton in his fantasy poem *Polyalbion* of 1622, which employs the conceit that England's historic sites are warring amongst themselves to claim title to be the Wonder of the Land. The accompanying maps are equally and delightfully fantastical. It makes no matter that on

PLATE 35 (*left*)   The earliest-known illustration of Stonehenge, in a fourteenth-century manuscript.

C ils sunt as portes aixes
M ...rer deuant et de traners
B iens ont en poingte et bon bote
e t bien retradt et bon trole
b ...e par force a la menom
A e purrent fair grendre un torn

T irahez uous dit celstuy en uus
A par force ne ferez plus
O ...tortez ...engine et demon
M enl... ...tu de cozp aller
S ...ut alast auant en bestuot
e ...tour ...dast le leue ...ut
C ...hde ge fist grestan
S e ...il ...ilt ...ni...ons
...ut as les ...retius rapeler

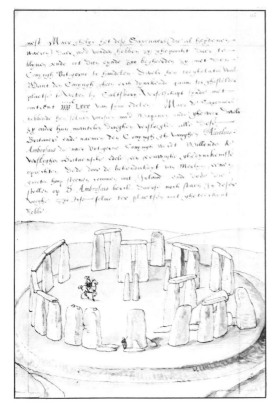

PLATE 37

PLATE 38

these maps Stonehenge looks more like a dolmen than a circle or even a Trilithon (a dolmen would have been a familiar sight to any of these draughtsmen): its recurrence in maps of Wiltshire bears witness to its fame.

We are indebted, as Part 1 has shown, to that inquisitive and energetic monarch Charles II for our first views of Stonehenge approximately as it stood. At his request the architect Inigo Jones visited the site, and left us the somewhat dry but doubtless faithful impressions later published in his book *Stone-heng Restored*, 1665. The King's reaction to these is not recorded, but it is a fact that he requested John Aubrey (like Inigo Jones, a member of the newly-founded Royal Society) to continue the study; in 1663 it is recorded that he 'took a review for the King' and sketched it. In fact Aubrey had been visiting the site for many

years, and his painstaking work resulted not only in the first detailed knowledge of the site, but also in numerous watercolour sketches in which the awkward attempts at accuracy are enlivened by the inclusion of figures in a charming 'naïve' style. It must have been a subject of some regret to Aubrey that not only could he not stay on his horses, he could not

PLATE 36 (*left*)   The second earliest-known representation of the monument, showing Merlin advising upon its construction, in accordance with the legend initiated by Geoffrey of Monmouth.

PLATE 37   One of the first detailed drawings of Stonehenge, in a manuscript by the Dutchman Lucas de Heere, dated 1574.

PLATE 38   An engraving in the 1660 edition of William Camden's *Britannia Descriptio*, which was based on the 1571 engraving by 'R. F.'

draw the animals either. His manuscripts with these drawings are now preserved in the Bodleian Library.

Following enthusiastically in his footsteps came William Stukeley, whose work is discussed elsewhere. The sketches he made during his surveys in the 1720s, although more accomplished than Aubrey's, have much of the same primitive charm – somewhat lost in the engravings in his invaluable book on Stonehenge published in 1740. These must however have had a wide circulation and influence among topographical artists of the period and in subsequent years; the factual approach reinforcing the style popularised by the well-known engraving (sometimes known as 'The Bustards') by David Loggan, c. 1690 (Plate 39). Presumably any number of amateur artists recorded the scene in the simple, even clumsy

style of Edmund Prideaux in 1716, but in the main the views taken of Stonehenge during the mid and late 1700s were simple records made for the studies of the antiquarians of the period.

In the late eighteenth century artists in watercolour began to visit the monument, and to make studies which were not related to any

PLATE 39 'Prospects' of Stonehenge from the west (top) and south (below), engraved by David Loggan, c. 1690. Bustards, then a familiar sight on Salisbury Plain, are seen in flight.

PLATE 40 A severe study by Paul Sandby, c. 1755, who was at one time a draughtsman for the Ordnance Survey.

PLATE 41 An elegant watercolour by Samuel Prout, made in 1805; large fragments of stone can be seen in the foreground.

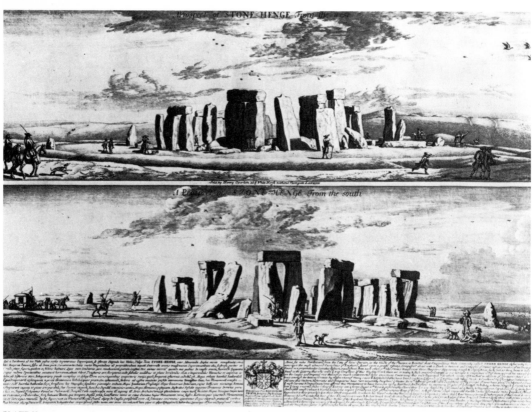

PLATE 39

PLATE 41 ▽

illustrative purpose but for paintings in their own right. In the mid eighteenth century Paul Sandby made the straightforward sketch one might expect from an Ordnance Survey draughtsman, as he was at the time, although it does appear that he has tidied up the scenes somewhat (Plate 40). The solidity of his stones is in marked contrast to the drunken dancers of Thomas Rowlandson's sketch, c. 1784, in which the passing carriage, almost as tall as the Trilithons, serves to further reduce any vestige of grandeur in the scene. Other late eighteenth-century and early nineteenth-century water-colourists worked much in the tradition of Sandby, giving more or less accurate renderings of the state of the site, with or without the traditional flock of sheep, and often following the widely-circulated view in John Britton's *The Beauties of Wiltshire* of Stonehenge from the South-West, directing the eye through the Trilithon in which the summer solstice sun rises. Examples of this are Samuel Prout's watercolour of 1805 (Plate 41), Philip Crocker's view c. 1812, and George Engleheart's of 1820. A slightly different but equally popular view-point is seen in James Malton's watercolour exhibited in 1800 (Plate 42); substantially accurate, it includes the Trilithon behind the leaning stone which fell in 1797, being based on his own sketch of the previous year. The dry topographical approach to the site was still popular at the start of this century, as can be seen in the coloured woodcut by W. Giles.

More talented artists, however, were viewing Stonehenge in the full glare of the Romantic response to 'the Sublime', in which context it was described by William Gilpin as 'awfully magnificent . . . it is not the elegance of the work, but the grandeur of the idea that strikes us' (Gilpin 1798). Artists such as Thomas Hearne, c. 1785, and Thomas Girtin in 1794 strove to convey this impression of Sublime

PLATE 42 A charming and yet precise view by James Malton, based on sketches done in 1796, the year before the fall of stones, and exhibited in 1800.

PLATE 42

Grandeur, and even Gothic dread, by bringing the elements to the aid of art. Lines from Wordsworth's *Tintern Abbey* (written in 1798) are recalled:

'. . . And I have felt
A presence that disturbs me with the joy
Of elevated thoughts; a sense sublime
Of something far more deeply interfused
Whose dwelling is the light of setting suns,
And the round ocean and the living air,
And the blue sky, and in the mind of man:
A motion and a spirit, that impels
All thinking things, all objects of all thought,
And rolls through all things.'

Artists' use of overcast or storm-tossed skies to create the desired atmosphere of wonder foreshadows the studies of the two greatest painters of the Romantic era, John Constable (1776–1837) and J. M. W. Turner (1776–1851). Both painted Stonehenge from close by, and from the fork in the main road, a view also chosen by William Turner of Oxford, very probably in imitation of his great contemporaries. In this view as seen by Constable (1820) and by Turner (1811–13), important differences are revealed. In 'Stonehenge, Sunset' details of landscape are subordinated to the subtle effects of the sky, and in 'Stonehenge, Daybreak' (Plate 43) Turner gives as much weight to the waggon and shepherds with their flock, as he does to the silhouette of stones on the skyline. In Constable's study however (reproduced in the mezzotint version by David Lucas, Plate 44), the site dominates the picture in spite of its distance, owing to the novel addition of the sun setting behind the Heel Stone. In this way, even though Turner's sky in this view is the more expressively dynamic, Constable's eye for detail – including a faithfully exact setting down of the stones' positions – gives his painting the greater force. This is even more true of the comparison between the two close-up views, Turner's of 1828 and Constable's of 1835.

Turner's view, shown in the engraved reproduction for his 'England and Wales' series of 1827–38 (Plate 46), invokes the Sublime with a vengeance. The melodramatic storminess of the sky is echoed in the theatricality of the sheep and shepherd struck down in the foreground; the stones themselves are placed according to Turner's imperious design rather than in their actual positions. The whole effect is one of fiery grandeur, well fitting the elemental ferocity of current folklore about the monument and its obscure past. Constable's study, however, takes as its starting point his careful and sober pencil sketch of 1820, from sketches made on the spot on 15 July that year (Plate 47). The sketch of 1820 and the final impassioned version of 1835 reveal how far his sense of the mystery and even doom evoked by Stonehenge had deepened in his years of bereavement since the death of his wife and two closest friends. The disposition of the stones remains true to life; the sky, however, which he had earlier described as 'The keynote . . . and chief Organ of sentiment' has been transformed by the departing storm and double rainbow into a force almost alive, by which the stones themselves are bowed, and man rendered insubstantial. He certainly avoids here what he describes as the general approach to Stonehenge: 'Its literal representation as a stone quarry has been often enough done.' 'Clearly, Constable has given us the most compelling and evocative rendering of Stonehenge in Britain,' wrote Louis Hawes in his catalogue (to which I am indebted) to the Victoria and Albert Museum's 1975 exhibition 'Constable's Stonehenge' (Plate 45).

Other artists have taken inspiration from Stonehenge to use as they will. The greatest of these is the visionary William Blake (1757–1827), who characteristically absorbs it, somewhat modified, into his own mythological system. Blake was apprenticed in his teens to James Basire who was the official engraver to the Society of Antiquaries, so he would have been familiar from an early age with current

PLATE 43 A mezzotint by J. M. W. Turner, after his 'Stonehenge at Daybreak', c. 1813.

PLATE 44 A mezzotint by David Lucas, published in 1845, after a lost study by John Constable.

△ PLATE 43

PLATE 44 ▽

theories concerning Stonehenge, and with its general appearance. (The connection of the Basire workshop with The Society continued into the next generation, incidentally, and it was the younger James Basire who engraved Philip Crocker's fine plates for Colt-Hoare's *Wiltshire*.) Blake strongly believed in the connection between Stonehenge and the Druids, and he associated the Druids with all that is negative, restrictive and destructive in humanity. For Blake, history has consisted of cycles, each ending in a pile of stones; Egypt and Mexico have pyramids crumbling to dust, Nineveh, Babylon, Tyre and Rome have their

ruined cities, and the Druids have left Stonehenge. For him Druidism is the most debased form of religion, associated with human sacrifice which in his work is also symbolic of spiritual repression; he wrote in *Jerusalem* (1804–20): 'I see a wicker Idol woven round Jerusalem's children.' In this people were burned alive – as shown in Plate 48, from Aylett Sammes's *Britannia Antiqua Illustrata* (Sammes 1676) – and with the repressive lawgiving inseparable from all organized religions, which destroyed the true Godhead of imagination in man. Only its unfettered power can bring us in touch with Divinity:

'If the doors of Perception were cleansed every thing would appear to man as it is, infinite. For man has closed himself up, till he sees all things thro' narrow chinks of his cavern.'

The correspondence here between the eye and the Trilithon as shown in *Jerusalem* (Plate

PLATE 45 (*previous page*)   This watercolour by John Constable, executed in 1835, is one of the most famous representations of Stonehenge.

PLATE 46   An engraving of his 1828 watercolour for J. M. W. Turner's 'England and Wales' series.

PLATE 46

49) is clear. For Blake, a stone is the ultimate symbol of opacity, and is therefore the ideal medium for conveying a reduction from the living to the deathly or Satanic – a symbolism pervasive throughout the Old and New Testaments – witness the rolling away of the stone of Christ's tomb. The Druidic association with mathematics, to Blake another symbol of limitation and rigidity – circumscribing the force of imagination – to him would be evident in the very shape of Stonehenge. In every sense the monument was for him the ideal poetic and figurative expression of evil, even to be evoked when describing the condemnation of Christ:

'Cold, dark, opake, the Assembly met twelve-fold in Amalek

Twelve rocky unshaped forms, terrific forms of torture and woe,

Such seemed the synagogue to distant view . . .'

In Blake's hands the stones, recognizably based on the Stonehenge Trilithons though shown separately or with the inspiration of Stukeley's Avebury 'serpent', take on a chillingly hard, cold, and threatening nature, deadening in their contrast with his usual exuberantly flowing line (Plate 50).

In the same period, artists in pursuit of the Sublime requisitioned Stonehenge as a prop for their essays in narrative painting. Thomas Jones, in his canvas of 1774 'The Bard', illustrating Gray's poem (Plate 51), again invokes the Druidic folklore of Stonehenge by placing it in the background of the painting in which the Welsh bard (Druidic no doubt) flees the British army in a suitably dramatic landscape. Jones has apparently here embarked on an experiment to prove his own observation on a visit in

PLATE 47

PLATE 48

PLATE 47   One of three pencil sketches made by John Constable on 15 July 1820, which were the basis for his dramatic 1835 watercolour (Plate 45).

PLATE 48   'The Ceremony observed in sacrificing Men to their Idols, in a Wicker Image . . .'; a plate in *Britannia Antiqua Illustrata* by Aylett Sammes, 1676.

Before the face of Albion, a mighty threatning Form.

His bosom wide & shoulders huge overspreading wondrous
Bear Three strong sinewy Necks & Three awful & terrible Heads
Three Brains in contradictory council brooding incessantly.
Neither daring to put in act its councils, fearing each other.
Therefore rejecting Ideas as nothing & holding all Wisdom
To consist, in the agreements & disagreements of Ideas.
Plotting to devour Albions Body of Humanity & Love.

Such Form the aggregate of the Twelve Sons of Albion took; & such
Their appearance when combind: but often by birth-pangs & loud groans
They divide to Twelve: the key-bones & the chest dividing in pain
Disclose a hideous orifice; thence issuing the Giant-brood
Arise as the smoke of the furnace, shaking the rocks from sea to sea.
And there they combine into Three Forms, named Bacon & Newton & Locke
In the Oak Groves of Albion which overspread all the Earth.

Imputing Sin & Righteousness to Individuals; Rahab
Sat deep within him hid: his Feminine Power unreveald
Brooding Abstract Philosophy. to destroy Imagination. the Divine-
Humanity A Three-fold Wonder: feminine: most beautiful: Three-fold
Each within other. On her white marble & even Neck, her Heart
Inorb'd and bonified: with locks of shadowing modesty, shining
Over her beautiful Female features, soft flourishing in beauty
Beams mild, all love and all perfection, that when the lips
Recieve a kiss from Gods or Men. a threefold kiss returns
From the pressd loveliness: so her whole immortal form three-fold
Three-fold embrace returns: consuming lives of Gods & Men
In fires of beauty melting them as gold & silver in the furnace
Her Brain enlabyrinths the whole heaven of her bosom & loins
To put in act what her Heart wills: O who can withstand her power
Her name is Vala in Eternity: in Time her name is Rahab

1769: '. . . I cannot help thinking, but that its Situation adds much to its grandeur and Magnificence, the vast surrounding Void not affording any thing to disturb the Eye, or divert the imagination. . . . Whereas, were this wonderful Mass situated amidst high rocks, lofty mountains, and hanging Woods . . . it would lose much of its own grandeur as a Single Object.' Similarly, Henry Thompson in his painting of 1811 'Salisbury Plain – Peasants in a Storm' also known as 'Distress by Land' (Plate 52), uses the site, balanced on the left by three burial mounds, to convey a bleakly ominous feeling of threat. The difference in effect is somehow enhanced by the careful painting of Stonehenge – careful as it would have to be for the cautious and literal-minded Sir Richard Colt-Hoare to have bought it.

Fanciful reconstructions in the background provide further instances of artists' appropriations of Stonehenge. James Barry (1741–1806), again invoking the Celtic - and Druidic - connotations of Stonehenge, placed it in the background, smaller and halfway up a hill, in his painting (dated between 1774–80) of the death of Cordelia from Shakespeare's *King Lear,* Act V, Sc. 3. This was undertaken for J. & J.

PLATE 49 (*left*)   A full moon seen through a stylised Great Trilithon, in Plate 70 of William Blake's *Jerusalem.*

PLATE 50   Stonehenge supplants Avebury as the focus of the 'dragon lines' (no doubt inspired by William Stukeley's theory), in Plate 100 of William Blake's *Jerusalem.*

PLATE 50

Boydell's series of engravings, known popularly as the 'Shakespeare Gallery', published in 1803 (Plate 53). A contrasting use of the circle reconstructed was by the American painter Thomas Cole (1801–1848), in the second of his panel series 'The Course of Empire' (1832–6). Whilst the structure is closely modelled on Barry's, there is no sense of threat in the panel which represents 'The Arcadian State'.

Fancy runs completely riot in two representations which purport to show how Stonehenge would have looked in its Druidical heyday. In a book by Samual Rush Meyrick and Charles Hamilton Smith, entitled *Costume of the Original Inhabitants of the British Isles,* published in 1815, we see Stonehenge transformed into an amphitheatre for the enactment of a ceremony which seems to include (in the foreground) a group of Morris dancers (Plate 54). W. O. Geller, in his apocalyptic version of 1830, makes one regret that John Martin did not tackle the subject.

Back in sober vein, Stonehenge was not ignored as a setting by Samuel Spode, a practitioner of that most English of genres, the sporting painting. His painting of 1845, 'Coursing at Stonehenge' (Plate 56), has a pleasingly

---

PLATE 51   This example of narrative painting is by Thomas Jones, 1774, and illustrates Thomas Gray's poem 'The Bard'.

PLATE 52 (*right*)   'Salisbury Plain – Peasants in a Storm', or 'Distress by Land', by Henry Thompson which was first exhibited in 1811. This painting was owned by Sir Richard Colt-Hoare, and still hangs in his former home, Stourhead House.

PLATE 51

accurate view in the background. This idea crops up again in a late nineteenth-century illustration of a hunt meeting in the *Illustrated London News*. Stonehenge was clearly a popular place for sporting events; witness the delightful sketch inscribed 'To the Gentlemen of the Stonehenge Club, this view of their ground, June 1831, is respectfully inscribed'. Illustrators also chose scenes set there for their engravings, such as those from *Tess of the d'Urbervilles* and *The Borgia Ring* (Plate 55). More recently the graphic artist E. McKnight Kauffer evokes a lonely stillness in her 'twenties' poster for Shell of Stonehenge by moonlight (Plate 56).

Surprisingly, few twentieth-century artists of stature have taken Stonehenge as a subject. Among the most notable are John Piper (who has both sketched and photographed it, and whose interest is shown by his entertaining article which appeared in the *Architectural Review*, September 1949), Paul Nash, and Henry Moore.

PLATE 53 The death of Cordelia in *King Lear*, overlooked from the hillside by a neat group of Trilithons; they make a powerful addition to this narrative illustration from J. & J. Boydell's *A Collection of Prints from Pictures painted for the purpose of illustrating the dramatic Works of Shakespeare by the Artists of Great Britain*, published in 1803. The original painting was by James Barry.

PLATE 53

PLATE 54

Nash visited the area in 1933 and found himself embarked upon what he described as 'The Adventure of the Megaliths'. Although his series of paintings resulting from this visit owe far more to the inspiration of Avebury than to Stonehenge, it is evident that the spiritual aura of the inter-related monuments of the entire area stirred a profound sense of mystery in him, so that he could not quite express, in his usual animistic figuration, their relation to the Wessex landscape around them or to man. In the event he resorted to a kind of symbolic abstraction – as in 'Equivalents for the Megaliths', 1935 (Plate 58) – but in other paintings such as 'Stone Forest', 1937, it is evident that he intuitively understood by then the theories concerning the 'male' and 'female' nature of the stones put forward by Alexander Keiller,

excavator of Avebury, whom he visited often.

This perception is shared by Henry Moore, whose lithographs in his 'Stonehenge Suite' of 1974 dramatically impart the sense of plasticity and of almost sinisterly anthropomorphised matter familiar to us from his sculpture. The attraction of the stones to him, as a sculptor, seems so obvious that it is a wonder so few have preceded him. Interestingly his initial reaction to the circle echoes almost exactly Paul Nash's; like him, Moore's first experience of the

PLATE 54   A coloured aquatint etched by R. Howell from Charles Hamilton Smith's drawing for one of the illustrations in the 1815 publication *The Costume of the Original Inhabitants of the British Islands.*

PLATE 55

PLATE 57

STONEHENGE
SEE BRITAIN FIRST ON SHELL

PLATE 56

PLATE 55 (*previous page*)   A scene from the drama 'The Borgia Ring', which once played at the Adelphi Theatre, London.

PLATE 56 (*previous page*)   'See Britain First On Shell': a poster by E. McKnight Kauffer, who portrayed Stonehenge as one of the country's tourist attractions in the 1920s.

PLATE 57 (*previous page*)   Cricket near the monument. The watercolour was captioned by the artist, 'To the Gentlemen of the Stonehenge Club, this view of their ground, June 1831, is respectfully inscribed.'

PLATE 58   'Equivalents for the Megaliths' by Paul Nash, 1935.

megaliths was at night. He described it in a letter to Stephen Spender:

'After eating I decided I wouldn't wait to see Stonehenge until the next day. As it was a clear evening I got to Stonehenge and saw it by moonlight. I was alone and tremendously impressed. (Moonlight as you know enlarges everything, and the mysterious depths and distances made it seem enormous.) I began doing the album as etchings, and only later decided lithographs would be better. Etchings are done with a point making a fine line, the technique isn't a natural one of representing the texture of stone. Also, blackness is more natural to lithography, and the night, the moonlight idea, was more possible.'

PLATE 58

Spender comments in his introduction to the album: 'The spectator looks at these scenes as though they had eyes which look back at him.' His further comment could serve for all the great artists who have studied Stonehenge: 'Such works have not been made into art-objects. The hand of man has only assisted to make them look more over-powering.'

PLATE 59　'Landscapes of the Megaliths', a lithograph by Paul Nash, 1937, which recalls West Kennett Avenue and Silbury Hill.

PLATE 59

Part 3
The Stones

Petrology – Shaping – Dressing
Transportation

An important moment in Stonehenge scholarship occurred in April 1923, when Dr Herbert H. Thomas, the Petrographer to H.M. Geological Survey, stood up before the Society of Antiquaries to read a paper. The proposals he made in it have never been seriously challenged since; they answered an embarrassing question which had puzzled researchers until then – where did the stones which were not of local sarsen come from? Dr Thomas's remarkable discovery was that they came from the eastern end of the Prescelly Mountains in north Pembrokeshire (now Dyfed), and moreover that they were to be found only in an area of about one square mile, between the outcrops there of Carn Meini and Foel Trigarn (Thomas 1923). The eminent petrographer (petrography is the science of the origin, chemical and mineral composition and structure, and alteration of rocks) added a very convincing point:

'It is probably more than a coincidence that this area, clearly indicated by geological evidence as the source of the Stonehenge foreign stones, should contain one of the richest collections of megalithic remains in Britain . . . the importance of the megalithic remains of the eastern portion of the Prescelly Mountains has been brought to our notice by the writings of the late Reverend W. Done Bushell. He described Prescelly as unique in this respect, and referred to it as a "prehistoric Westminster". Dolmens and the remains of stone-circles are extremely numerous . . . Bushell described the southern slopes as "a land of circles" and points out that in this limited area there were eight at least of which traces still exist!'

In fact it was very unwise of Thomas to accept Bushell's comments; there are only two circles in the area.

The surviving stones of Stonehenge could now (and can today) be conveniently classified into three main types. (1) The *bluestones* which comprise the stones of the Bluestone Circle and Bluestone Horseshoe. The term is a traditional one used at Stonehenge to describe a variety of volcanic and sedimentary rocks, most of which are bluey-grey in colour, especially when wet. (2) A single large block of *micaceous sandstone* known as the Altar Stone. (3) The large *sarsen* blocks consist of the two surviving station stones, the Slaughter and Heel Stones, the Sarsen Circle uprights and their lintels, and the Sarsen Trilithon Horseshoe.

PLATE 60   A bluestone, temporarily removed from its position during the 1958 excavations. Taken by Mrs H. E. O'Neil, the widow of the Chief Inspector during the early 1950s of the Inspectorate of Ancient Monuments in the Ministry of Works.

PLATE 61 Sarsen Stones (from the right) 29, 30, 1 and 2, with their linteis, seen from the north. The axis pointing along the Avenue, past the Heel Stone, is between Stones 30 and 1. The central area has now been grassed over again.

The word *sarsen* is usually accepted as deriving from *saracen*, a heathen: 'As the Saxons applied the term Saresyn to pagans or heathens in general, and as the principal specimens of these blocks of stones were perceived to be congregated into temples popularly attributed to heathen worship, it naturally came to pass that the entire geological formation acquired the distinctive appellation of Saresyn (or heathen) stones' (*Notes and Queries*, 1885). An alternative rendering may be from the Anglo-Saxon *sar* (troublesome) and *stan* (stone). Locally this type of stone has long been known as 'Grey Wethers' (the spelling varies). Colonel Richard Symonds, royalist and antiquary, was near Marlborough in the Civil War in November 1644, and recorded the fact in his diary: 'a place so full of grey pibble stone of great bignes as is not usually seen . . . the inhabitants calling them Saracen's stones; you may goe upon them all the way. They call that the Grey-weathers, because a far off they looke like a flock of sheepe' (Symonds 1644).

Over the years each of these different categories of stone, which make up Stonehenge as we see it today, has been studied in great detail, both in the hand-specimen and by thin section examination under the petrological microscope. This latter geological technique involves detaching small fragments (c. 10 × 10 mm) from the stones and then grinding them down until each sample is transparent; at this point the minerals which make up the different types of rocks can be identified by their optical properties under polarized light. This valuable method of analysis not only allows the positive identification of rocks from their constituent minerals, but also permits them to be 'characterized' by studying the 'texture' of those minerals – that is, their size, shape and frequency. Textural analysis makes possible the comparison of rocks with similar types of known origin, a particularly important point when identifying the source of the bluestones.

PLATE 62

PLATE 62 Some of the stone mauls, which were used for dressing stones, found during Professor William Gowland's excavations and restoration work for the Society of Antiquaries, which commenced in 1901. There had been a fall of stones on 31 December 1900. The mauls appear to be arranged on and beside Stone 12.

PLATE 63 Professor Richard Atkinson (left) and Professor Stuart Piggott at work in the north-east central area during the 1958 excavations. The size of the stone mauls in the foreground indicate the strength of their prehistoric handlers.

The majority of the bluestones (twenty-nine out of thirty-three still standing) can be classified as ophitic dolerite. This is a hard, medium-grained, basic igneous rock composed mainly of feldspar and augite. A common feature of most of the Stonehenge dolerite is the white or pinkish irregular grouping or 'spotting' of clusters of feldspar that occur throughout the rock giving rise to the descriptive term 'spotted dolerite' for these particular stones. Three of the dolerite standing stones appear to lack this distinctive 'spotted' feature, but are otherwise mineralogically very similar to the rest.

The other main type of bluestone, accounting for four of the standing stones and one buried stump, is a hard, flinty, bluish-green or grey stone. This has been identified as rhyolite, a fine-grained to glassy acid volcanic rock. Also to be classed as a bluestone, though no examples remain above ground, is a soft, slatey, greenish volcanic ash rock, five stumps of which have been excavated just below ground level.

Salisbury Plain is situated in a non-igneous region; clearly therefore, the bluestones could not have originated locally, and their source had to be located elsewhere. In the search for the place or origin it is fortunate that the 'spotted' aspect of the Stonehenge dolerite is, as Dr Thomas knew, such an uncommon feature of this type of rock. Thin section examination of the Prescelly dolerite has revealed that texturally it is virtually identical with the samples from Stonehenge. Examples of 'un-spotted' dolerite similar to those types at Stonehenge have also been found in the Prescelly Range. Moreover, it has been shown that the remaining bluestones, namely the rhyolites and volcanic ash stones, can be matched

PLATE 64 The central area as it was in the early 1860s. The figure (Colonel Sir Henry James?) is sitting on Stone 59b; the much larger Stone 59a lies behind him. The extent of the former lean of Stone 56, propped up by Stone 68, is evident. A picture dated 1574 shows it already leaning, and also Stone 59 fallen and broken into three pieces.

texturally with similar types of rocks that occur in this area of South Wales.

A South Wales source is also highly likely for the so-called Altar Stone, a bluish-grey micaceous sandstone containing abundant grains of quartz and glistening flecks of mica, set in a calcareo-siliceous matrix. This rock is quite unlike any of the other stones at Stonehenge apart from the below-ground stump of Stone 40g of the Bluestone Circle. The high amount of mica and the calcareous nature of the stones can both be paralleled in the Old Red Sandstone Beds of South Wales – more particularly in the Senni Beds which outcrop widely in Glamorganshire, and the Cosheston Group which occur in the Milford Haven district. A heavy mineral separation on a sample of the Stonehenge Altar Stone revealed the presence of a high content of garnet, a mineral which is known to be common in the Cosheston Beds. Another pointer to the possibility of the area around Milford Haven being one of the sources of some stones at Stonehenge is the similarity in texture noted between Stone 40g (a different type to the Altar Stone) and samples from near Llangwn to the west of Milford Haven.

The evidence for a source in South Wales for the bluestones has been recognized for some time now. However, the question of transporting these heavy stones from the area where they occur naturally to their present locality on Salisbury Plain is still a matter of debate. (Some eighty bluestones weighing up to seven tons each would have been required for the Double Bluestone Circle of Stonehenge II; the Altar Stone weighs about seven tons.) Were these stones deposited close to the site of Stonehenge by glaciation during the Pleistocene Age, there to be carried a comparatively short distance before erection, or were they moved by human endeavour all the way from Wales, a minimum journey of about 386 km (240 miles)?

Those who favour the former view point out that it was not necessary for the Stonehenge builders to travel to Wales for a durable stone, when large outcrops of equally suitable building stone were available less than twenty miles away in the form of great oolite limestone.

PLATE 66

Unless, of course, hard stones such as dolerite and rhyolite could be found closer to hand. Indeed, they drew attention to the unsuitability of the 'imported' soft volcanic ash stones to stand up to the rain and frost without slowly disintegrating, as *has* been the case at Stonehenge where only the stumps of this type of rock remain. This may also have been the case with other foreign rocks such as slate, greywacke and quartzite, which may once have been

PLATE 65 (*left*)   A photograph taken by the Ordnance Survey Department for the 1867 book by the Director-General, Colonel Sir Henry James. Perhaps it shows the author himself, seated on the mortised Stone 156 (the fallen lintel from Stone 56 behind him). At that time it was often called The Leaning Stone; it was set straight in 1901. The Altar Stone(80) lies beneath Stone 156, and Stone 55b (half of Stone 56's companion).

PLATE 66   The Heel Stone, which leans at a 24° angle. Some commentators consider that it was originally set in this leaning position.

part of the stone structure at Stonehenge and which are now represented only by small chips, the latter probably resulting from the dressing or destruction of the stones. It would certainly have been more practical for the builders of Stonehenge to have acquired these soft stones, easily prone to weathering, fairly locally than to have deliberately chosen and transported them for some great distance.

However, the fact remains that there is no clear evidence of glacially derived material in the Salisbury Plain area – such as one would expect to be left behind following the retreat of the ice. Moreover, apart from the foreign stones at Stonehenge, there are comparatively few examples of igneous erratics in the region. In view of this, the bluestones must have been moved from South Wales to their present setting by human effort.

The question as to why these stones in particular were chosen and transported some 135 miles by land and water, rather than stone from the nearby Cotswold Hills, is one of the most interesting and most puzzling of the mysteries surrounding Stonehenge. I cannot provide a solution to it, yet I do not like to ignore it completely.

The earliest reporters of the folklore of this region have recorded a hint, which, indeed, may not represent the beliefs of the builders of Phase II of Stonehenge, but is at least suggestive. This hint attributes magical healing powers to the stones.

Geoffrey of Monmouth, who, as I mentioned earlier, is the earliest significant source of information about Stonehenge—if the somewhat vague comment of Diodorus Siculus about the Hyperborean Temple to Apollo is disregarded —stated, 'There is not a stone there which has not some healing virtue.' John Aubrey, in the seventeenth century, also recorded a local belief that the stones had such healing powers.

Can we assume that the ancient builders of Stonehenge, Phase II, shared in this belief, and that Stonehenge, in addition to its other possible functions, was some sort of center for primitive, magical medicine?

It may not be entirely chance that similar medical properties are often attributed to the dolmens and menhirs of Britanny by the local Celtic peasantry. Water gathered from depressions in the stones is believed to have curative powers. Similar traditions have been reported about megalithic monuments elsewhere.

This does not, of course, answer the question why the bluestones per se should be associated with this belief, any more than the other stones, or local stone.

It is also possible, of course, that the importation of the bluestones was not connected with primitive healing. The reason may have been socio-economic: the local inhabitants may not have had the skill to work the local stone, which is an oolitic limestone, or there may have been some question of tribute from Wales. Transportation of stone monuments, whether as finished products like the Egyptian obelisk in Rome, or as raw material, was not unknown in premodern times.

Was the quarry in Wales a sacred area in itself? Was there a "revelation" that the bluestones, through color, were most fitting to be used in a lunar calendar? In all probability, we shall never know. In any case the bluestones were quarried in the third millennium BC or so, taken from their sacred source which was 112.6 km (70 miles) east of Ireland (Geoffrey of Monmouth's source), and 363·3 m (1195 ft) above the sea-level which lay 12·8 km (8 miles) down the circuitous valley of the River Nevern. The mystifying origin of the word Prescelly is 'Pris(g)-seleu' (Solomon's Bush), or possibly 'Pre-Seleu' (Solomon's Hill), according to Professor Atkinson (Crampton 1967, p. 113), but I have no speculation on the matter.

The most likely of four possible routes for the transport of the bluestones was overland in the first instance from Prescelly to Canaston Bridge by Milford Haven on the coast; the probable source of the Altar Stone and at least one other form of sandstone present at Stonehenge in the form of chippings. Then they were no doubt taken by some form of craft (or hung between two or more) around the coast of South Wales and across the mouth of the Severn to the Bristol Avon, down that river and also the

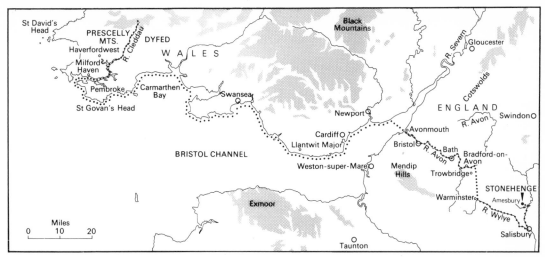

FIGURE 16

PLATE 67

Frome, then overland 9·6 km (6 miles) to the River Wylye at Warminster and along the river until it joins the Avon at Salisbury; and finally 3·2 km (2 miles) overland to Stonehenge (see Figure 16). The distance on land by this route, when the stones would probably have been drawn by sledge, is about 38·6 km (24 miles), and a further 347·7 km (216 miles) by water. The distance as the crow flies is 217·3 km (135 miles).

A famous experiment by the B.B.C. in 1954 utilized the energies of teams of boys from Bryanston and Canford Schools to move a

FIGURE 16   The probable transportation route of the bluestones, from the Prescelly Mountains in South Wales to Salisbury Plain.

PLATE 67   Four boys from Bryanston School ferry three 'barges' bearing a concrete replica of a bluestone along the River Avon, near Stonehenge. The total load was about 3,600 lbs, and this experiment (for BBC Television) proved that the 'primitive craft' could in fact have been propelled by only one person.

concrete replica of a bluestone by both land and water. It was found that thirty-two were needed to haul the sledge overland (twenty-four if a system of wooden rollers placed under the sledge was used), while a crew of four boys were all that were required to propel a raft on which the concrete slab was strapped up the Avon. Professor Gerald Hawkins has calculated that 209,280 man-days were needed to bring the bluestones to Stonehenge (Hawkins 1966). Before leaving the subject of transportation and the lengths of time it required, mention must be made of one of the major mysteries of Stonehenge which is very far from being resolved. There is evidence to show that the bluestones were not in fact brought *directly* to Stonehenge, but might have formed part of a circle or circles near Warminster, Wiltshire, which is about 18·5 km (11½ miles) west-north-west) of Stonehenge, soon after 3000 BC and certainly around the time of the beginning of Stonehenge I! A block of bluestone, weighing about three-quarters of a ton, has been found in the neolithic earthen long barrow called Boles Barrow and it is now in Salisbury Museum.

The other stones at Stonehenge, and visually the most striking, are of course the sarsens. These huge boulders (some weighing up to fifty tons) are Tertiary sandstones of fine to medium-grain size, and have a colour which varies from brown to yellowish grey. These sandstones consist predominantly of sub-angular quartz grains strongly cemented together with silica, which gives the stones a coarse 'sugary' appearance.

This type of stone can be found scattered unevenly over the greater part of the Wessex region, with a concentration on the Marlborough Downs, about 32 km (20 miles) to the north of Stonehenge. Indeed, given the size and numbers of sarsens present at Stonehenge, it is probable that these were obtained from the area of the Marlborough Downs, where even today similar though smaller boulders are to be found lying on the ground. In view of this it is probable that the Stonehenge boulders were obtained by little, if any quarrying. Herbert Stone reports in his book (1924, p. 50) that 'these boulders are to be found in considerable numbers near East Kennet, Lockeridge Dene, Piggledene Bottom, Overton Down, Manton Down and Barton Down. But they occur in the greatest profusion and in the widest extent in the area above Clatford Bottom, extending in a north-westerly direction from the Devil's Den towards Totterdown.' I quote his opinion because it remains accurate to-day, although distribution was markedly different when A. C. Smith published his guide to the area (1885).

Despite the shorter distance, the task of transporting more than eighty of these enormous boulders from the Marlborough Downs to Stonehenge was undoubtedly greater than that which involved the removal of the bluestones from Prescelly. It has been estimated that the task may well have taken 1,242,300 man-days (or 3,413 man-years) to dress and shape the sarsens, prepare haulage equipment and transport them to Stonehenge (Hawkins 1966, p. 101): one may speculate (forgetting the organizer's time!) that this occupied 1,000 men for 3·42 years, 500 men for 6·83 years, or 250 men for 13·65 years (in *man-day* terms). My own assessment, using Professor Hawkins' base figures, is that 500 men spent about 13½ years, working, say, 12 hours per day. Professor Atkinson estimates that 1,500 men took 5½ years just to transport the stones (Atkinson 1956, p. 115).

'Give me a place to stand on, and a lever, and I will move the world,' said Archimedes. I imagine that the sarsen transport teams found things a bit more complicated! The first-ever overhead photograph of an archaeological site was taken of Stonehenge (another in a long list of 'firsts') by Lieutenant P. H. Sharpe from a balloon in 1907: the picture I would prize would have been taken some 5,000 years earlier

PLATE 68 The second sarsen Trilithon (Stones 53/54), with the fragmented Stone 55a lying in the foreground. The elegant sculpture of the uprights and lintel of the Trilithon are clearly shown.

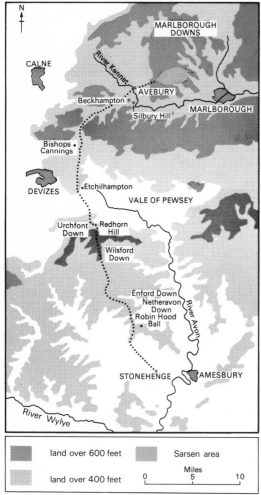

land over 600 feet   Sarsen area

                     Miles
                     0   5   10
land over 400 feet

FIGURE 17

of those transportation teams. I am not mentioning teleportation theories in this book, but there are those who believe in the controlled projection through the air of bodies and matter. (And I am not speculating upon the potential strengths of those rumoured giants of the day.)

One of the first commentators to address himself to the problems involved, was, appropriately, an engineer, E. Herbert Stone; his 1924 book on Stonehenge ably discusses the subject; J. H. Hutton's 1929 article on Assam megaliths

in *Antiquity* is full of relevant information on what can actually be achieved by man today; and Professor Atkinson's *Stonehenge* (1956) has a full discussion of possible transportation techniques (see also Figures 16 and 17). Always to be borne in mind when evolving one's own concepts of the methods used in the transportation of the bluestones and sarsens, is that capstans, windlasses and perhaps pulleys were not available around 3,000 BC; but there were levers and rollers of shaped tree-trunks, ropes and (as we know from several sites) a knowledge of the use of inclined planes . . . and one-piece, disc-like wheels have been found in Danish peat bogs, *dated at 3,000 BC* (Hodson 1974). I would also be interested indeed to read responsible speculation on the uses, during the transportation of the stones, of water to reduce friction, of ice surfaces during winter months (however long they might have been), and of animals.

One estimate (Myra Shackley 1978) has been that a total of 3,000 men were involved in the transportation of all the stones; my own feeling is that less than half that number were used. As I discuss in Part 4, the one factor which cannot be entered into such calculations is motivation – and I believe it was the most powerful of all.

It seems unlikely that the builders of Stonehenge were faced to any great degree with the problem of quarrying for either the bluestones or the sarsens, because even today large boulders of each of these types can be found lying scattered on the ground in their respective source areas. However, it is obvious that stones of a particular size would have been sought after, and this undoubtedly involved splitting larger boulders to pre-set requirements. In this respect an additional attraction of the sarsens

FIGURE 17   The probable route along which the sarsen stones were dragged, from the Marlborough Downs to Stonehenge, a distance of about 32 km (20 miles).

PLATE 69   An artist's impression of how the huge blocks of sarsen stone might have been moved from Marlborough Downs to Stonehenge.

PLATE 70

PLATE 71

may have been their tendency to occur naturally in tabular blocks. Any reduction in size would have been accomplished by applying hot and cold stresses to the break line, and by direct pounding and placing wooden wedges into the cracks. A great deal of the shaping of the sarsens was probably done in the source area, thereby reducing the weight of the stones for transportation. Each upright of the Sarsen Circle and the Sarsen Trilithon Horseshoe were slightly shaped – and this work is mentioned in detail in Part 4.

With the exception of the Heel Stone and Station Stone 91, a few of the bluestones show distinct evidence of dressing, that is, a deliberate smoothing of the natural coarse surface of the rock. Much of this work evidently took place at Stonehenge—sarsen sand abounds there. E. H. Stone's and Professor Atkinson's books go into technical details of the minor quarrying, dressing and shaping. It was, basi-

cally, done by direct pounding of the stone, using very hard sarsen mauls, many of which have been recovered from Stonehenge. The technique seems to have been to first work longitudinally on the stones, producing long shallow grooves, the ridges of which could be removed later by sideways pounding. Again, we must be vastly impressed at the sheer organization and design factors involved in the massive enterprise we now call Stonehenge.

PLATE 70   The first aerial photograph of Stonehenge. It was taken from a war balloon on 17 April 1907 by Lieut. P. A. Sharpe, and shows the prominent cart tracks running through the area.

PLATE 71   The majesty of Stone 56 is well shown in this tranquil photograph of the monument. Stone 16 is in the left foreground, with the Trilithon 57/58 between them.

Part 4
The Construction of Stonehenge

Builders – Society – Phases
Dates – Erection– Carvings

Stonehenge is frustrating. We know some answers to some questions certainly – but equally certainly we don't yet know all of the *right* questions. The monument is emotionally breathtaking – and all that is actually *known* about its construction is equally confounding.

There is no 'date for Stonehenge' of course; we will see how it evolved through six separate Phases – from being a simple, though fairly unusual, causewayed henge monument, to the grand, beautiful and unique thing that existed long before the Romans. Since the days of John Aubrey there has been a curiously spasmodic piecing together of its intricate history. This process has been greatly hastened during the last eighty years – started perhaps by the investigations of Lockyer and Penrose. The pace really quickened with the publication in 1956 of Professor R. J. C. Atkinson's now classic book, *Stonehenge,* to which every student of Stonehenge is deeply indebted.

The enquiring public's inquest into what Aubrey Burl has called 'this ravaged colossus' took a new and for a time strange direction in 1966 when Professor Gerald Hawkins published *Stonehenge Decoded;* it was a challenging yet confident title which seemed to offend the establishment of the academic archaeological world. 'Tendentious, arrogant, slipshod and unconvincing' was how one reviewer thought of it, but it greatly excited readers throughout the world.

By this time the great surveying work of Professor Alexander Thom and his family was under way, and it was to have a crystallizing

PLATE 73

PLATE 72 (*opposite*)   The tooling on Stone 16 achieved with heavy stone mauls. (This is the stone that has the O. S. bench mark 338.9).

PLATE 73   Professor Richard Atkinson with his theodolite, during the 1958 excavations.

and then a shattering effect. His first book *Megalithic Sites In Britain* attracted much public interest in 1967, which belied its scholarly presentation by Oxford's Clarendon Press, and his cause was taken up by John Michell (1966, 1973, 1974) and other authors who were on or beyond the fringe of what slowly became known as the New-Archaeology (a more recent branch is astro-archaeology). The stones of Stonehenge, which we examine in the following pages, were and are at the heart of the matter as far as the general public is concerned – the admission figures there clearly indicate it. They have put away for ever the notion of those woad-covered and wholly ignorant ancestors who peopled Victorian British history books with the implication that they were incapable of anything more creative than killing to survive. When manned space flights commenced there was a perceptible freshening of appetites for speculative and often loony theories about the real origins of man and his prehistoric existence and achievements. This period may now have passed, and it was typified to both stimulated readers and grateful booksellers by Erich von Daniken, who wrote in *The Chariot Of The Gods* (1971, p. 117): 'It even seems as if the ancient peoples took a special pleasure in juggling with stone giants over hill and dale . . . our remote ancestors must have been queer people.' Let's see for ourselves.

PLATE 74   A view from the west.

The end of the Ice Age, about 10,000 BC, brought new survival factors to the lives of wild animals which Old Stone Age man hunted all his days. Formerly living a nomad's life, following herds to their successive grazing grounds, he now found he was gradually and more easily able to capture, stock and breed his own animals for food and covering. With more knowledge of the one place he had chosen he observed the changing seasons and their effect upon plant growth, and so he came to primitive agriculture, sowing and reaping, and eventually storing his own food supply. These changes took about six thousand years to approximately 4,000 BC (in Britain), about the end of the Mesolithic Age. During this period the semi-nomads, probably in packs, gangs or tribes of 35–50 members and under some sort of leadership and authority, were also making tools for cutting and shaping timber, the antlers of red deer, and skins; they were made of flint and stone, and a trade in them grew up, over hundreds of miles. Journeys were no longer without end, for Mesolithic man was also becoming a builder.

Most of southern England was covered in forests, and with the habit of settlement came clearance with heavier tools. We know from the size of post-holes how large the timbers were that needed felling and shaping and erecting according to previously worked-out plans. The chalk and limestone areas with their lighter vegetation, which included Wessex, were most attractive to the earliest immigrant settlers who had come (*if* you accept the old diffusionist theory) via either the Western Sea Route or the Danubian route with more sophisticated stock breeding and agricultural practices. They also settled in Ireland, and on the western mainland coasts and hinterlands in the north as well, avoiding the Midlands (as any distribution map of prehistoric monuments shows), and gradually spread the influences of a culture that still had established roots, via Greece and the Balkans, in the evolving cities in the Euphrates and Tigris valleys in the Near East.

In Wessex the earliest neolithic settlers have been called the Windmill Hill people, simply

PLATE 75

because their main characteristics have been found at this great 21-acre causewayed enclosure site not far from Stonehenge. It is accounted for, briefly, in Part 5. Although there must have been more, seventeen enclosures are known in south and west England; the one on top of Windmill Hill is the largest of all. They used to be called 'causewayed camps', until it was realized that they have no defensive

PLATE 75 This is how the Dutchman Lucas de Heere (1574) imagined the early inhabitants of Britain at the supposed time of the 'construction of Stonehenge'. From a manuscript in the British Library.

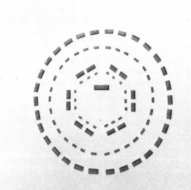

INIGO JONES.

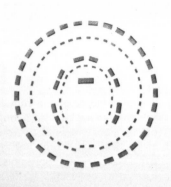

STUKELY.

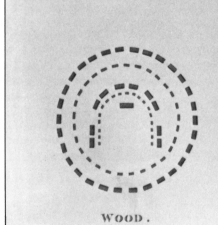

WOOD.

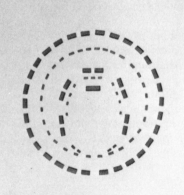

SMITH.

FIGURE 18

characteristics and were perhaps never permanently inhabited – which introduced something of a mystery. Further, it was then found that, over a period of centuries, their ditches were dug out and sometimes partially filled again by throwing back some of the bank: but (and therefore) the ditches have yielded a great deal of artifacts and information about lifestyles and the possible pattern of the primitive society of those days, between six and five thousand years ago. They were shortly to lead directly to the beginning of the construction of Stonehenge.

The farming of the Windmill Hill people was mixed: cattle, goats, pigs, sheep (useful for forest clearance too), and dogs; wheat was grown and stored; fish and shellfish were gathered on the coasts. The causewayed enclosures, with their banks, ditches and gaps, were not used for penning livestock or as habitation settlements: they were, it appears, used for ritual or ceremonial purposes, possibly involving the sacrifice of animals.

At the time of the first Stonehenge construction Phase (commonly known as Stonehenge I), the 180 or so megalithic monuments in the Cotswold-Severn Group were being constructed (one of the first and most complete is the West Kennett Long Barrow which is discussed in Part 5). The causewayed enclosures evolved into henge monuments with their ceremonial and celebratory functions intact. It was the users of Rinyo-Clacton and Grooved Ware, who undertook this conversion – but there was *still* no sign of domestic settlements becoming established in or around them in Wessex. In fact this situation was to continue until as late as the Early Pre-Roman Iron Age in about 500 BC, with the exception of, for

PLATE 76

instance, the Orkneys (Skara Brae) and the Shetlands (the Benie Hoose on Whalsay). The domestic pattern of life seems to have remained semi-nomadic to the extent that smallish tribes, of perhaps only 25 to 50 people, moved on to fresh grazing grounds every 10 to 15 years. Each territory probably contained its own tomb, which might have been built in phases, as time and food gathering activities allowed. I possess a very early French engraving with a long-chambered tomb denoted as a 'purgatoire' – but such megalithic monuments were more probably for safe shelter and, later on, burials of the family heads or chiefs. And often amid celebrations and feasting. It would not over-simplify to state that there were possibly about 180 social centres in Wessex in about 2,900 BC, when Stonehenge I was commenced.

The stone axe heads brought from far away as gifts at funerary celebrations were no doubt welcome to the succeeding Beaker folk (from

FIGURE 18   The ground plan of a 'restored' Stonehenge, according to four antiquaries. This engraving by Philip Crocker appears in Colt-Hoare's *Ancient Wiltshire* (1812).

PLATE 76   This aerial view shows the excavations and restoration in the summer of 1958. The Larkhill Army Camp is at the top right hand side, and Salisbury Plain stretches away to the horizon.

near the mouth of the Rhine, where there are very many timber circles of the same period), who were perhaps responsible for transferring the techniques of working wood to the shaping dressing, transport and erection of stones. These offered bulk (to make a good impression was doubtless important among these small farming communities) and precaution against fire. That Neolithic farming communities, living barely above subsistence level, could erect such structures as the Sarsen Circle and Trilithon Horseshoe centuries *before* the Great Pyramid was built used to puzzle archaeologists. It is now however generally accepted that the extraordinary concentration of megaliths on the Atlantic-facing coastal regions of Western Europe was the natural end-result of the spread of the Neolithic farming economy from the Near East. It had continued until it could, as it were, go no further, exactly at the time when the Mesolithic indigenous populations were themselves hunting and gathering – *and* (earlier in Britain than Europe) building with stone. The Mesolithic site at Beg an Dorehenn, Finistère, in Brittany, is dated as far back as 5,500–5,000 BC, and the earliest passage graves there date from c. 4,600 BC. So we must suppose that in fact it was the sudden growth in local populations, that necessitated a higher degree of organization, the need for boundaries to community territories and a concentration in ambitions to create more and more impressive structures. This provides the context for the stunning achievement of, for example, Silbury Hill (2500 BC). To whatever uses it may later have been put and whatever it came later to represent in myth, belief and reality, it was probably visualized, when the digging began, just as 'something different and bigger'. Professor Atkinson has estimated it took 500 men 15 years to make (Hodson 1974). The effort was primitive, yet it is completely understandable; for the result was an increase in pride and common purpose. Perhaps the chief legacy of the arrival of the Neolithic farmers was 1,500 years of megalithic architecture, which had started as a community social expression and ended providing instruments of

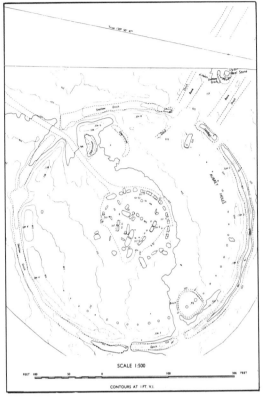

FIGURE 19

power – with neither cities nor writing known to the builders who were thus, by convention, 'uncivilised'. It would appear that the greater the number of members in a community, the higher the art involved in the construction and decoration of megalithic monuments, because the chiefdom hierarchy produced a high enough degree of economy management and viability to allow specialization in crafts and

FIGURE 19 A contour map of Stonehenge. The contours are drawn at 1 foot vertical intervals. (0·5 m [15·7 ins] of the chalk surface has been weathered away since Late Neolithic times).

FIGURE 20 The distribution in the British Isles and North-West Europe of stone circles (with and without centre stones), stone alignments and burials in stone and timber chambers.

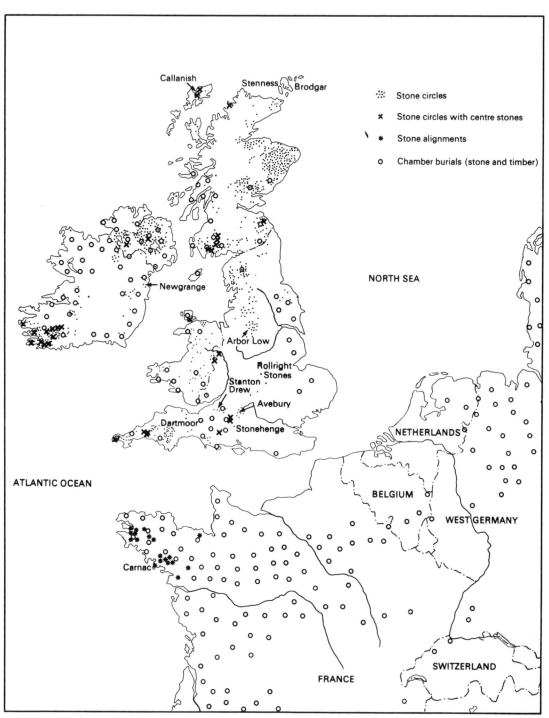

Callanish
Stenness Brodgar

⠶ Stone circles

✕ Stone circles with centre stones

✳ Stone alignments

○ Chamber burials (stone and timber)

NORTH SEA

Newgrange

Arbor Low

Rollright
Stones

Stanton
Drew

Avebury

Dartmoor

Stonehenge

NETHERLANDS

ATLANTIC OCEAN

BELGIUM

WEST GERMANY

Carnac

FRANCE

SWITZERLAND

FIGURE 20

related arts: the decorated monuments in Malta and parts of Brittany are examples. All this was due, therefore, *not* to the old-fashioned theory of the diffusion of cultural influences with their origins in the Near East, but to the simpler factors of population increase and social organization among indigenous peoples.

Before returning to the Stonehenge site to await the arrival of the Beaker People, note should be taken of one craft of particular importance to the workmen in that chalky landscape. It has been established that an oak tree of 30 cm (12 ins) diameter can be cut down in 30 minutes by one man using a flint axe (J. Coles, *Archaeology by Experiment,* 1973), and so the earliest timber structures, such as huts and mortuary houses, were not hard to put up. The earliest flint mine known in Britain is in Sussex and dated at 4,300 BC. Miners went down through no less than ten layers of unsuitable flint in Spiennes, Belgium, to reach the kind they wanted – and all this in tunnels with self-supporting arches roofing its galleries; the later but more accessible Grimes Graves in Norfolk attest to such engineering feats. Factories produced the rough shapes of axes and axe-heads, and they were probably finished into their finial-shapes at the sites where they were needed, after the conduct of trade, by barter and exchange no doubt, over surprisingly large distances. And so the Beaker People had many skills to call upon when they arrived from the continent in about 2,500–2,300 BC with their own skills for working with copper and then the bronze that gave its name to the Age they ushered in.

Their name comes from their pottery drinking vessels, which were generally 151–202 mm (6–8 ins) high and 126–151 mm (5–6 ins) wide, and heavily decorated; these have often been excavated with inhumations (not cremations). With the Beaker People (or Folk) came battle axes, flint daggers, barbed-and-tanged flint arrowheads, and copper and bronze daggers. Forest clearance continued, great areas were exposed and became grassy; shepherds began to watch the sun, moon and stars as well as their flocks, noting their movements in the

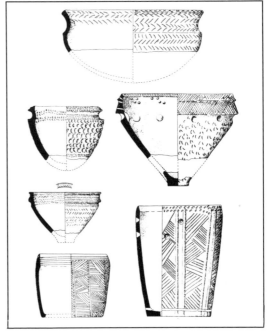

FIGURE 21

new and permanent grazing grounds. Salisbury Plain was probably now in existence.

The era of great prehistoric engineering feats was commencing. The Dorset Cursus was 10 km (6·2 miles) long, the circular earthwork at Avebury enclosed 12 hectares (29·7 acres), 8·75 million cubic feet of earth, chalk and rubble was being piled up to make Silbury Hill, the largest man-made mound in Europe – all with red deer antler picks, cattle shoulder blades and rough baskets.

We know from the work of Professor Thom that alignments in or from stone circles correspond with sun and moon risings for between 2,000–1,700 BC, and this was roughly when the earth-moving Beaker people were building stone circles. It is paradoxical that

FIGURE 21 Late Neolithic pottery.

PLATE 77 The 'Stonehenge Urn' found in one of the barrows near the monument. It is 55·9 (22½ ins) high and 38·1 cm (15 ins) in diameter.

PLATE 78 A drinking vessel, from Barrow 93.

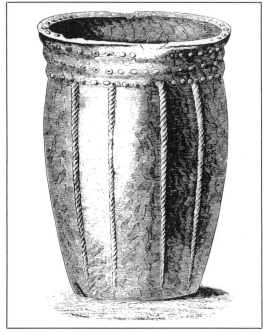

PLATE 77

PLATE 78

although there are some 900 stone circles without henge banks and ditches in Britain, only 30 to 40 of them are in South-West England, excluding rings of kerbstones. Mathematical knowledge was being written down in Egypt in about 1,600 BC (the Rhind papyrus); the Beaker People recorded theirs in a different way – in a living language of stones, positioned over generations of recorded observation which is only now perhaps being deciphered, in a long process which started perhaps with Dr John Smith's prognostication in 1771. It appears that they had their own unit of measurement too. The techniques for moving and erecting large megaliths (Greek: '*mega*', large '*lithos*', stone) were invented and evolved in north-west Europe: the tombs in Brittany were the earliest constructed. The Great Menhir at Locmariaquer is no less than 20·3 m (21·9 yds) long, and weighs an incredible 340 tonnes (334 tons), and Professor Thom has suggested that this could have been a foresight erected for observations over 16 km (10 miles). Some 8 km (5 miles)

away to the north-west, near Carnac, the Menec alignment was built: 1,100 stones in 11 rows over a distance of 1,200 m (1,312 yds). Possible transportation techniques are examined towards the end of Part 3.

Stonehenge students have long been fascinated by passages, preserved by Diodorus Siculus, from the lost *History of the Hyperboreans* by Hecataeus of Abdera (c. 300 BC), in which he wrote of 'this island . . . situated in the north . . . inhabited by Hyperboreans . . . there is also on the island both a magnificent sacred precinct of Apollo [the Sun] and a notable temple which is adorned with many votive offerings and is spherical in shape. Furthermore there is a city there which is sacred to this god, and the majority of its inhabitants are players on the cithara; and these continually play on this instrument in the temple . . .' Whether or not this account refers to Britain, and therefore to the Iron Age inheritors of the traditions of the astronomer-priests who constructed Stonehenge is constantly debated.

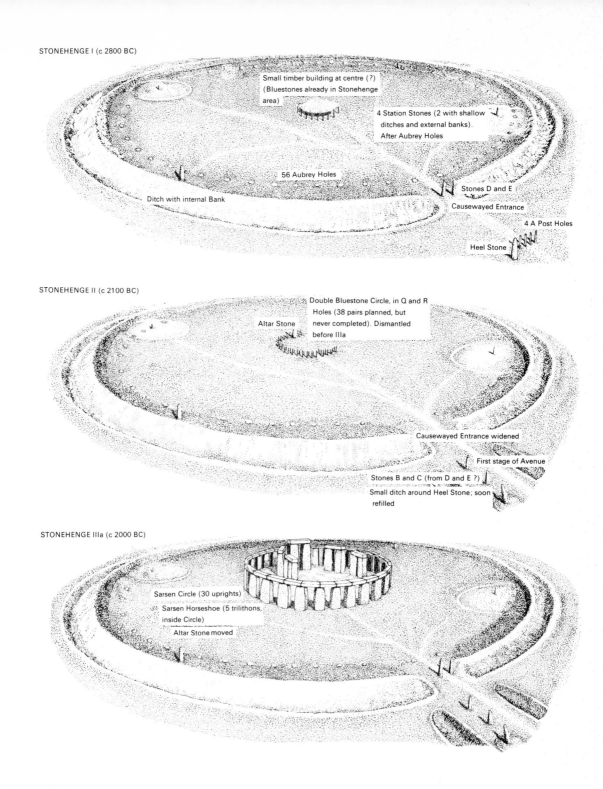

STONEHENGE I (c 2800 BC)

Small timber building at centre (?)
(Bluestones already in Stonehenge area)

4 Station Stones (2 with shallow ditches and external banks).
After Aubrey Holes

56 Aubrey Holes

Stones D and E

Causewayed Entrance

Ditch with internal Bank

4 A Post Holes

Heel Stone

STONEHENGE II (c 2100 BC)

Double Bluestone Circle, in Q and R Holes (38 pairs planned, but never completed). Dismantled before IIIa

Altar Stone

Causewayed Entrance widened

First stage of Avenue

Stones B and C (from D and E ?)

Small ditch around Heel Stone; soon refilled

STONEHENGE IIIa (c 2000 BC)

Sarsen Circle (30 uprights)

Sarsen Horseshoe (5 trilithons, inside Circle)

Altar Stone moved

FIGURE 22   The construction Phases of Stonehenge, as revised by Professor Richard Atkinson at the end of 1978.

STONEHENGE IIIb (? date)

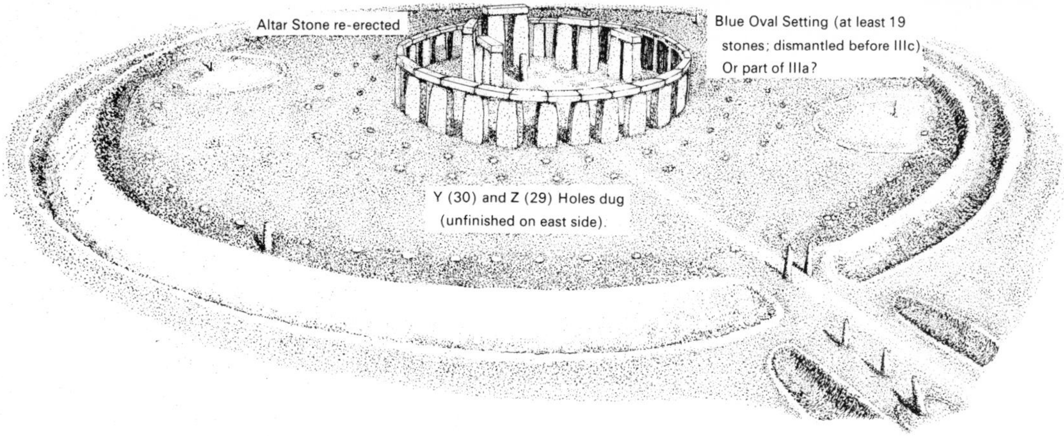

Altar Stone re-erected

Blue Oval Setting (at least 19 stones; dismantled before IIIc). Or part of IIIa?

Y (30) and Z (29) Holes dug (unfinished on east side).

STONEHENGE IIIc (c 1550 BC)

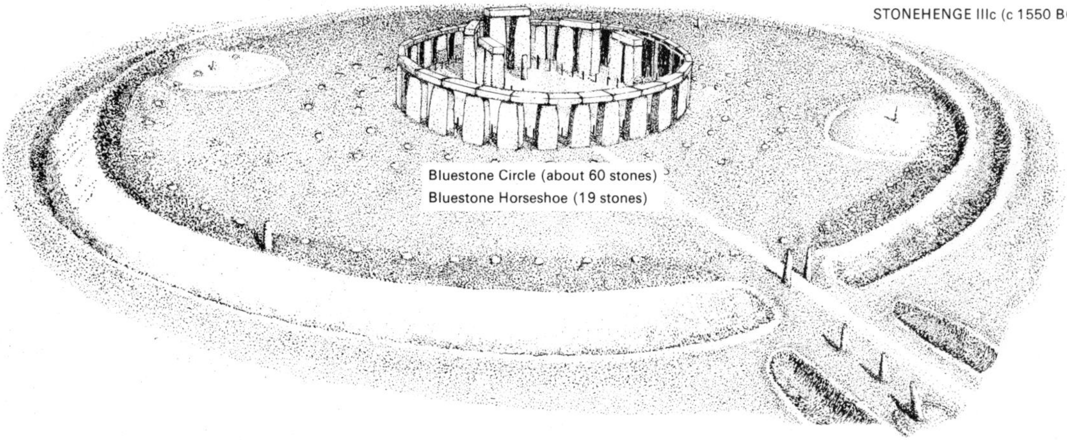

Bluestone Circle (about 60 stones)
Bluestone Horseshoe (19 stones)

STONEHENGE IV (c 1100 BC)

N

Avenue extended from Stonehenge Bottom, eastwards, then south-eastwards towards River Avon

The construction of Stonehenge is now thought to have occurred during a period of about 1800 years, and in six separate phases. These are shown in Figure 22, to which constant references are made in the following pages. The identification of these phases has been one of the very many results of excavations and publications by the eminent archaeologists, Professor Atkinson, Professor Piggott and the late Dr J. F. S. Stone, to all of whom I am greatly indebted. Mention should also be made of the work earlier this century by O. G. S. Crawford, Colonel R. H. Cunnington, Professor Gowland, Colonel Hawley, Sir Norman Lockyer, R. S. Newall, and E. H. Stone. The stones of Stonehenge were given their numbers by Sir William Flinders Petrie in his book on the monument (which included highly accurate plans) published in 1880.

PLATE 79   Professor Stuart Piggott (left) and Professor Richard Atkinson, beside Stone 160b, in 1958.

PLATE 80   Dr J. F. S. Stone.

PLATE 79

PLATE 80

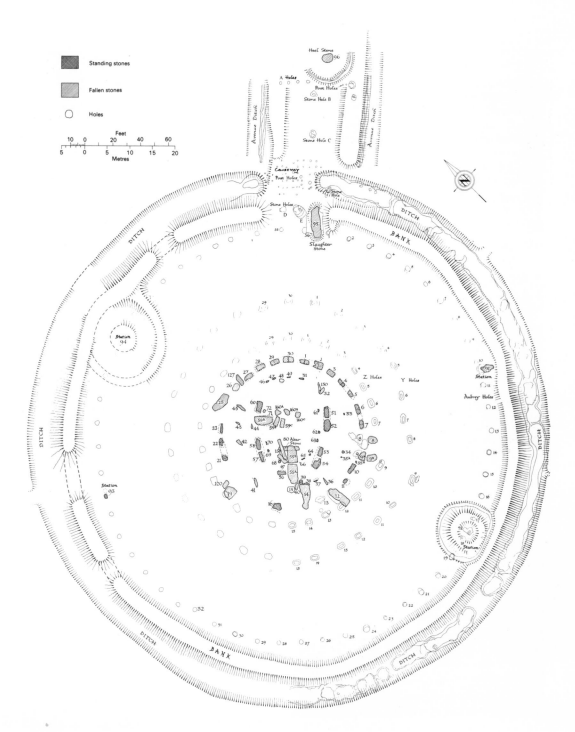

FIGURE 23

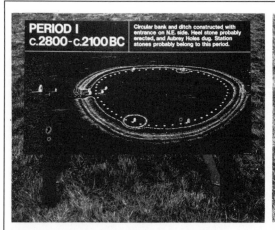

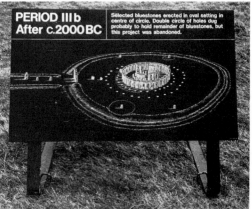

PLATE 81 I photographed this series of five information boards around the perimeter of the newly erected fence in March 1978. They are inaccurate in places – and Professor Richard Atkinson has since announced a sixth Phase, Stonehenge IV.

Phase I
(c. 2800 BC)

The *Ditch* surrounding the monument is irregular and as at so many henges, not defensive; it was simply a quarry for the 2700 cubic m (3,500 cu. yds) approximately of chalk rubble which make up the bank inside it, which, according to one estimate, required 30,000 man-hours to dig (Burl 1976, p. 303). Now if there were capable fit men, each working at intervals of 1·82 m (6 ft) around the (approximate) 320 m (1,050 ft) circumference of the ditch bottom, then 175 men, shifting ·76 cu. m (1 cu. yd) per day, would take 20 days to complete the job; or 28,000 man-hours, through eight-hour days. My figures (omitting administrators) greatly contrast with Aubrey Burl's statement (but not his total) that the digging of the Ditch must have taken as many as 500 people 'weeks of effort'. I mention again at this early stage the subject of the possible manpower necessary for the construction of Stonehenge, because of its perennial fascination and thus wild speculations it provokes.

The Ditch's depth varies from between 1·8 m (6 ft) and 1·4 m (4½ ft), and it is 3·7 m (12 ft) wider at the bottom. Being merely a quarry, chalk rubble was left at the bottom; this has yielded two shards of grooved ware which is interesting because it has also been found in the enclosures at Durrington Walls, Mount Pleasant and Marden, and in Woodhenge and Maumbury Rings (and as far away as Stenness in the Orkney Islands). Many dressed flints have also been excavated, many red antler picks and, in the layer above the rubble, some fragments (only, as always)

△ PLATE 82

PLATE 82   Stone 91, one of the Four Stations. This slightly worked sarsen is about 2·7 m (9 ft) long, and has no mound (as Stones 92 and 94 do). The astronomical significance of the Station Stones is discussed in Part 1. It can be seen that the Ditch is not a defensive construction; it served merely as a quarry for the chalk rubble bank inside it.

PLATE 83   The Heel Stone (96), seen from the north-west. The 'cavity something resembling the print of a man's foot' (John Aubrey 1666) is clearly visible. This famous stone beside the A344 main road has variously been known also as the Hele Stone, the Bowing Stone, the Index Stone and The Friar's Heel.

PLATE 83

of Beaker pottery; above this have been found the usual workmen's rubbish of the period: hammer stones, broken tools and bones. Cremation holes from Phase I have been also discovered in the Ditch.

It is very unusual indeed to find a *Bank* at a henge monument inside its Ditch, but once again Stonehenge surprises us, for this is the case here. It measures about 97·5 m (320 ft) from crest to crest, was about 1·8 m (6 ft) high and lies about 30·4 m (100 ft) from the nearest stones, which were to arrive some 650 years later. The causewayed entrance was and is to the north-east, and beyond it the famous *Heel Stone* was placed. It has been called the Bowing Stone (Gridley 1873) and the Index Stone (Barclay 1895).

This is the only extant stone erected in Phase I (there was a pair of stones in Holes D and E in this Phase, and *possibly* the Four Stations as well), and being so prominently positioned, at the entrance to the earth circle, and beside a trackway that was to become the far too busy A344, it was natural for the first public turnstile for paid admission and the custodian's hut to be very near it. The Heel Stone also has a bench mark, and fifty feet away lay a mile stone. It is 78 m (256 ft) from the middle of Stonehenge, stands 4·8 m (16 ft) above the ground, and 1·2 m (4 ft) below it. The Stone is local sarsen (of which more under Phase III a), of 2·4 m (8 ft) maximum thickness and is almost pointed at the top. It is generally believed to be of a natural and untouched shape. However, Edward Duke was first to claim (1846, p. 145) that its top could have been shaped to make it coincide with the skyline as it appeared to an observer standing in the middle of the henge, as he waited for the midsummer solstice sun to rise over it. This famous alignment (which is discussed in Part 1) has helped Stonehenge to its present controversial status – but E. H. Stone damply pointed out in 1924 that the sun will not in fact rise truly over the Heel Stone until the year 3,260 (Stone 1924)! And when the Stone was put there, the sun rose just to the west of it. The possible connection between '*helios*', the Greek word for sun, and Heel Stone has been discounted by philologists, and so has any relation of the Gaelic '*clach na freas heol*' (*heol*: street or road), or '*helan*' which is the Anglo-Saxon for 'to hide' (ie: the sun). It has also been called Hele, a familiar Devonshire place-name by itself, and also found near Stonehenge (*cf*, Hele House). It is interesting to note that the Old English word '*healh*' means 'corner' (in which the Stone

PLATE 84

could be said to be). Alternatively, we should perhaps ponder upon the Old English '*heah*' which meant high and was mostly used as a prefix: now if, for the sake of conjecture, it was ever connected to '*tūn*' (which meant 'enclosure' and is never found alone as a place-name – nor its descendant 'town' – and very rarely as a prefix), then we would have 'high enclosure'. All a diverting possibility of course, because the forests were cleared some 2,000 years ago over many wide local areas (*eg*, Windmill Hill, Durrington Walls) and presumably around Stonehenge too, because the astronomical alignments required their distant markers. Only if these were along wooded avenues, with marker ropes hung across them, could my diversion become less than

PLATE 84   The Heel Stone, seen from the south-east. The barbed wire behind it is in place and ready for the annual Druidic summer solstice ceremony.

playful. Extraordinary is the variety of names to which Stonehenge itself has been subjected! A report on the Spring 1978 excavation by Professor Atkinson has confirmed that the environment of the henge *was* grassland when it was constructed (Dr John Evans, *The Times*, 23 August 1978).

Dr John Smith refers to the Stone as the Friar's Heel in *Choir Gaur*, published in 1771 (in which he was probably one of the first to point out that it indicates 'the sun's greatest amplitude' at the summer solstice) and so does Sir Norman Lockyer as late as 1906. The appellation seems to have occurred because John Aubrey (see Part 1) refers in his famous manuscript to a stone that 'hath a cavity something resembling the print of a man's foot.' He was referring to the recumbent Stone 14, which indeed has a large natural cavity resembling a footprint. But the Heel Stone has a much larger one on its south-west face, and the name must have transferred in the telling of the legend which has the angry or jealous Devil throwing the stone at a friar whose heel print remains to this day. I suspect that the present name arises from the fact that it 'heels over' towards Stonehenge – and perhaps always has. And could it have been put up simply as a sort of travellers' guide-post to the more or less contemporary henge, as was perhaps the King Stone at Rollright?

Perhaps the most mysterious feature of the Phase I construction period is the group of *Post Holes* between the Ditch ends in the causewayed entrance gap. I am inclined to think of the making of these as Stonehenge Ia, with the rest of Stonehenge I as Stonehenge Ib. Analyses (Atkinson 1956 and Newham 1966) of the positions of these fifty-three post holes, in eleven rows by six, which were discovered by Colonel Hawley, has offered convincing evidence that, even during the first Phase, it was being used for precise and constant observation and the recording of the extreme northerly risings of the moon for a hundred years or more. The dating of a ditch antler at c. 2,900–2,600 BC (Burl 1976, p. 305) firmly indicates the age of a Stonehenge actually in use for midsummer and midwinter rituals. Long established indeed were those 'pagan religious practices'.

Three more (undated) post holes, marked today in concrete in the hideous car park to the north-west across the road, may be contemporary with 'the 53'. Each about 76 cm (29·9 ins) across, Newham has suggested (Newham 1972, p. 24) that they might

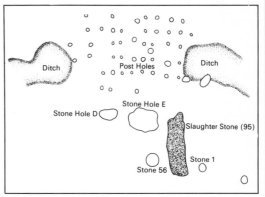

FIGURE 24

have been markers on midwinter moonset and midsummer sunset alignments. The role of observation platforms is frequently mentioned by Professor Alexander Thom, and he has suggested that these posts holes could have been for supports.

It has also been suggested by many archaeologists, noting evidence of post holes there, that there may have been a *small timber building* at the centre of the henge, perhaps in the manner of Woodhenge nearby.

The lively and inquiring John Aubrey was the first to notice a ring of what he called 'cavities', set just inside the Bank. R. S. Newall remembered this reference during the Society of Antiquaries official excavations in 1919–26, and suggested a search for them. And so it was that the sites of the fifty-six *Aubrey Holes*, as they were dubbed (after being designated X Holes – thus the Y and Z Holes within), were finally discovered. Just how important this event was did not become apparent until some forty years later, when Gerald Hawkins pronounced them to be eclipse predictors in his famous second paper in *Nature* in June 1964. This function is discussed in Part 1.

Thirty-two of the Holes are indicated today on the ground by those white markers which show up so well in aerial photographs. They were set in a circle 86·7 m (284½ ft) in diameter, and with such precision that none of the centres of them deviates more than 482 mm (1 ft 7 ins) from this circle. Their edges are some 4·9 m (16 ft) apart and again are remarkably

FIGURE 24 The causewayed entrance post holes.

precisely placed. The average diameter of the Holes is 1·06 m (3 ft 6 ins), and the depth 762 mm (2 ft 6 ins). They were evidently all made at the same time, but the excavation of thirty-four of their numbers has not helped searches for conventional functions; it has been shown, for instance, that they have never held stones or wooden posts (as at Woodhenge). We now suspect their astronomical function; was this extraordinary instrument perhaps in use before the calibrated date of about 2,200 BC on the evidence of a sample of charcoal found in Hole 32? The Holes have yielded cremation remains (some secured perhaps in pinned bags), flakes of flint, a stone mace head, ash, and an earthenware cup. It is also clear that after they were dug they were refilled with chalk rubble, then small holes were dug out again – and finally refilled with the rubble, wood fragments and burnt soil. Rituals involving cremation burial must have taken place – and perhaps over the period of its use as an eclipse predictor. Could the two have been connected? Stonehenge's mysteries are in layers as well as degrees.

PLATE 85   Some of the Aubrey Holes can be clearly seen, indicated with white markers, in this aerial view of the excavations on 31 July 1958.

PLATE 86 (*right*)   Three prominent figures in the Stonehenge story, standing between the recumbent Stone 55a and Stone 56 during the 1958 excavations and restoration work. R. S. Newall (left), Professor Stuart Piggott, Dr J. F. S. Stone (centre).

PLATE 85

We take leave of Phase I with notice of two odd facts. That enormous construction, The Cursus, was going up (see Part 5), with incalculable manpower involved, for a still unknown purpose, some time after Phase I, but before Phase II. Secondly, although we meet the bluestones in Phase II, it is believed that they were actually in the area during the period of Stonehenge I; a large block of spotted dolerite has been found in Boles Barrow, which is 18·5 km (11·5 miles) west of the monument and is on the supposed route from Prescelly to Stonehenge. Perhaps it was from a sample brought for the testing of still unknown properties, or perhaps – and this theory has some support – there was a 'bluestone henge' once set at either the western end of the Cursus or in the Warminster area at Boles Barrow.

PLATE 86

Phase II
(c. 2100 BC)

This second stage in the assembly of Stonehenge is the one that raises a very common question: why were the stones brought from so far away? As we will see, by no means all of them were, but the bluestones which form the *Double Bluestone Circle,* the centre-piece of Stonehenge II, were indeed transported with prodigious effort over some 386 km (240 miles) of mountain, valley, sea, river and downland plain. This is peculiar because no other known British stone circle is of anything but local stone – and yet these bluestones, most of them dolerite, do not appear to have any properties essential to their supposed functions. The theory that glacial action brought them to the Plain (Kellaway 1971) has now been discounted as we see later, although it had an eminent supporter in Colonel Sir Henry James, Director General of the Ordnance Survey, who wrote of 'the agency of ice' (James 1867).

Eighty-two of them, weighing up to four tons each, were somehow brought down from the Prescelly Mountains, Dyfed (formerly Pembrokeshire), in South Wales, where they may just possibly have formed part of a circle and some more were collected from Milford Haven on the coast; they were shipped east along the Bristol Channel, and up the River Avon (see Figure 16). The Stonehenge Avenue (see Part 5) was once believed to have been created in this Phase from the banks of the Avon, and the huge stones to have been brought along it to the Stonehenge site with some ceremony and celebration.

The bluestones were set up in the Q and R Holes in two concentric circles 1·8 m (6 ft) apart, with an entrance on the north-east side, where there were extra stones within. On the western side this Double Bluestone Circle was probably not completed. A big pit was dug on the north-west which might have been for a very large stone – perhaps even for the present Altar Stone (III b).

Geoffrey of Monmouth wrote that the bluestones came from Mount Killaraus in Ireland. But it is more likely, as a study of pottery and certain Irish stone circles tell us, that it was just the idea or inspiration that came from across the Irish sea – via the Beaker folk's trading route, and so by the awe-inspiring Mountains (Atkinson 1956, p. 175). That idea for a bluestone circle was magnificently realized in its achievement and use, as we have seen in Part 1.

The north-east *Causeway* was widened during Phase II by some 7·6 m (25ft) at its eastern side. Additional prominence was awarded the Heel Stone by enclosing it with a ditch – but this was filled in again almost immediately with chalk (which had bluestone chips in its upper layer, and a rhyolite flake in the original filling). Stones D and E, erected at the original entrance during Stonehenge I, were also removed, possibly to Holes B and C.

The *Altar Stone* (Stone 80) was set in place within this Phase. It was named by Inigo Jones, but John Smith (1771) showed that it could never have been used for sacrifices as it cannot take fire – so perhaps its position bespoke it. It is the largest of the 'foreign' stones at Stonehenge, and is 1·0 m (3 ft 4 ins) wide. 0·5 m (1¾ ft) deep, and 4·9 m (16 ft) long. It now lies

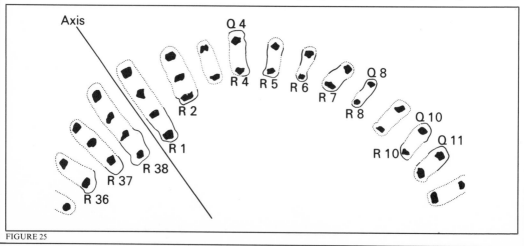

FIGURE 25

FIGURE 25   The Q and R Holes which contained bluestones in the eastern section, as they were in Phase II (after Atkinson 1956).

recumbent, mostly buried and probably across its own stone hole, with its present upper surface nearly buried, under the pressure of part of Stone 55 and Stone 156 (both from the Great Trilithon in front of which it might once have stood, on the Axis). The petrology of the Altar Stone is unique at Stonehenge: it is of pale green micaceous sandstone, but with minute traces of garnet, and this composition indicates its source as Milford Haven on the bluestone route from the Prescelly Mountains to Salisbury Plain.

These characteristic changes of Stonehenge II were related to the creation of a new alignment (the Axis) from the central pit, through the newly widened entrance and past the Heel Stone to the point of the summer solstice sunrise. The changes have also, however, been shown to be involved with lunar rather than solar prediction (Newham 1972, p. 7), but without doubt both were intended to enable predictions to be made for the exact timing of ceremonies or rituals associated with the process of regeneration, perhaps both animal and vegetable. To refer to 'pagan acts of worship', as many commentators on the period have done, is slighting to the perpetrators of acts of natural magic which were sustained by ever-refined use – and, presumably, results!

The arrival of the bluestones at the henge marks a transition of planning, from circle of timbers in holes to stones in holes; we see this also at The Sanctuary (an account of which is in Part 5). So we face the odd fact that on the chalky Salisbury Plain there were concentric stone circles, and yet in the stony Cornish lands to the south-west there are none to be found. It was the craft of the Wessex carpenters who had responded to the fresh and far more sophisticated needs of their Late Neolithic Beaker leaders who were evolving into astronomer priests of great power.

PLATE 87

FIGURE 26

PLATE 87   The shattered Altar Stone (80) lies fully revealed during the 1958 excavations, as viewed from the north-east. Stone 55b lies on one end of the larger part, and Stone 156 rests on the other. The Altar Stone probably belongs to Phase 11 and was named by Inigo Jones; it is the largest of the 'foreign' stones at Stonehenge, being 4·9 m (16 ft) long.

FIGURE 26   Sir Richard Colt-Hoare's plan of the stones made in 1810, and engraved by Philip Crocker. From his magnificent *History of Ancient Wiltshire: South* (1812).

Phase IIIa
(c. 2000 BC)

The *Four Stations* are (clockwise) Stones 91, 92, 93 and 94, and their prominent former siting is shown in Plate 88. Stone 91 is about 2·7 m (9 ft) long, recumbent, without a mound and is an undressed sarsen; Stone 92 is missing from within a ditch which overlays Aubrey Holes 17 and 18; Stone 93 is 1·2 m (4 ft) high as it stands above the ground; it is also of slightly dressed sarsen and has no mound; Stone 94 is also missing. Thus we see that they were so placed after the final digging of the Aubrey Holes, and we also know that the Four Stations were erected before the Sarsen Circle and the Horseshoe, which comprise the principal features of Phase IIIa. This is because the intersections between Stones 91–93 and 92–94 could not otherwise have been mutually sighted . . . and yet it is now certain that in fact they once were. This is due to the discovery of C. A. 'Peter' Newham in 1963 of the geometric relationship of the Four Stations to the latitude of Stonehenge, which is described in more detail in Part I. The importance of this discovery by Newham, who died in 1974 (although it was slightly anticipated, unknown to him, by Charrière), is commemorated by the name of Peter's Mound, a feature on the north-eastern skyline which Alexander Thom was to find very significant in 1974.

Sometime just before or after the placing of the stones of the Four Stations, there was a crucial change of plan at Stonehenge. The *Double Bluestone Circle* erected in Phase II was dismantled in something of a hurry: it was part of a determined effort perhaps to create a monument to rival nearby Avebury. Whoever guided the design of this Phase – the last of the Beaker folk or Early Bronze Age merchants of the Wessex culture – they certainly evolved a truly majestic structure.

Perhaps even whilst the Double Bluestone Circle was being taken down (and the stones left, as we know, lying around nearby), 77 huge sarsen stones were being dragged about 32 km (20 miles) to the site, destined for roles in the *Sarsen Circle* and *Sarsen Horseshoe*. They were selected from among the hundreds of blocks on the Downs outside what is today the town of Marlborough. The sarsens for both the Sarsen Circle and the Sarsen Horseshoe in the middle were roughly dressed at their original sites, and it must have been an astonishingly laborious task, the testing for internal flaws, the cutting, the rough shaping and then the endless pounding with harder

PLATE 88   The monument seen from beyond the Bank and Ditch to the east. Station Stone 91 is on the left. Of the Four Station stones, Stone 93 also survives, but Stones 92 and 94 are missing.

stone hammers or balls, to smooth the surfaces to their final simple elegance. Maximum efforts at refinement were concentrated on the surfaces facing inwards, and on the extraordinary tapering and curving which becomes startlingly evident if you stand (if you are allowed to!) in the centre and look up at the calm integration at their curvilinear joins and edges. Imagine the degree of organization required for all this work to be undertaken so far from Stonehenge – over 4,000 years ago! After incredible feats of transportation (which I discuss later) the uprights were set into position in the Circle and Horseshoe, and presumably allowed to settle into their chalky, rubble-packed foundations. After this their tops were dressed by cutting, more pounding with the mauls, leaving tenons or knobs ready for their lintels to be raised up and lowered directly, mortises to tenons, on to them.

The height, in every sense, of the achievement of Stonehenge, was reached with the construction of the Sarsen Horseshoe of Trilithons. The five groups of giant dressed stones were so named in 1740 by William Stukeley (Greek: '*Tris*', three, '*lithos*', stone) in his book on Stonehenge. The Horseshoe opens to the north-east, directly along the Axis, and its pairs of uprights are set only a foot or so apart. Trilithons

PLATE 89

PLATE 89   The 23 cm (9 ins) high tenon on the top of Stone 56, part of the Great (or Central) Trilithon.

PLATE 90   The lintel of the Great Trilithon, Stone 156, with its two mortises clearly shown. It is lying in front of Stone 68, with Stone 56 towering behind.

PLATE 90

51/52 and 53/54 are standing intact. Stone 55 fell inwards sometime before 1574, broke in two and its lintel (Stone 156) still lies across the so-called Altar Stone; the third stone (56) in the mighty Great or Central Trilithon still stands. It was leaning for centuries until straightened in 1901 by Professor William Gowland: a flake which broke off then is in Devizes Museum. An antler pick found in a construction ramp of this trilithon has been dated at 2120 ± 160 BC (Burl 1976, p. 312). Continuing clockwise, Stones 57 and 58 and their lintel (158) fell outwards on 3 January 1797, but were re-erected in 1958. Stone 59 fell inwards long ago and lies in three pieces; its lintel (160) is also in three pieces, but their companion, Stone 60, still stands. The highest Trilithons are Stones 55 and 56 at 6·6 m (21 ft 8 ins) or 7·7 m (25½ ft) to the top of their lintel, from ground level; Stone 56 is known to be set 2·4 m (8 ft) into the ground. Lower are Stones 53/54 and 57/58, measuring 5·4 m (17¾ ft), or 6·4 m (21¼ ft) to their lintel tops; smallest are the ends of the Horseshoe, Stones 51/52 and 59/60 which are 5 m (16½ ft) high, or 6 m (20 ft) to their lintel tops. The inside edges of the lintels are beautifully shaped to incline inwards in a concave curve, the outside edges similarly incline inwards in a convex curve (which is not so of lintels in the Sarsen Circle) and their uprights are tapered to give the slightest bulges to their girths.

The Sarsen Circle has a diameter of 29·6 m (97 ft), and was originally made up of thirty stones all with lintels. Seventeen of the uprights are standing today

FIGURE 27   The first published Ordance Survey of Stonehenge, carried out by Colonel Sir Henry James in June 1867.

FIGURE 27

PLATE 91

uprights are now recumbent but complete (Stones 12, 14, 25); parts of five of them remain (Stones 8, 9, 15, 19, 26) and five are missing (Stones 13, 17, 18, 20, 24). Stone 22 and its lintel fell on 31 December 1900 and were re-erected in 1958. Stone 23 fell in March 1963 and was restored to its position in 1964. Their average height is 4·1 m (13 ft 6 ins) above the ground – a further 1·2–1·5 m (4–5 ft) lies underground – they average 2·1 m (7 ft) in width, and stand 3 m (10 ft) apart (measuring centre to centre). The heaviest sarsen in the Circle weighs about 28 tons, though the average is 26 tons.

Only five of the 30 dressed lintel stones remai (Stones 130, 101, 102, 105, 107); the lintels were numbered by William Flinders Petrie by taking the number 1, and adding to it the greater of the two stone numbers below them. Parts of Stones 120 and

(Stones: 1–7, 10, 11, 16, 21–3, 27–30). It is immediately noticeable that most of the damage is on the south-west, where, according to one commentator, the Deluge hit the Circle! Three of the

PLATE 91   Colonel William Hawley (left) examining chalk rubble sifters' finds during his 1919–26 excavations. It was then that the Aubrey Holes were re-discovered and so-named.

PLATE 92 (*below*)   The raising of Stone 56 during Hawley's excavations (he is right of centre). Note the police constable on the far left, keeping well clear of the somewhat primitive lifting gear.

127 survive, but the remaining twenty two lintels are missing. They average 1·0 m (3½ ft) wide, 0·7 m (2½ ft) thick and 4·0 m (10½ ft) in length. Each is mortised twice beneath it as we have seen, all are tongued and grooved each end as well, all are rebated or dished and gently curved to rest gracefully (or rather did, and we should assume the Circle was completed) upon their supports, which taper slightly upwards in the ancient Greek manner which so delights the educated eye.

The Sarsen Circle is constructed with such precision that there can be no wonder at the continuity of its popularity through the ages; this has of course been connected for over 200 years with the Axis. The entrance to the Circle is between Stones 30 and 1 where the gap is 3·05 cm (1 ft) wider, and this is absorbed by smaller gaps either side of it. The lintel above it is thicker than the rest, but its up-rights are not lower (see Plate 61) note that the upper surfaces of the lintels all remain level because the undersides of lintels 130 and 102 are carefully rebated; it is this feature that has caused some researchers to hint at a possible function for those upper surfaces. Reference is made in Part 1, for instance, to Professor Brinckerhoff's discovery of a significant pattern of 'wand' holes there.

Although it has no tenon, and was probably not intended for a place in a lintelled circle, there is one more dressed sarsen stone at Stonehenge, which is presumed to have been brought to the site during Phase IIIa with the rest of the sarsen blocks. For some unknown reason it is called the *Slaughter Stone* (95), and it lies between Aubrey Holes 56 and 1 at the south-east side of the Causeway, with its upper surface almost level with the ground. It is 2·1 m (7 ft) wide, 0·9 m (3 ft) thick and 6·4 m (21 ft) long, and was probably one of a pair. The other was the now lost Stone E and stood opposite its fellow, at the other side of the Axis.

During this Phase the building of the barrows in

PLATE 93

PLATE 94

PLATE 93 Heavy steel lifting tackle being employed during the restoration work in June 1958.

PLATE 94 An unusual view of the monument (from the top of the Heel Stone), looking over the Slaughter Stone (95). This dressed sarsen stone was probably one of a pair (to Stone E), and lies between Aubrey Holes 30 and 1 (the white disc on the left); it belongs to Phase IIIa.

the area around Stonehenge (mostly to the south, as in a churchyard) also commenced; some 460 of them have been identified. The eight Barrow Groups, which form an integral part of the Stonehenge story, are described in Part 5.

Phase IIIb

(date uncertain)

You cannot 'see' most of this Phase as it must have been intended – which only emphasizes the completed grandeur of Stonehenge IIIa. Professor Atkinson proposed in his *Stonehenge* (1956) a hypothesis that links the Dressed setting, the Altar Stone and the Y and Z Holes, and also the last Phase settings of the Circle and Horseshoe: it can be shown as follows:

Phase IIIa
Stones from
dismantled Double
Bluestone Circle
(II)   82

Phase IIIb		*Phase IIIc*
		19 used in Bluestone Circle
		2 used as lintels in Bluestone Circle
		1 became the Altar Stone
Stones in Dressed Bluestone Oval (longest used)	22 →	22
Y Holes (intended for stones)	30 ⎫	
Z Holes (intended for stones)	30 ⎭	60 missing
	82	82

The Y and Z Holes could be assigned to Phase IIIc, but for the coincidence indicated above.

The exact location of the nineteen stones in the *Dressed Bluestone Oval* is not known, but it was certainly inside the Sarsen Trilithon Horseshoe, and very approximately followed the line of the later Bluestone Horseshoe though spaced differently. Stone holes J, K and L could well belong to the Oval, on account of this spacing. Four stones survived into Phase IIIc. Two are tongued-and-grooved and once stood together; they became part of the Bluestone Horseshoe and are Stone 66 (now a buried stump beneath part of the broken Stone 55) and Stone 68 (which stands upright). Two lintels from at least two former Trilithons survive; they are Stones 36 and 150, both of which became uprights in the Bluestone Circle and are now recumbent.

PLATE 95

The irregular concentric circles of *Z and Y Holes* form the third characteristic of Stonehenge IIIb and are not indicated on the ground today. They are so-called and in this order because the Aubrey Holes outside them were once known as X Holes. The 29 Z Holes vary in their distance from the Sarsen Circle from 1·5–4·6 m (5–15 ft); the 30 Y Holes are some 10·6 m (35 ft) away from the Circle . . . too many surely for them to be roof support post holes, as has been suggested? They were discovered during the 1923–4 excavations, and compounded the mystery of the Bluestone Oval – because they were never used and not even filled in after they were abandoned. Fillings of sarsen and bluestone chips, pottery, flint chips and chalk rubble occurred naturally over the years, although five deer antlers have been found in the bottom of one Hole. They average 889–1016 mm (35–40 ins) deep, 1·06 m (3 ft 6 ins) wide, and 1·8 m (6 ft) long. Stonehenge IIIb is the 'official' Phase for the occurrence of the Z and Y Holes – but do they in fact belong to the final Phase of all? I find it difficult indeed to believe that about 76 stones of the later Bluestone Circle and Bluestone Horseshoe were

PLATE 95   This photograph of a stump of a bluestone, uncovered during the 1958 excavations, shows a violent break.

PLATE 96

manoeuvred into position past 59 holes, shallow or otherwise, outside them. It is certain on the other hand, as I have shown in the calculation above, that they were intended for bluestone uprights: but then the plan changed: their spacing, from Z29 and Y29 (round clockwise) became ragged; Y7 was not finished, and Z8 was not dug out at all. Did the knowledge and traditions of one astronomer-priest suddenly succeed another; were different gods to be appeased with his coming? What exactly happened about 1,500 BC on Salisbury Plain to ensure such a dramatic change of plan? This is just another mystery of Stonehenge that will never be solved – but at least the archaeological facts are being pieced together to form a coherent sequence of events.

PLATE 96   The renovation and grassing of the central area began in March 1978, soon after the fence was erected in order to protect the stones from hundreds of thousands of annual visitors. Coke was uncovered, in the right foreground.

PLATE 97   My March 1978 photograph shows the bases of stones set into concrete. This precautionary work was done in 1964, and the ground level can be clearly seen.

PLATE 97

Phase IIIc
(after 1550 BC)

This final Phase evidently followed soon after the last; the Dressed Bluestone Oval was dismantled, and the Z and Y Holes' plans abandoned, as we have seen.

The *Bluestone Circle* was erected between the Sarsen Circle and the Sarsen Trilithon Horseshoe, in a very irregular circle of about 23 m (76 ft) in diameter. Its remaining stones are all untooled or undressed, with the exception of two: Stones 36 and 150. These are usually assigned to an original place in the Double Bluestone Circle of Phase II – but as undressed stones.

Eleven of the stones remain more or less upright (Stones 31–4, 37–9, 46–9): eight of them have fallen (Stones 36, 40–45, 150); Stone 35 is now just a visible stump, and seven have only stumps or fragments left below the ground surface. There were probably 60 stones, or 59 if one was omitted, to form the entrance, in the Circle originally; excavations have revealed evidence of five more stones between 32 and 33 (Professor Atkinson, Piggott and Dr Stone), six more between 33 and 34 (Colonel Hawley) and eight more between Stones 40 and 41 (Colonel Hawley). The Circle entrance was no doubt between Stones 31 and 49 (damaged but upright), which are set slightly into the Circle and further apart than others.

The *Bluestone Horseshoe* is, like the Sarsen Trilithon Horseshoe which encloses it, open along the line of the Axis, and its inner circle has a diameter of 11·9 m (39 ft). It was originally made up of 19 fully

PLATE 98

PLATE 98   Custodian Griffiths in front of Stone 58 in March 1978, the week after the fence went up. The four metal rods indicate the position of a stone which is buried encased in lead to preserve it.

PLATE 99   A section of the Ditch on the north side, roped off in March 1978, in preparation for the excavations carried out during the next months by Professor Richard Atkinson and Dr John Evans, both from University College, Cardiff.

PLATE 99

dressed stone pillars, 1·6 m (5½ ft) apart, centre to centre. Of these six remain upright (Stones 61–3, 68–70); two stumps are visible (Stones 64, 65) and one more is buried (Stone 66). The fallen stones are 67 (the central pillar) and Stones 71 and 72 (now known to be the broken halves of the same stone); the rest of the bluestones are now missing. They are all of spotted dolerite, except Stone 62 which is unspotted. After the manner of the Sarsen Horseshoe, the tallest are at the centre; Stone 67 stands 2·4 m (8 ft) high above the ground, and weighs about 4 tons, whilst Stone 61, at one end, is only 1·9m (6 ft 2 ins) high. The stones are finely tooled and generally taper upwards, with the sides and faces slightly expanded at the girth, though strangely and for no reason even guessed at, their form *alternates*—first a parallel sided pillar of square cross sections and then a markedly tapering obelisk of oblong cross sections. Their tops are flat and no lintels were intended for this Phase construction, except possibly for two of them, where the tenons have not been removed. Among other noteworthy features are the tongued-and-grooved sides of Stones 66 and 68. Of the original nineteen stones in this Horseshoe it is probable that only six or seven came from a former bluestone structure.

Phase IV
(c. 1100 BC)

Professor Richard Atkinson announced this sixth phase in December 1978. The Avenue (see Part 5) was extended from Stonehenge Bottom so that it passed over the hill eastwards and from there southwards to the River Avon. This means that Stonehenge was still 'in use' for some purpose unknown about 1100 BC.

Erection

As we have seen in Part 3, most of the stones were only roughly dressed at their source; no doubt to lose excess weight, but keeping until their eventual arrival at Stonehenge the careful organization and the astonishingly intricate designs. Their transportation to Stonehenge is also mentioned in Part 3. At the site, the placing of the uprights in their prepared holes would not have been too difficult: Figure 27 shows methods. The placing of the lintels on their tops – mortises and tenons exactly matching – must have been a much more difficult task. There is no evidence that chalk rubble (from the top of the surrounding bank for instance) was used, and opinions vary as to whether a timber structure was erected around each pair of stones for the purpose, or whether earth was brought to the site so that ramps could be built up the sides – and used for making the early Bronze Age barrows afterwards.

The possible techniques of erection of the stones are discussed thoroughly in the engineer E. H. Stone's *The Stones Of Stonehenge* (1924), and also summarised, 'with additions and variations' by Professor Atkinson (1956, pp. 125–35). Figures 27 and 28 display perhaps better than in words the most commonly accepted erection theories.

FIGURE 27   How the sarsens were erected?

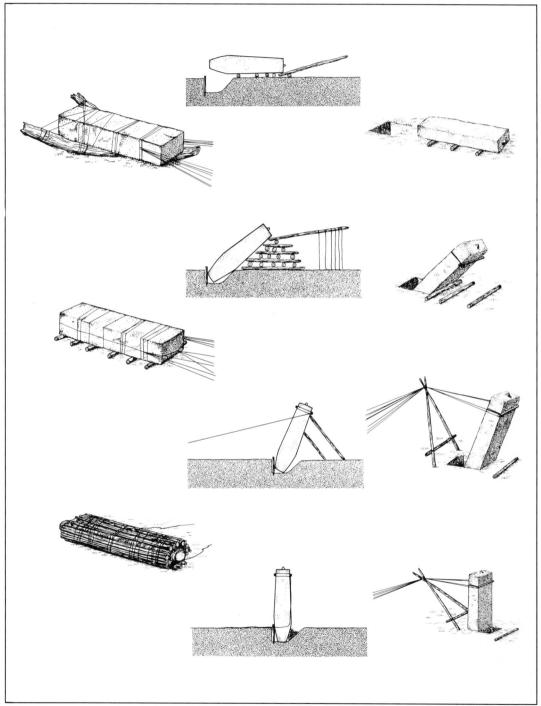

FIGURE 27

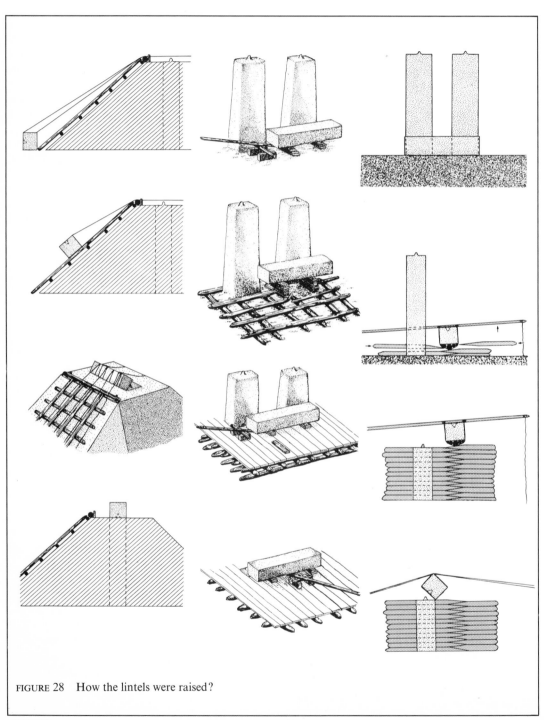

FIGURE 28   How the lintels were raised?

FIGURE 28

The Carvings

Jones, Aubrey, Stukeley, Wood, Colt-Hoare, Duke, Petrie, Barclay, Lockyer, Hawley, Stevens, Cunnington, Stone – all these eminent contributors to the Stonehenge story missed a remarkable but simple, and now of course obvious, fact, which appropriately fell to Professor Atkinson to discover. While photographing the inner face of Stone 53 in the Great Trilithon Horseshoe during the late afternoon of 10 July 1953 he found himself looking at a carved representation of a hilted dagger. Moreover it seemed to be of the type found in Shaft Grave 6 at Mycenae which was dated at about 1,600–1,500 BC. Was this the proof that the diffusionist theory of the spread of Mycenaen cultural influences to Britain was correct? Was this the actual mark, or 'monogram' of the architect of Stonehenge? It must have been a 'heady' moment.

Ten days later, David Booth, the 10-year-old son of a helper at the official excavations, found no less than twenty-five further carvings of what appeared to be Early Bronze-Age-type axe-blades on the outer face of Stone 4. As so

PLATE 100 This was the sight which must have met Professor Richard Atkinson's gaze into the view-finder of his camera on the afternoon of 10 July 1953; he had been intending to photograph the seventeenth century carved initials *above* the hilted Mycenaean-type dagger which he discovered at that moment.

PLATE 101 A contoured cast made by R. S. Newall, c. 1954, of 'Atkinson's Dagger' (as I call it), on the inner face of Stone 53.

PLATE 100

PLATE 101

often happens in the case of a discovery, more are made immediately: one knows what one is looking for. Near 'Atkinson's Dagger' were also four Early Bronze Age axes, one of them crescentic, indicating that its model was metal. On the outer face, Mr Barratt, a custodian of the day, found three incised axe heads. On the inner face of Stone 53 there were rough representations of about twelve Early Bronze Age axe blades. And in the same year R. S. Newall found most unusual marking on the inner face of Stone 57; it was named by O. G. S. Crawford the 'Box Symbol', and consists of an irregular quadrilateral of faintly incised grooves, 114 cm (45 ins) high: this same shape has been found on megaliths and in chambered tombs in Brittany in quantity, and it is believed to be associated with a cult of the mother or earth goddess, which is mentioned briefly in the account of West Kennett Long Barrow in Part 5. A more doubtful hilted dagger was found in August by Brian Hope-Taylor on the west face of Stone 53, just 14 cm (5½ ins) top to bottom.

On the first day of 1954, O. G. S. Crawford, still the editor of *Antiquity* (which he had founded more than twenty-five years previously), found further carvings. On the south side of Stone 23 there was a dagger without a hilt, and on Stone 29, also on the south side, he found (and named) what he detected to be the shape of a Torso; he also thought he saw markings on Stones 30 and 55a.

Finally brief mention of some apparent cup marks on Stone 9b – but these are likely to be natural occurrences – and of the initials I O H : L V D : D E F E R R E, which may stand for the untraceable Johannes (John) Ludovicus (Louis) de Ferre, who probably carved his name (just above Atkinson's Dagger) in the seventeenth century. The L V enclosed by a loop on the (now) west face of Stone 156 has been shown to be of nineteenth century origin.

The surprise discovery of these carvings immediately provoked academic debate; in the ensuing years enthusiasm for the Mycenaen link faded (and radio-carbon dating despatched it completely although Atkinson's hilted dagger could indeed have been carved

PLATE 102

PLATE 103

PLATE 102 Professor Richard Atkinson (left) and Dr J. F. S. Stone examine a latex rubber mould of 'Atkinson's Dagger'.

PLATE 103 R. S. Newall (right) and Dr J. F. S. Stone (beside him) watch a latex rubber mould being made of the 'box symbol' on the inner face of Stone 57. It is recumbent here, but was re-erected in 1958. The symbol was first identified by Newall in 1953 as being similar to carvings in Brittany, and it is probably connected with a cult of the mother or earth goddess. The ladder behind Newall was specially designed by Atkinson for archaeological photography.

later by an Eastern hand: it is an accurate description): today more attention is given to the British-Breton connection, the nature of the earliest metal trade, and whether some kind of axe cult helped it flourish. We only know three things for certain: the weather has obliterated some carvings and changed the appearance of others, that they were made at Stonehenge and not at the source of the stones – and that old habits don't change.

PLATE 104   Brian Hope-Taylor sitting near the excavation hut whilst discussing a point with Professor Piggott during the 1958 season.

PLATE 105   Modern carvings photographed in March 1978 – hopefully the last there will be, now that the stones are closed to visitors.

PLATE 104

PLATE 105

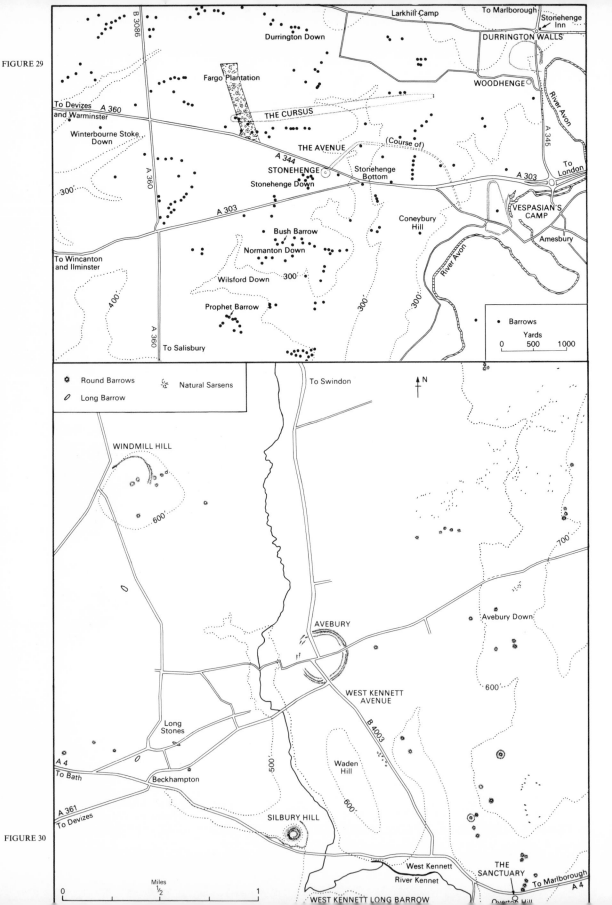

FIGURE 29

FIGURE 30

Figure 29 (top map):

To Marlborough
Larkhill Camp
Stonehenge Inn
Durrington Down
DURRINGTON WALLS
Fargo Plantation
WOODHENGE
THE CURSUS
River Avon
To Devizes and Warminster A 360
A 345
Winterbourne Stoke Down
THE AVENUE
(Course of)
A 344
Stonehenge Bottom
STONEHENGE
To London
A 303
Stonehenge Down
Stonehenge Down
300'
VESPASIAN'S CAMP
A 360
A 303
Bush Barrow
Coneybury Hill
Amesbury
Normanton Down
River Avon
To Wincanton and Ilminster
Wilsford Down   300
300'
300'
400'
Prophet Barrow
A 360
To Salisbury

• Barrows
Yards
0   500   1000

Figure 30 (bottom map):

Round Barrows
Natural Sarsens
Long Barrow

To Swindon
N

WINDMILL HILL
600'
700'

AVEBURY
Avebury Down

WEST KENNETT AVENUE
600'
Long Stones
B 4003
A 4
To Bath
Waden Hill
Beckhampton
500'
A 361
To Devizes
600'
SILBURY HILL

West Kennett
River Kennet
THE SANCTUARY
To Marlborough
A 4
Overton Hill
WEST KENNETT LONG BARROW

Miles
0   1/2   1

Part 5
Twelve local Prehistoric Sites

Avebury – The Barrow Groups – The Cursus
Durrington Walls – Old Sarum – The Sanctuary
Silbury Hill – Stonehenge Avenue
West Kennett Avenue – West Kennett Long Barrow
Windmill Hill – Woodhenge

PLATE 106

Britain possesses, in Christopher Marlowe's words 'infinite riches in a little room.' Surely most of them are concentrated in those areas of ancient Wessex around Stonehenge and Avebury, which afford as exciting a week of walking, and contemplation of the very beginnings of our society, as one could find anywhere in Europe? As I mentioned in my Preface, superlatives abound: the sheer scale of activity within a period of some 1,500 years matches, in the ratio of men: effort, the NASA space programme in its entirety.

These are twelve of the most prominent sites, and all of them, just as Stonehenge does, have their own mysterious facets.

FIGURE 29   The area around Stonehenge.

FIGURE 30   The area around Avebury.

PLATE 106   'A Prospect from Abury Steeple'. This is one of William Stukeley's engravings from his book *Abury, A Temple Of The British Druids* (1743). Many of the plates in it are still respected as references today.

Avebury

O.S. Map Reference: SU 103699
A Property of the National Trust (the village and monument), and the Department of the Environment have the guardianship of the monument.

John Aubrey 'discovered' Avebury whilst out fox hunting, as he recorded in his journal for 7 January 1648; he was 'wonderfully surprized'. So would I have been, for it is the mightiest stone circle in the British Isles; and Aubrey noted that it 'does as much exceed in greatness the so renowned Stoneheng as a Cathedral doeth a parish Church.' It is as well that we have on record comments from the past, because today the Great Circle contains roads, half a village and few of the stones.

Avebury was built between c. 2,500 and 2,200 BC, even while the camp on Windmill Hill nearby and above it was perhaps in use. The Hill is described later in this Part, and so are The Sanctuary and the West Kennett Avenue which connects it with Avebury.

The outer bank, between 4·2 m (14 ft) and 5·4 m (18 ft) high, encloses an area of about 11·5 hectares (28½ acres), and is made from 3,950,000 cu. ft of chalk dug with antler picks from the ditch inside it, which went 9 m (30 ft) below ground level. There were four causewayed entrances (only one at Stonehenge). Just inside, the main circle of almost 100 stones was erected, and within it in turn were set not one but two further stone circles – separated today by Green Street! In the centre of the northern circle, which had a diameter of 97 m (320 ft) and twenty-seven stones (only four left visible today), stood three stones (two left), which have become known as the Cove (its equivalents are found at Stanton Drew and Arbor Low); and there may have been a second ring set closer in towards it. In the middle of the

PLATE 107

southern inner circle, which had a diameter of 103 m (340 ft) and twenty-nine stones (five left), was placed a single stone 6·3 m (21 ft) long, which became known as the Obelisk; it was broken up by the time William Stukeley got to Avebury. Between the Obelisk and the western arc twelve smaller stones were placed, which have become known as the Z feature; and between the southern and the outer circles stood the Ring Stone, the stump of which remains.

Although the sarsen stones of Avebury are certainly erected with a certain giant elegance, and by a most complicated geometry (according to Professor Alexander Thom's surveys), they do not rival the appearance of the dressings of the sarsens of Stonehenge. This majestic site has suffered badly at least twice; in the Middle Ages many of the stones were levered into pits and buried, to hide away the natural rivals of the church. In the early eighteenth century the building trade had a go at them: 'Stone-Killer' Tom Robinson heated the sarsens that he managed to pull down, or were already there, and ... let William Stukeley describe the ghastly scene of predators at work:

'The barbarous massacre of a stone here with leavers and hammers, sledges and fire, is as terrible a sight as a Spanish Auto de fe. The vast cave they dig around it, the hollow under the stone like a glasshouse furnace or baker's oven, the huge chasms made through the body of the stone, the straw, the faggots, the smoak, the prongs, and squallor of the fellows looks like a knot of devils grilling the soul of the sinner.'

William Stukeley's oblique aerial reconstruction drawing of Avebury, or Abury, of 1724 (his last year of field work there) is one of the most complete; our debt to Stuke-

---

PLATES 107 The circles at Avebury as they may have appeared on completion (from *The Celtic Druids* by Godfrey Higgins, 1829).

FIGURE 31 A ground plan of the village and the circles.

FIGURE 32 'Temple At Abury': an 1829 engraving.

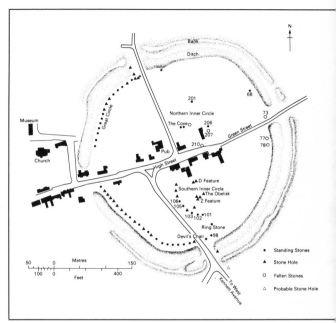

△ FIGURE 31

FIGURE 32 ▽

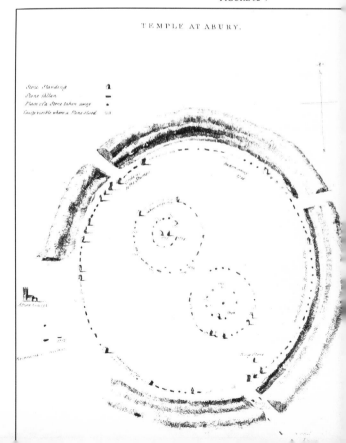

ley is considerable, and perhaps covers his claim to have found a double line of stones, like West Kennett (I have adopted the O.S. spelling) Avenue, going westwards from Avebury to the village of Beckhampton: this, as his fine illustrations show, gave him the shape he wished to discern. In June 1730 he confided its meaning to his friend Roger Gale:

'The form of that stupendous work is a picture of the Deity, more particularly of the Trinity, but most particularly what they anciently called the Father and the Word, who created all things. . . . A snake proceeding from a circle is the eternal procession of the Son, from the first cause . . . My main motive in pursuing this subject is to combat the deists from an unexpected quarter, and to preserve so noble a monument of our ancestors' piety, I may add, orthodoxy.'

PLATE 108   PLATE 109 ▽

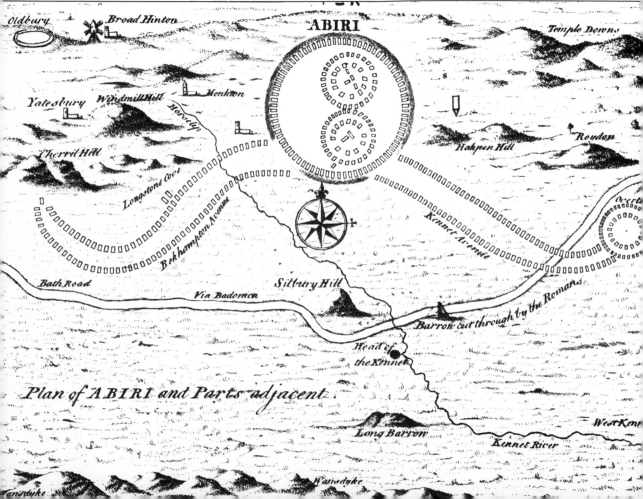

In 1743, William Stukeley published a companion volume to his *Stonehenge*. It was called *Abury, A Temple Of The British Druids,* and we should be grateful indeed for it, snake's head, wings and all. *The Mirror* of 15 November 1828 included the following comment, in an article on Avebury: 'The grand total of stones, included in the temples and avenues, was 650; in the original temples 188. . . . In Aubrey's time, 73 stones. . . . In Dr Stukeley's time, 29 stones. . . . In 1815, 17 stones.'

Fortunately the figure of seventeen stones has been increased by the discovery of some forty buried ones, by the Scotsman Alexander Keiller during his excavations of 1934–9. He had just bought most of Avebury village and some of the West Kennett Avenue (he already owned Windmill Hill). He then founded the Morven Institute of Archaeological Research (having moved his museum from Charles Street, in London's Mayfair), and after an appeal, enough money was raised for Avebury village to be transferred to the National Trust. The monument itself was put into the care of what was then the Ancient Monument Inspectorate of the Ministry of Works. The result of his great generosity, allied to sensitivity, gift for friendship and scholarship, is a fine small museum at the village, the restored stones, and many publications: these, and Dr I. F. Smith's 1965 book are his memorial.

Aubrey Burl has a detailed and enthusiastic account of Avebury in his comprehensive book on British stone circles (1976), and the Vatchers' small official H.M.S.O. guide-book (1976) precludes the necessity for further description by me of this very beautiful place. The pub in the middle is all plastic and piped music.

PLATE 110

PLATE 111

PLATE 108 (*left*)   The south-west quadrant of the Great Circle.

PLATE 109 (*left*)   Another plate from Stukeley's *Abury*; the Beckhampton Avenue may never have existed, but it served the author's conception of the dragon pattern in the landscape north of Silbury Hill.

PLATE 110   Alexander Keiller (1889–1955), a great benefactor of the monument and village of Avebury.

PLATE 111   Part of the eastern section of the bank and ditch (from which about 3,950,000 cubic feet of chalk rubble was removed). This photograph was taken in 1897 by W. Jerome Harrison, compiler of the great Stonehenge bibliography (1901).

The Barrow Groups

(OS References omitted, but see detailed map below)

The National Trust owns parts of some Groups' Access: see latest OS maps for rights of way.

Allowing the Reverend William Gilpin to set the scene as it was some two hundred years ago:

'The plain on which Stonehenge stands, is in the same style of greatness as the temple that adorns it. It extends many miles in all directions, in some not less than fifty. An eye unversed in these objects is filled with astonishment in viewing waste after waste rising out of each new horizon.

> Such appears the spacious plain
> Of Sarum, spread like Ocean's boundless round,
> Where solitary Stonehenge, grey with moss,
> Ruin of ages, nods.

'The ground is spread, indeed, as the poet says, like the ocean; but it is like the ocean after a storm, it is continually heaving in large swells. Through all this vast district, scarce a cottage or even a bush appears . . . . Regions like this, which have come down to us rude and untouched, from the beginning of time. fill the mind with grand conceptions, far beyond the efforts of art and cultivation. Impressed by such views of nature, our ancestors worshipped the god of nature, in these boundless scenes, which gave them the highest conception of eternity. . . . All the plain, at least that part of it near Stonehenge, is one vast cemetery. Everywhere, as we passed, we saw tumuli or barrows, as they are called, rising on each hand . . . that they are mansions of the dead is undoubted.' (Gilpin 1798)

No hard roads, wire fences or the works of tractor and plough: a ceremonial burial must indeed have been a remarkable scene, and it is a pity that no fine artist has attempted to recreate one. The barrows are well worth visiting, for unlike Stonehenge (now), they are steadily deteriorating. They are not rare for the nature of their individual structure or their contents (such as remain and as far as we know), but they certainly are for their (probably) unique grouped and dense distribution – particularly as it occurs around one of the great wonders of the world. And they are of course an

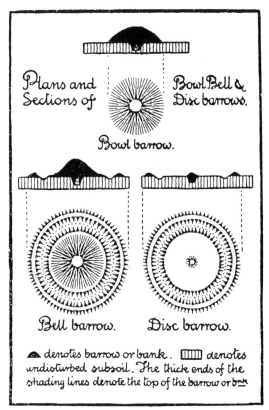

FIGURE 33

integral part of Stonehenge's story.

The coincidence – which L. V. Grinsell points out in his invaluable booklet *The Stonehenge Barrow Groups* (1978) – that there were about 460 barrows in the area around Stonehenge, which is the number of Geoffrey of Monmouth's warriors slain by Hengist, can be treated lightly.

FIGURE 33   This illustration of bowl, bell and disc barrows is taken from an early official guide-book *Stonehenge: Today and Yesterday* by Frank Stevens (Rev. Ed. 1929; page one: 'Stonehenge was erected about the year 1700 BC'). The sgraffito diagram is by Heywood Sumner (1853–1940), who was a leading figure in the Arts and Crafts Movement in the late 19th century, and in his later life deeply interested in archaeology.

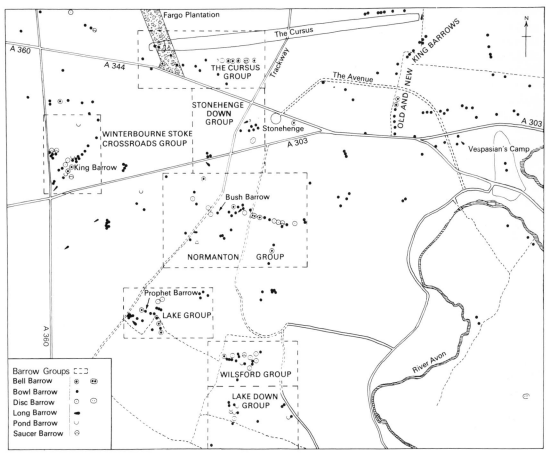

FIGURE 34

What cannot be is the very unhappy state of so many of them. Modern agricultural machinery has in the last thirty years done more damage than looters over the previous four thousand years. And planned excavations since Stukeley's day have been strangely few, as we shall see.

There are six different types of barrows to be found in the area: bell, bowl, disc, long, pond and saucer. These are illustrated in Figure 33. They are mostly within the following main groups seen in Figure 34, going west to east and north to south:

Group one   The Cursus Group

Group two	Old and New King Barrows
Group three	Winterbourne Stoke Crossroads Group
Group four	Stonehenge Down Group
Group five	Normanton Group
Group six	Lake Group
Group seven	Wilsford Group
Group eight	Lake Down Group

Outside these Groups, there are about six long barrows, a few bell, disc and saucer

FIGURE 34   The distribution of the eight Barrow Groups (based on L. V. Grinsell 1978).

barrows, one or two pond barrows and about eighty-four bowl barrows, often clustered. Most of these are discussed in as much detail (with numbering, here omitted) as is generally available, by Colt-Hoare and by L. V. Grinsell in his booklet, published by Salisbury Museum, to which I am greatly indebted. Artifacts discovered are also given by them, but I set out Thurnam's details of them below.

Before proceeding, let us add statistics to names. In 1880, before the depredations of twentieth-century men and machines struck Wiltshire, Sir William Flinders Petrie published the following table (Flinders Petrie 1880, p. 26):

Within-miles	No. barrows	No. per sq. mile
$\frac{1}{2}$	17	22
$\frac{1}{2}$ to 1	89	38
1 to $1\frac{1}{2}$	92	23
$1\frac{1}{2}$ to 2	66	12
2 to 3	74	4·7
3 to 5	87	1·7

He was trying to make the point that the barrows would be thickest on the ground nearest Stonehenge if they referred to it, but this need not be true at all.

One of the earliest commentators on the barrows, as he was upon so many diverse subjects, was John Aubrey. William Long (Long 1876) gives us this passage from Aubrey's unpublished manuscript *Monumenta Britannica*: 'At Stoneheng one may count, round about it fourtey five Barrowes. I am not of the opinion, that all these were made for burying the dead that were slayne herabout in Battels: it would require a great deale of time and leisure to collect so many thousand loades of earth: and soldiers have something els to doe flagrante bello: to pursue their victorie, or

PLATE 112

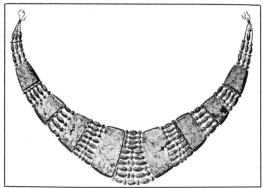

PLATE 113

preserve themselves pursued: the cadevera remained a feast for the Kites and Foxes. So that I presume they were the Mausolea or Burying places for the great Persons and Rulers of those times' (Aubrey c. 1666). This may have been the case; and is indeed suggested by many of the grave goods found in them; Stonehenge was as famous in Aubrey's time as much for its looters, cut-throats and vagabonds as it was for its bustards.

William Stukeley, who visited Stonehenge for the first time in May 1719, was fascinated by the barrows . . . 'it is no small entertainment for a curious person, to remark their beauties, their variety in form and magnitude, their situation'

PLATE 112 'Normanton Twin Barrow'; a mid-19th century water-colour by J. Bridges.

PLATE 113 A collar of amber (restored), found in a Lake Group barrow.

(Stukeley 1740, p. 43). How the Reverend Doctor would love to have known that the heads of both primary and subsequent inhumations (burials) were almost always faced to the north! He considered that the Druids built Stonehenge and used it for 360 years; enough time for nineteen kings' reigns according to his friend Sir Isaac Newton's theory . . . 'and there seems to be about that number of royal barrows (in my way of conjecturing) about the place' (Stukeley 1740, p. 66).

Stukeley, funded by the Earl of Pembroke, opened barrows in Groups One, Four and Five. He went carefully about it, as his notes show: 'After the turf taken off, we came to the layer of chalk, as before, then fine garden mould. About three foot below the surface, a layer of flints, humouring the convexity of the barrow . . . This being about a foot thick, rested on a layer of soft mould another foot; in which was inclos'd an urn full of bones' (Stukeley 1740, p. 44).

The next on an astonishingly brief list of excavators is William Cunnington (1754–1810), an amateur geologist from Heytesbury, who spent the last ten years of his life among the Stonehenge barrows. He was a reasonably conscientious excavator and recorder of bone and grave-goods detail, but he was unfortunately not very interested in pottery shards, although on 27/28 May 1802 he and the Parkers discovered the Stonehenge Urn (see Plate 77). In April 1804 Sir Richard Colt-Hoare took over the funding of Cunnington's work, and thereafter often joined him on digs, together with his superb surveyor and

PLATE 114

PLATE 114   William Cunnington (1754–1810) of Heytesbury, painted by Samuel Woodforde and engraved by James Basire. Sir Richard Colt-Hoare (1758–1838) sponsored Cunnington's barrow excavations towards the end of his life, and this portrait is the frontispiece to Colt-Hoare's *Wiltshire* (1812).

FIGURE 35   The Winterbourne Stoke Crossroads Group (from Colt-Hoare's *Wiltshire*).

FIGURE 35

draughtsman, Philip Crocker (1779–1840). Sir Richard Colt-Hoare's magnificent *Ancient Wiltshire, Volume One, South* appeared as testimony to the lasting value of their excavations, in 1812, whilst William Cunnington's notebooks are in Devizes Museum, Wiltshire, and The Society of Antiquaries, London. It is interesting to note that the Reverend E. Duke – later to write a stirring book (Duke 1846) – lived at Lake House, near Stonehenge, and joined a dig in Group Six, The Lake Group, during 11/15 November 1806, when 'in perfect weather' they opened Prophet Barrow (French prophets were reputed to have preached from it a hundred years previously).

In 1808 Cunnington reached the primary interment in Bush Barrow, in Group Five which is one of the finest round barrows in Wessex; it is some 37 m (120 ft) in diameter and was then about 3 m (11 ft) high. In this particular case it was found that the skeleton was buried with the head to the south which is very unusual for the area; further, his thigh bone was a tremendous 51 cm (20½ inches) long, and he was estimated to have been some 2 m (6 ft) tall: a giant indeed for his time, which is estimated at c. 1600/1550 BC (Grinsell 1978).

The next prominent excavator (and indeed the last one until after 1950) on that tranquil heath was the medical superintendent for the Asylum at Devizes, Dr John Thurnam (1810–73); he was mainly after skeletons, from 1850 onwards; and has left some intriguing details in his analyses of Cunnington's and Colt-Hoare's excavations of primary interments in what he called 'that great necropolis' (see table below); they encapsulate much that this brief account requires.

*In a contemporary twin-barrow (H15 and H16) in Group Three, one primary and one secondary interment were found by Colt-Hoare; reasons for non-cremation remain unknown. **These were all complete. ***Twelve of these were without any artifacts at all. ****68 of these (25%) were in urns.

Class of Barrow	Skeletons	Cremations	Totals
*Bell** (named by Stukeley)	**10 (25%)	***30 (75%)	40
Bowl (most common in Britain)	71 (26%)	207 (74%)	278
Disc (perhaps of women)	1 (0·2%)	35 (98%)	36
	82 (23%)	****272 (77%)	354

Artifacts found in Bell, Bowl and Disc Barrows	Skeletons	Cremations	Totals
Urns or other fictile vessels only	17	67	84
Implements of bone	2	14	16
Implements of stone	7	5	12
Implements of stone and bronze	4	1	5
Implements of bronze, awls, blades	14	58	72
Ornaments only	9	20	29
Total with objects	53 (65%)	165 (61%)	218 (62%)
Total without objects	29 (35%)	107 (39%)	136 (38%)
	82	272	354

PLATE 115

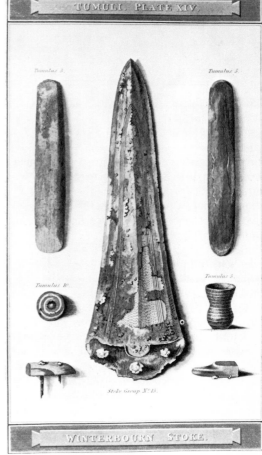

PLATE 116

Among prominent excavators in the flurry of interest in the barrows, in the face of the encroachments of farmers after 1950, were Paul Ashbee, Mrs P. M. Christie, Miss E. V. Field (now Mrs Proudfoot), Ernest Greenfield, W. F. Grimes and the late Mrs F. de M. Vatcher.

I conclude with two more mysteries in the Stonehenge story: Dr Thurnam records that no skeleton in any primary interment in Wiltshire has been found in any other but the contracted posture *and,* in almost every case, with the head facing north; whereas many secondary interments are in the extended posture. It would be interesting to ascertain the date for this change of habit, and to see whether it relates to that of a Stonehenge, Silbury, or Avebury construction phases. When did the idea depart, that a body should regain its foetal position in preparation for its journey back to the bosom of the Earth Mother?

The average height, derived by Dr Thurnam from fifty-two skeletal samples, was 1·68 m (5 ft 6ins) for long barrow men, and 1·75 m (5 ft 9 ins) for round barrow men. The difference is a surprise, but so are the heights in either case.

PLATE 115   Grave goods from barrows in the Winterbourne Stoke Crossroads Group (Plate XIII, engraved by Philip Crocker, in Colt-Hoare's *Wiltshire*).

PLATE 116   Artifacts from Barrows 5 and 10, in Plate XIV.

The Cursus

OS Map Reference: from SU: 109429 (west) to
SU: 133432 (east)
Car Parking: Stonehenge Car Park (free)

This is another mysterious construction near Stonehenge. It is an earthwork made up of two parallel banks which runs roughly east to west for more than 2·8 km (1¾ miles), 91·4 m (100 yds) apart, about ·804 km (½ mile) north of the monument.

It was discovered on 6 August 1723 by William Stukeley who thought it might have been a race course and gave it the name it has today; there were domestic horses in Western Europe about 4,500 years ago. The Rev. William Cooke, writing in 1754, was evidently attracted by Stukeley's theory: 'The west end of it, towards which are many considerable barrows, is curved into an arch, for the conveniency of turning the contending chariots. Its eastern termination is shut up with a long bank or huge mole of earth, where the judges of the race are supposed to have sat; and whence they had a distinct view of all that was transacted within the compass of this magnificent course' The Rev. James Ingram, wrote

Britton, 'considers Stonehenge to have been intended for a heathen burial place, and the courses adjoining as the hippodrome on which the goods of the deceased were run for at the time of the burial. This opinion is entitled to some consideration, from the vast numbers of barrows and other earthworks which abound in this part of the plain' (Ingram 1807).

There are about twenty similar constructions to The Cursus in Britain (none is known outside it, incidentally); it is the second longest and probably predates Stonehenge I. Some are aligned to long barrows, and perhaps at some time between Phases I and II, funerary rites occupied them because the long barrow at its eastern end, now badly damaged, has yielded the part-skeleton of a child. Cremations have been found in barrows between the western end and the A344 road; other artifacts are in the Devizes Museum.

Jacquetta Hawkes has mentioned a suggestion that the bluestones were first brought to the Stonehenge area for some construction related to The Cursus. If this is correct it magnifies the importance of this strange little length of Wessex, through which (but for vigorous protests of the Society of Antiquaries) a railway line would have been driven in 1883.

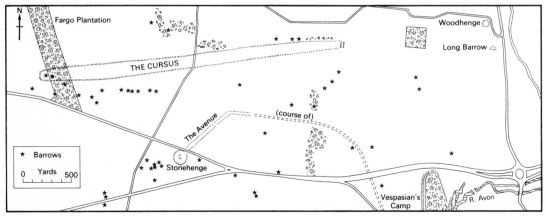

FIGURE 36

Durrington Walls
OS Map Reference: SU: 150437
Mostly accessible at all times

This enormous Late Neolithic henge monument lies either side of the A345 road from Salisbury to Marlborough, about two miles north of Amesbury, a few hundred yards north of Woodhenge (and just south of the Stonehenge Inn!). Only to the north-east is the earth bank still clearly visible; the whole bank is in fact 524 m (1,720 ft) in diameter east to west and crest to crest. Between its banks, which have their ditch on the inside and have suffered badly from natural erosion and farming, lie some 12 hectares (30 acres) which make Durrington Walls even larger in area than Avebury. Once upon a time there were two causewayed entrances through the banks, but they too can barely be spotted. Not much to see you may think – but this oddly named monument is very much part of the Stonehenge story.

Before the henge was built, the Avon valley in which it stands was cleared of woodland and cultivated, probably by the Windmill Hill people. The monument was begun about 2550 BC (a few hundred years after Stonehenge) and it was a truly massive undertaking. It has been estimated by Geoffrey Wainwright and I. H. Longworth (Wainwright and Longworth 1971), that it required 900,000 man-hours to construct: the banks were 27 m (90 ft) wide and 3 m (10 ft) high. Across the berm inside, which was up to 43 m (140 ft) wide, the ditches were 18 m (60 ft) wide, 6 m (20 ft) deep and 6·7 m (22 ft) across the bottom. Professor R. J. C. Atkinson has suggested that the so-called megalithic yard was not a unit of measure in use at Durrington.

Inside the banks two circular buildings were constructed in the manner of Woodhenge

PLATE 117

nearby, and nothing can be seen of them on the surface today. The northernmost circle was made up of four large posts, with small posts around them; they were approached from the south by a short avenue of posts which started from the façade off them. Such avenues are also found as far away as Lugg, Dublin and Kilham, Yorkshire, and they may be more important than we think at present.

The second circle was larger and lay to the south of it, almost opposite the eastern causewayed entrance, about 61 m (200 ft) from the River Avon. Here the first phase structure consisted of four concentric rings of posts, with four more posts around the central circle. There was also a straight façade of posts set against a section of the circle as if to protect it from the entrance to the enclosure. These were succeeded in a second phase of building, this time with six circles of larger posts, with two even larger ones (set as much as 3 m (9 ft) into the

FIGURE 36   A plan of The Cursus.

PLATE 117   An aerial view of Durrington Walls.

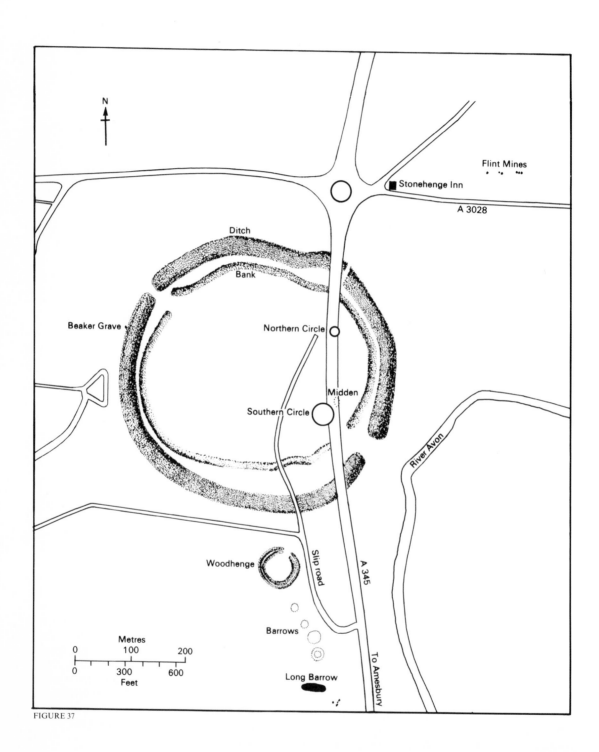

N

Flint Mines

Stonehenge Inn

A 3028

Ditch

Bank

Beaker Grave

Northern Circle

Midden

Southern Circle

River Avon

Woodhenge

Slip road

A 345

Barrows

Metres
0   100   200

0   300   600
Feet

Long Barrow

To Amesbury

FIGURE 37

chalk foundation) either side of the apparent entrance on the south-east. A chalk and flint platform was put up opposite where burning evidently took place; excavators have found animal bones, flints and broken pottery on top, and these are now in Salisbury Museum. There was also a rubbish dump just to the north-east of this southern circle and now known as the Midden, which has yielded large quantities of pottery shards, worked flints, animal bones, etc. There was a flint mine near Stonehenge Inn.

These two circles were probably roofed and thatched, and used for both ceremonial and trading purposes. Their sheer size (over 260 tons of wood were used for the larger building, according to one estimate) and a lack of defence characteristics (the inside ditches for example) urge this view. Celebration and feasting on a community or tribal scale is easy to picture – but why and how often? Just for pleasure ... each day or night or quarter day? Part of a Cornish greenstone axe has been found in the southern circle, similar to those found elsewhere in Wiltshire: that was a long journey. Grooved Ware has been found here (and at Stonehenge) – but also 'within' The Lios, Co. Limerick, and Stennes in the Orkney Islands, which are roughly contemporary – a tremendous geographical spread of incidence. And why have astonishingly few animal skulls been found? Perhaps they were used for some ritual purpose elsewhere, or was it that only meat was required for feasts, which is fair enough but implies an unexpected degree of organization. Many basic questions about the possible uses of Durrington Walls remain, and perhaps further excavation within these giant banks will give us more clues to the enigmas. Smaller buildings are suspected to be there, which would imply occupation on a domestic scale; and almost a

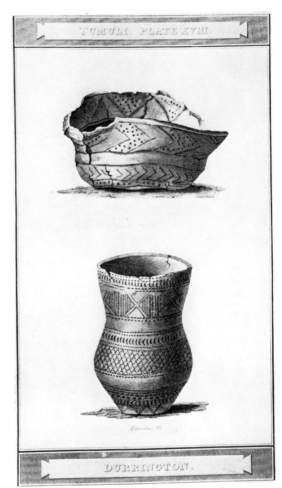

PLATE 118

FIGURE 37   A plan of Durrington Walls.

PLATE 118   Reconstructed pots from Durrington Walls. Plate XVIII in Colt-Hoare's *Wiltshire* (1812).

hundredweight of broken pottery has so far been recovered, which also indicates this. The habit of breaking drinking vessels during celebrations survives to this day of course, *but*, as Evan Hadingham points out (Handingham 1975, p. 47), 'not even a single complete vessel could be reconstructed' from all that broken pottery. Odd, isn't it? Perhaps we should pay more attention to the pattern of concentric circles, or 'occuli motif', found on four of the vessels found within the Walls.

PLATE 119

Old Sarum

OS Map Reference: SU: 137327
In the care of The Department of the Environment.
Car park and conveniences within the outer bank (free). Bus stop at Old Castle Inn, opposite entrance from main road.

Exactly six miles south-east of Stonehenge as the crow flies, and on the line (or ley) which continues a further two miles to the present Salisbury Cathedral and then three miles to the Iron Age fort at Clearbury Ring, lie the vast and crumpled ruins of Old Sarum. One favourite approach by car is from the north-east along Port Way, the Roman road that runs from Silchester; another is directly from the east on the Roman road from Winchester. John Constable's favourite view was looking across Stratford-sub-Castle and the water meadows of the River Avon to the north-east and Old Sarum's mighty form 73 m (240 ft) high.

It was first of all an early Iron Age hill fort, constructed by removing the chalk neck which connected this natural promontory with Bishopsdown just to the east (today the A345

PLATE 119 An aerial view of Old Sarum.

runs through it as well). Then a motte and surrounding ramparts were raised around it, to enclose an area of 12 hectares (29½ acres): compare with Avebury's 11 hectares (28½ acres) and Durrington Wall's 12·1 hectares (30 acres). Later the site may have been the Roman posting station of Sorviodunum, but some authorities think that this was to the west or south, in spite of the convergence of these Roman roads and also the discoveries of pottery, the remains of a Roman building on the original hill surface and some tiling and plasterwork.

After the Romans left Old Sarum it was probably more or less abandoned until the end of the ninth century when the great ramparts were repaired. This marked the start of a new era which is unique to a British hill fort because of the scale of activity and building there (the henge at Knowlton in Dorset for instance just has the church inside its banks) and also because of its later complete decline into the desolate (though very tidy) condition in which we find it today. So important did it become that Edgar (944–975) held a court there in 960, and even several decades later its great defences and natural position saved it from foreign raids. It was by then a thriving West Saxon community; it had its own mint and there were buildings that even extended beyond its ramparts.

St Etheldreda's Church was built below the banks to the north-west, and could possibly superimpose one of pre-Norman origin. A wooden castle rose on the motte soon after William the Conqueror was crowned, and by 1092 a cathedral in the Romanesque style was also completed, surrounded we imagine by public buildings, barracks, the bustle of trading activities and presumably private houses as well. The new Norman king took care to centre cathedrals within the hubs of commercial and military activity, and so our great cities were created.

In 1085, William I had summoned all English landowners to Old Sarum to swear allegiance to him, and perhaps they worshipped in the unfinished cathedral of the Blessed Virgin in this large and important diocese. Soon after it was finished, though, it was almost completely destroyed in a storm. St Osmund, its creator, died in 1099, and his successor, Bishop Roger, built a larger cathedral on what was left of the previous one. This was demolished in 1331 and a new one was constructed, as one of the most beautiful buildings in the world, in New Sarum to the south, or Salisbury as we now know it.

Just how cathedrals are sited may well be governed by an ancient tradition which is not likely to be revealed by Church authorities, and general as well as academic interest in the subject seems to be confined to historical associations, architects, the bishops, and so on. But there remains the mystery of that fascinating fact with which this account opened. Namely, that the centre of Stonehenge, the well within the inner Old Sarum banks, the Chapter

PLATE 120

PLATE 120   The timeless beauty of Salisbury Cathedral.

PLATE 121   The remains of the Great Tower, from the east.

PLATE 121

House in Salisbury Cathedral, and Clearbury Ring fort to the south-east, are all connected by a dead straight line. This is what Alfred Watkins called a 'ley', but this particular alignment was noticed before his time by Sir Norman Lockyer, and the phenomenon is discussed in Part 1. It may or may not be coincidence that the distance between Old Sarum and the Cathedral is precisely one third of the distance between Stonehenge and Old Sarum (see Figure 14). And so in many ways Old Sarum is also part of the Stonehenge story.

PLATE 122   A view from the outer bank, looking east across the car park to today's entrance.

PLATE 122

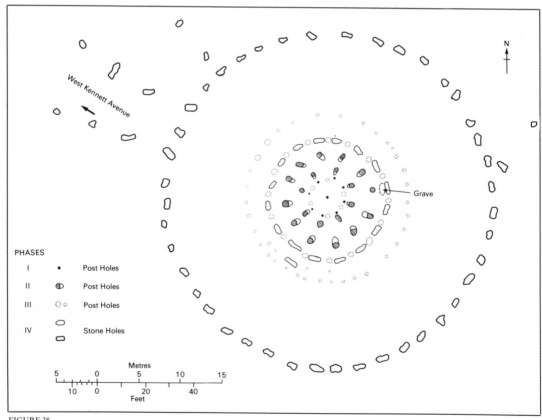

PHASES

I	•	Post Holes
II	◐	Post Holes
III	◌ ○	Post Holes
IV	▭	Stone Holes

West Kennett Avenue

Grave

N

Metres

FIGURE 38

The Sanctuary

OS Map Reference: SU: 119680
In the care of The Department of the Environment
At the start of The Ridgeway Path.

FIGURE 39

The West Kennett Avenue (described later in this Part) once ran, complete with about a hundred pairs of undressed stones, south-east from the Great Circle at Avebury to connect with The Sanctuary, which lies just south of the A4 (Bath to Marlborough) on Overton Hill. Aubrey Burl effectively summarises its context: 'The Sanctuary does not excite the casual visitor. The A4 roars past its iron railings, a lorry-loaded transport café faces it, and the greying concrete blocks and cylinders marking the positions of the former posts and stones do little for the uninstructed imagination. Yet this site is almost a chronicle of the history of stone rings in Wiltshire, their origin, their modifications, their destruction, their quiet mysteries.' (Burl 1976). William Stukeley first drew it on 8 July 1723; strangely his later finished plan showed the circles to be ovular when he clearly knew otherwise.

The construction of The Sanctuary probably took place in four phases, and in this it differs from Woodhenge:

Sanctuary I
6 post holes, 4·1 m (13 ft) in diameter

This was probably a hut circle, with smaller post holes in the middle, built before 2500 BC. It was first used by the Windmill Hill people from the nearby hill camp to the north-west and by people familiar with the Long Barrow at West Kennett which is only three-quarters of a mile to the west. Remains perhaps indicate a thatched roof; this would have been desirable if we assume from the absence of

animal bones that The Sanctuary had a ritual or ceremonial use, and not a purely or even temporary domestic one.

Sanctuary II
12 post holes, 9·8 m (32 ft) in diameter

Two further rings of posts were constructed outside those of the first phase.

Sanctuary III
34 post holes, 19·7 m (65 ft) in diameter

The buildings of Sanctuary I and II were replaced by an even larger edifice – still by Late Neolithic people and thus earlier than the Avebury stone circles. It may have had an open smoke hole at its centre, and the building rested on three circles of wooden posts. In the middle of them was set a circle of stones, 13·72 m (45 ft) wide; near one stone a skeleton has been found, together with Beaker pottery which has been dated at c. 2000 BC.

Sanctuary IV
42 post holes, 39·3 m (129 ft) in diameter

A second stone circle was constructed (probably at about the same time as the West Kennett Avenue), outside the Sanctuary III building, from which the Avenue leads off to north-west, about 6·10 m (20 ft) wide at that point. It was the remnants of Sanctuary IV that John Aubrey reported seeing in about 1670 – but within fifty years they were gone.

The proposal that The Sanctuary was continually in ritualistic use is strengthened by the fact that, as Aubrey Burl notes, in each successive phase either the diameter of the rings of holes or the number of the holes themselves more or less doubles its predecessor (Burl 1976). The Sanctuary's tantalizing plan can be found on the pillar on the south side.

FIGURE 38 A plan of The Sanctuary.

FIGURE 39 How The Sanctuary may have looked on completion.

Silbury Hill

OS Map Reference: SU: 100685

In the care of the Department of the Environment

Parking on the Avebury-Beckhampton road (free)

This vast and silent hill lies in considerable majesty beside the Roman road we now know prosaically as the A4, which connects Marlborough with Bath, and runs a mile south of Avebury. It has its role in the strange story of Stonehenge for many reasons, one of the more definite ones being that the first stage of its construction occurred at about the time of Stonehenge I; indeed John Michell has pointed out (Michell 1966, p. 156 and 1973, p. 108) that Silbury Hill is exactly 6 megalithic miles from Stonehenge. It has defied attempts to fathom (in one sense literally!) from its bulk a purpose, a point for its existence. But attempts and responsible speculations must continue: it really would be fun to understand why, about 4,600 years ago, approximately 500 people worked for an estimated 15 years (according to

Professor Atkinson) in order to add about 8·75 million cubic feet of earth, chalk and gravel to the 3·75 million cubic feet already there – and thus create what is still Europe's largest man-made mound.

The construction of Silbury Hill can be divided into four continuous stages according to the most recent understanding of it. The large chalk spur was already there, and during *Silbury I* (the first stage) there was raised over it a conical mound of layered gravel taken from the valley around it; at the core of this mound were downland turves. The new cone was 36 m (120 ft) in diameter and 5 m (16 ft) high. This primary stage has been dated at 2660 BC (Vatcher & Vatcher 1976), just after the time of Stonehenge I.

PLATE 123   A view of Silbury Hill, from the path leading up to West Kennett Long Barrow. 8·75 million cubic feet of earth, chalk and gravel were added by man to a natural mound, to create what is still the largest artificial mound in Europe.

PLATE 123

During *Silbury II* chalk was taken from a new ditch, with an internal diameter of 107 m (350 ft); this was dug around the existing mound and incorporated into a method of construction also known to the pyramid builders at Giza. A succession of layered chalk block walls were made, infilled with local rubble and with occasional internal walls or buttresses directed to the centre; each was of course smaller than the previous one, and they rose to form a sort of stepped cone. During this stage a third one was suddenly envisaged – the height of the mound had to be increased. So the ditch was carefully filled in to prevent later subsidence, and covered by the larger base of *Silbury III*; this was made of chalk rubble from the new ditch, of which parts remain today, and a new cone was created up to today's height. The new ditch sides were secured with chalk rubble and wooden posts. *Silbury IV* brought the Hill to today's familiar pudding shape: five of the 'steps' ringing the cone were filled in, 'smoothed over' as it were, to present the even-sided profile. But the top 'step' was, for some reason not yet understood, left uncovered, some 5 m (15 ft) from the summit (where fragmenta of greenstone all the way from Cornwall has been found).

If you take the delightful path up from the A4 to West Kennett Long Barrow (described elsewhere in this Part), and turn about, half way there, you will see perhaps the finest view of Silbury Hill. The base spread out below you is 167 m (550 ft) in diameter; the summit is 30 m (100 ft) wide and is about 40 m (130 ft) from the base which squats on some 5½ acres (2·2 hectares) of Wiltshire. The slope is a pleasing 30° from the ground level.

Several major excavations have taken place in Silbury Hill. In 1776/77 a team of hardy Cornish miners, directed by the Duke of Northumberland and his friend Colonel Drax, sank a shaft about 30 m (100 ft) down from the centre of the summit, to reach the original hill top. In 1849 John Merewether, the Dean of Hereford, and Henry Blandford, a railway engineer, led a group which fruitlessly drove a small tunnel from inside the south ditch up

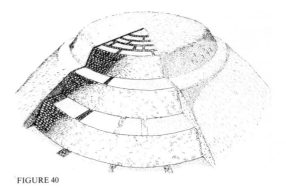

FIGURE 40

FIGURE 40   How Silbury Hill is constructed.

through an angle conforming to the outer surface to the Hill's centre. Pits were sunk into the ditch in 1886 to ascertain its original depth. In 1922 Sir William Flinders Petrie searched for an entrance in the east causeway to a burial chamber, but without success.

During 1967/70, Professor R. J. C. Atkinson (whose name is closely connected with Wessex monuments) led a large televised excavation to find information he thought would be somewhere inside (Atkinson 1956, p. 165). He drove a horizontal tunnel higher up the hill from the 1849 entrance, to connect with the previous inclining tunnel; he also explored the ditch, slopes and summit platform with modern equipment. But no hidden secrets were revealed. Said Magnus Magnusson, 'We are not quite clear that the burial, if any, was at the centre.'

So the tunnels were filled in again. Apart from the discovery of pottery shards, animal bones, antler horn picks and a Viking interment, little has resulted from all these efforts. We do, it is true, know now how it was constructed, and approximately when – but the ubiquitous Wessex question 'why' remains.

Less elaborate attempts to provide answers to this question have been attempted and suggested as well of course, and interest in Silbury Hill has been increasing steadily in recent years. But it was in 1867 that the Wiltshire Archaeological Society tackled what it thought to be a fundamental subject; they explored the eastern side of the Hill to find out if the Roman road from Mildenhall (Cunetio) to Bath (Aquae Sulis) continued on its straight course beneath the mound. It did not, thus confirming to sceptical early Victorians that Silbury Hill was of course there first! But is J. R. L. Anderson right when he writes (Anderson and Godwin 1975, p. 56) that 'Silbury Hill has come down to us as the most massive folly in Europe. It is simply a man-made hill with a flat top, of the sort children make with buckets of sand'?

PLATE 124   A view from the Devizes road, from *The Celtic Druids* by Godfrey Higgins (1829).

PLATE 124

In all likelihood not, but we may never know. And Robert Southey made a telling point two centuries ago, in his *Inscription For A Tablet At Silbury Hill*:

'This mound in some remote and dateless day
Rear'd o'er a Chieftain of the Age of Hills,
May here detain thee, Traveller! from thy road
Not idly lingering. In his narrow house
Some warrior sleeps below, whose gallant deeds
Haply at many a solemn festival
The Scauld hath sung; but perish'd is the song
Of praise, as o'er these bleak and barren downs
The wind that passes and is heard no more.
Go, Traveller, and remember when the pomp
Of Earthly Glory fades, that one good deed,
Unseen, unheard, unnoted by mankind
Lives in the Eternal register of Heaven.'

The mystery of Silbury Hill is likely to remain unsolved for some time to come. But it really is too convenient to close the 'case' with the proposal that it was a rather successful attempt to get savage celebrants as near to their gods as possible; that its flat top (the Great Pyramid has one too) was used only for ceremony, feasting, sacrifice, games, dancing, coronations, meetings or worship. We certainly cannot ignore the fact that, as a sanctuary, it is remarkably secure from any but air attack. The Hill seems not dead but merely asleep; it just must be more than the largest barrow in Europe, concealing the doubtlessly contracted skeleton, head northwards, of the founder of Stonehenge, as some researchers have suggested.

Many believe that mounds are sighting points. The meridian line from Silbury goes through the church at Avebury; and on to the church at Berwick Bassett; the same line runs south through the earthwork on Milk Hill and then to the church at Wilsford; coincidence? Or perhaps not, in which case the prehistoric trackway must have been of tremendous importance – and it is not connected with Stonehenge in this manner.

Perhaps the successive 'sills' or 'steps' around the cone were for the observation of the sun, moon or stars; if so, why the sudden Silbury III construction phase? Perhaps a very tall pole stood on its summit, to cast seasonally shifting shadows to the north. The Rev. E. Duke, writing in 1846, reckoned that the solar prediction system covering most of Wiltshire 'pivoted on Silbury Hill, 16 miles distant from Stonehenge.' This surely is nearer the truth of the matter?

The Stonehenge Avenue
OS Map References: from (west) SU: 123423 to (east) 142416 (end is lost)

The first part of the Avenue leads away from Stonehenge, from the north-east earthwork entrance, its parallel banks being 21 m (70 ft) apart. 663 m (726 yards) from the centre it runs due east for about 786 m (860 yards) to the top of a hill and then drops gradually southeastwards towards the River Avon, always along the easiest gradients.

The Stonehenge Avenue was noted by John Aubrey (who had noticed the Hole sites) but one of the father figures of Stonehenge archaeology, Dr William Stukeley – perhaps on 6 August (when he found The Cursus), but certainly in 1723 – re-discovered and named it. He correctly foretold that much of it would disappear under the plough, and it was not until exactly 200 years later, in 1923, that aerial photography revealed most of the latter part of its course. The first part had been visible to Sir Richard Colt-Hoare who mapped it in 1811,

A direct View of Stonehenge from the union of the two Avenues.

PLATE 125

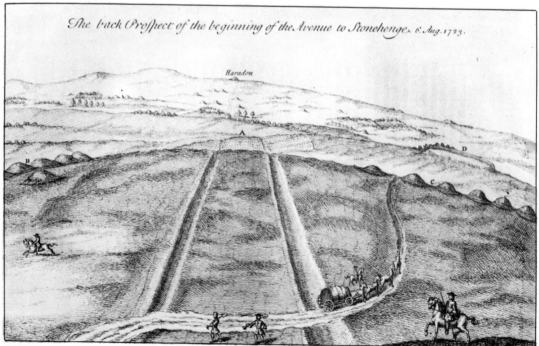

The back Prospect of the beginning of the Avenue to Stonehenge. 6. Aug. 1723.

PLATE 126

and indeed the Ordnance Survey did so six years later.

Stukeley thought that the Avenue connected Stonehenge with the River Avon, at 'an ancient ford of the River Avon', Ratfyn, which has long been thought of as the landing place for the bluestones, on the last part of their long journey from the Prescelly Mountains. If this is so, and there is much evidence to support the theory (quite apart from the Devil's carelessness in dropping one of the stones near Bulford which has since been found), and if the Stonehenge Avenue was a processional way, then the arrival of the bluestones was a highly important event. West Kennett Avenue was probably such a way, but along this Avenue no evidence of former standing stones has been discovered yet. Perhaps the places to look for holes or burials are where the Avenue changes direction. An avenue of stones was hinted at by a friend of one Stonehenge researcher (Long 1876, p. 91).

What does seem certain is that the Avenue has no astronomical significance. The famed archaeologist, O. G. S. Crawford, put it this way writing about the re-discoveries from the air: 'In the first place, it puts out of court once and for all the fanciful astronomical theories of the late Sir Norman Lockyer and others. An avenue which splits into two branches, one leading to a racecourse and the other to a river (and neither branch straight) cannot be regarded as orientated to the rising sun for purposes of worship' (Crawford 1923).

At the end of 1978 Professor Atkinson announced a sixth Stonehenge Phase; Stonehenge IV marks the extension (about 1100 BC) of the Avenue from Stonehenge Bottom onwards along the course described.

PLATE 125 'A direct view of Stonehenge from the union of the two Avenues' runs the caption to William Stukeley's engraving for this *Stonehenge* (1740). He shows one 'wing' going to 'Radfin' and the other to the Cursus (which he so named).

PLATE 126 Another of Stukeley's *Stonehenge* plates – looking along the Avenue (as he saw it) from Stonehenge; beyond the Kings' Barrows on the right, Vespasian's Camp (which is outside Amesbury) can be seen.

West Kennett Long Barrow
OS Map Reference: SU: 104677
Parking on a lay-by on A4

This dramatic site must not be missed. As the map shows, it lies about 2·4 km (1½ miles) south of Avebury, and remember to take a torch. It is happily not accessible by car, and cannot even be seen from the A4 Bath road where you have to park as best you can. As you start to climb the signposted footpath, about half a mile south-west of West Kennett village, from the meadow where the River Kennett rises from its springhead, the largest chambered tomb in England and Wales slowly comes into view, as Silbury Hill falls away below and behind you.

Its mound (and strangely no one seems exactly agreed on the first dimension) is about 104 m (340 ft) long, 23 m (75 ft) wide at its larger eastern end and some 2·5 m (8 ft) high; you can walk along its chalk and grassy spine to gain a vivid idea, before you even enter inside it, of the enormous and cohesive labour involved in collecting, transporting and erecting the rude or unworked sarsen boulders from the surrounding hills and valleys to construct its core, capstones and corbelling and interior walls, and also in bringing the dry-stone panel stones from the Frome and Calne districts. At its eastern end lies the tomb itself (a bare eighth of its length), which you can enter, past the three huge upright façade stones, which originally sealed it up; the largest of these stands 3·5 m (12 ft) above the ground and weighs 16 tons. Ahead of the semi-circular open forecourt inside, lies the main passage, from which two chambers open on each side, before it reaches the larger polygonal chamber at the middle of the west end. The stones are all undecorated.

The skulls and bones of forty-five skeletons have been found, but they were certainly not buried at the same time; according to excavators, the tombs were in use for about a thousand years, with remains constantly being replaced during or for a ritual which remains obscure. Then all the chambers were completely filled up with chalk rubble, and the

PLATE 127

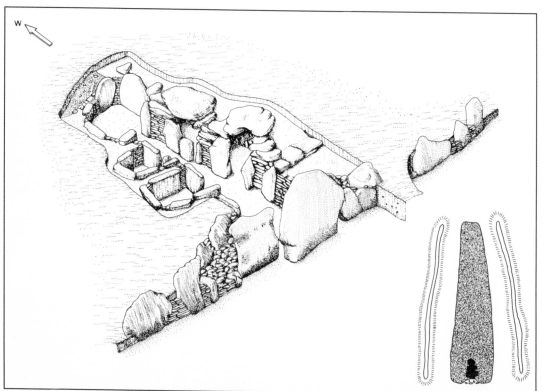

FIGURE 41

forecourt was sealed off with boulders and three huge facing stones outside and two inside, at right angles to the central and largest one, which completed the line of the main passage.

The Long Barrow (perhaps the best known of some 260 in Britain, of which 148 are in fact in Wiltshire) suffered considerable damage in the seventeenth century, notably at the hands of Dr Toope of Marlborough in about 1685, who needed human bones for the making of his 'noble medicine'. 4·5 m (15 ft) of the passage and the western chambers were explored by John Thurnam in 1859 when sherds of Peterborough ware and late beakers were found. But

it was the excavation in 1955/56 by Professors Stuart Piggott and R. J. C. Atkinson which dramatically revealed the four intact side burial chambers; the considerable restoration to its present state was completed in 1957. Artifacts

PLATE 127   West Kennett Long Barrow.

FIGURE 41   A plan of the eastern end of the Barrow (after Piggott).

PLATE 128 (*below*)   The largest façade stone, which stands 3·5 m (12 ft) above the ground and weighs 16 tons.

found during excavations are in Devizes Museum.

When first constructed, estimated at 3600 BC (as Stonehenge I was c. 2800 BC), the mound was enclosed all the way round by a kerb of stones (as John Aubrey's c. 1670 drawing shows), but these have long since vanished and, partly as a result of this, the two long ditches both about 12 m (40 ft) from each side have silted up.

Early Neolithic pottery sherds of the Windmill Hill people have been found in the Long Barrow, so their arrival was to result in the construction of this most impressive megalithic monument, one of the finest of its kind in Europe. But, was it really just a cemetery?

Michael Dames, in his original and challenging book *The Avebury Cycle*, 1977, raises a fundamental question about the West Kennett Long Barrow – why was it so long? No past or living authority has successfully answered this. Dames writes:

'Long barrows are long because they show the Winter goddess as gigantic, and that is probably why in Germany, Denmark and Holland the name Giant is still attached to prehistoric tombs – a pattern confirmed in southern England where "Neolithic long barrows tend to be called after giants" [he quotes from G. I. Dalton's "The Loathly Lady" in *Folklore*, vol 82, 1971]. Each singular giant was a version of the Great Goddess. In Wiltshire we find Giant's Grave, Dowton, Giant's Cave, Luckington, and Giant's Grave, Milton Lilbourne. Further examples in Hampshire and Cornwall also represent the vestiges of a once universal attribution.'

Dames proposes that the Neolithic people were worshippers of the Great Goddess, whose seasonal aspects were commemorated with appropriate constructions in the Avebury area; he likens a ground plan of the chambers in the Long Barrow to a squatting harvest goddess. in her Old Hag guise, from which the long goddess, a Stone Age deity, seasonally came and to which she returned. The regularity and amazing refinement of the design of this chambered tomb (it is, as Piggott has shown, an almost perfect isosceles triangle, the base façade of the stones being north-south and half the length of the east-west axis), and its similarity with so

PLATE 129

many others far away, certainly infers a prescribed use of the *total* area of the Long Barrow more than 5,000 years ago. The earliest constructors of Stonehenge would have been aware of it surely.

It has been claimed by a leading dowser in the 1930s (Boothby 1935) that all long barrows had an underground stream running their length. In referring to the West Kennett Long Barrow, among others, in his book *The Pattern of the Past* (Underwood 1969), another prominent dowser, Guy Underwood, writes: 'The justification for the chambers is that the central geodetic [his word for Earth Force] line inside the barrow has thrown out branch or "habitation" spirals on one or both sides. The chambers are set at the end of these spirals. It appears that the existence of such a spiral made a site auspicious either as a habitation for the living or as a grave for the dead.'

The East Kennett Long Barrow (OS Map Reference: SU: 116699), a little larger than its neighbour a mile to the north-east, is covered in trees, and has traces of sarsen stones at the south-east end which indicate an exciting excavation prospect one day.

PLATE 129 The interior of West Kennett Long Barrow, looking west. A side-chamber entrance can be seen on the left; the four chambers were not discovered until the 1955/56 excavations (led by Professor Richard Atkinson and Professor Stuart Piggott).

The West Kennett Avenue

OS Map Reference: from SU: 103697 (Avebury) to SU: 118680 (The Sanctuary)

There were once some two hundred stones comprising the Avenue which links the circles at Avebury with the Sanctuary (both described already in this Part). 'In the year 1720 I saw several stones just taken up there' (Stukeley 1743, p. 30). They were rude, or unshaped, stones, set in pairs, with diamond shaped and narrow ones alternating for some unknown reason, which may be important to our ultimate understanding of the meaning or role of avenues. They were at an average of 15 m (49 ft) apart, across the Avenue, with 24 m (80 ft) between the pairs. Mostly between 2 m–4 m (7–12 ft) high, they ran an erratic course over 2340 metres (2560 yds). At the Avebury end the route remains obscure because it does not seem to run directly up to the southern entrance of the Great Circle; it surely should have because they were constructed at about the same time? Grave goods, pottery sherds, burials and flint flakes found under and around some of the stones confirm a Late Neolithic date.

The West Kennett Avenue (double 'tt' is per latest OS 1:50,000 map) must have been some kind of processional way of importance and indeed permanence, because no mere post holes have been discovered along it. Perhaps Avenues were designed just to impress, just as ours are today in the centre of capital cities!

PLATE 130   Looking along West Kennett Avenue.

PLATE 131   The world's most famous stone alignments, at Carnac, in Brittany.

△ PLATE 130

PLATE 131 ▽

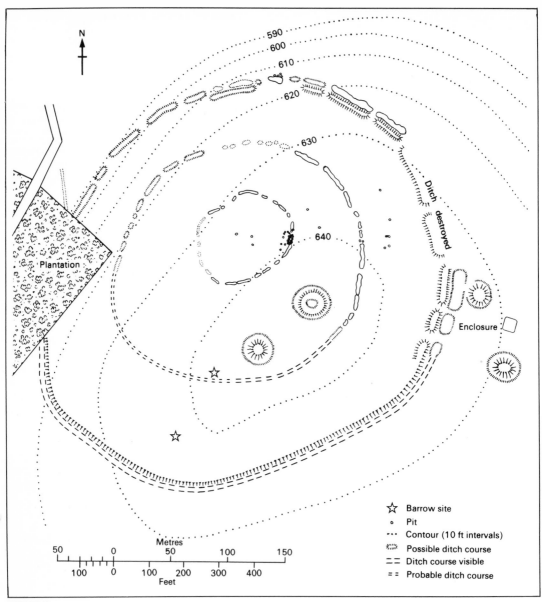

FIGURE 42

Windmill Hill
OS Map Reference: SU 087715
A property of the National Trust

This broad bald hill (which you can approach by car to within three-quarters of a mile) which lies about 2·4 km (1½ miles) to the north-west of Avebury, has given its name to the earliest known Neolithic colonist-farmers who spread over southern England from the Continent some time (estimates vary on this) around 4000 BC. They practised a form of primitive agriculture and cattle-raising which was soon to usurp the earliest ways of life in Britain, which until then involved survival of the fittest simply by hunting and fishing food for immediate consumption. As the newcomers' habits spread, and though life was still semi-

FIGURE 42   A plan of Windmill Hill.

nomadic, the earliest discernible patterns of primitive society were being laid. A more extended account of this period is given in Part 4, with reference to construction abilities.

About 3250 BC, a causewayed enclosure or camp (but it must have been much more than this and was hardly defensible) of three concentric circles of banks and ditches – the largest about 365 m (1200 ft) in diameter – covering about 21 acres (8 hectares) (which makes it the largest found in England), was built around its top, over the evidence of previous occupation. Much of the enclosure has now gone, through natural erosion and under the plough, but the ditches yielded deposits (including more than 1,300 pottery vessels) to excavators between 1925 and 1929 which indicated a ceremonial or tribal centre of some importance; indeed it continued in occupation after the Great Circle at Avebury was finished. It is because this enclosure was the first large camp to be excavated in the south of England (by Alexander Keiller) that the hill became the type-site and thus its earliest identifiable occupants acquired their name.

There is no direct evidence to connect the Windmill Hill people with the early Stonehenge constructors themselves, but the presence in the same area of so many barrows, the Avebury Circle and the Avenue indicate an area of special significance and sanctity, which in turn implies organization on a tribal scale. Within the hilltop enclosure enough evidence has been discovered to suggest its continuous use (though not perhaps permanent settlement) for over 1,000 years; the ditch tops have been dated to 2000 BC. Some of the broken pottery (now in the Avebury Museum) found in the ditches came from Devon and Cornwall, which again confirms the importance of the site, and the ditches yielded evidence in 1957/8 of a hunting, farming, domestic and indeed trading life. Cornwall also supplied axes to the hill people, as did Wales and Westmorland far to the north. The round barrows there came later of course, during the early Bronze Age.

We very nearly lost Windmill Hill before Keiller's excavations in fact: a scheme was proposed for a Marconi wireless station to be erected on it in 1924/5. The Neolithic earthworks had just been rediscovered there – sensational news at the time – and Alexander Keiller, a wealthy and scholarly though then untrained Dundee jam magnate, bought most of the Hill. He bought the rest later – and the whole of Avebury as well.

Woodhenge
OS Map Reference: SU 150434
In the care of the Department of the Environment
Car parking: in a slip road off the A345
Entrance free

The existence of Woodhenge as we see it today was only revealed in 1925 by Squadron Leader Insall's aerial photography; it had formerly appeared to be just a ruined disc barrow. During the following three years it was excavated by Mr and Mrs B. H. Cunnington, and it was they who gave the evocative name to this rather desolate place, a mile north of Amesbury. A visit will be short, but it will be however an important one for followers of the Stonehenge story.

The excavations showed that this was a Late Neolithic henge with a single entrance at the north-east. Within the banks – which are 77 m (252 ft) across – and the quarry ditch inside there are six concentric elliptical settings of wooden post holes, which could be earlier or later date than the earthwork. One reconstruction of Woodhenge shows them to be holes for wooden timbers to support a thatched roof; a hole would have been in the centre for the release of smoke. Or the observation of the sun, the moon or the stars? The ground holes are

PLATE 132

today marked on the site with concrete cylinders, and a plan of them is on permanent open-air display.

Finds at the site have included Beaker shards, Neolithic pottery, axes, arrowheads and flint scrapers: Devizes Museum holds them. Some debris indicates that Woodhenge (c. 2300 BC) superimposes an earlier settlement. Excavators in 1928 pointed out one of the most interesting aspects of Woodhenge: that the skull of a crouched three-years-old child found among the circles had been split before interment. This, he says, 'was evidently a dedicatory deposit, and is one of the very few pieces of evidence for human sacrifice in prehistoric Britain.' (Atkinson 1976, p. 34). A pile of flints now marks this revelatory spot, and we would do well to ponder the implications of this surprising fact.

The popular researcher John Michell has claimed an extremely sophisticated purpose for Woodhenge in his book *The View over Atlantis*; it was 'a stringed musical instrument laid out according to the plan of the universe, the outer bank representing the crust of the firmament, the moat within it providing the water layer which the ancient astronomers saw as the lining behind the zodiac' (Michell 1969, p. 122). It was, he wrote, constructed on the square of Mercury to invoke that God's influence through the music of the spheres, and Professor Thom's surveys of Woodhenge are in accord with the geometry claimed to this exciting pre-Pythagorean idea, which was apparently known also to the builders of the Great Pyramid and Stonehenge.

PLATE 132   The site of Woodhenge today.

Part 6

Stonehenge and the Public

Official Attitudes – Private Feelings

'Every age has the Stonehenge
it deserves – or desires.'

Professor Jacquetta Hawkes, 1967

Stonehenge has always been too popular for its own good. The volume of visitors in recent years has grown to such an extent it was obvious that something had to give – something had to be done to protect what is left of the finest megalithic monument in Europe; it came on 15 March 1978 when a fence was erected around the stones (by chance I had been among them only the week before), after much careful official deliberation. This was contrary to a Deed of Gift made with the presentation of Stonehenge to the nation in 1918 – but it probably had to be done.

The matter was discussed in the House of Commons on 20 December 1976; Parliamentary Under-Secretary Mr Kenneth Marks said: 'The density of crowds in summer and at fine weekends throughout the year is such that the custody staff cannot control them. There is no

room within the circle to fence off corridors within which large numbers of people can shuffle round in a queue.' He was right – the area within the stones is only 30·5 m (100 ft); how can 2,500 visitors an hour be stopped from

---

PLATE 133   The notice that went up near the admission point on 15 March 1978.

PLATE 134   I took this photograph early in March 1978; a week later the stones were fenced in.

PLATE 135   The desolate approach to the monument from the car park.

PLATE 136   In March 1978 I photographed this model of Stonehenge (as it exists today), placed about a hundred feet from the monument itself. Whose idea was it? What was the point? (Note: *it* is fenced off too; so you still can't see inside!)

PLATE 133

PLATE 134

PLATE 135

PLATE 136

climbing on recumbent stones, scratching their initials on them, marking them with the gravel attached to muddy shoes, and fingering and rubbing the important carvings and marks? Some think to harm the ones they love – perhaps there is the same attitude to venerable objects like these mute stones, which have been attacked since the days of the Romans. Only a hundred years ago hammers were hired out in neighbouring Amesbury so that visitors could chip off souvenirs. Long before then reputed medicinal properties attracted invalids and their friends to the scarred surfaces. The passage of thousands of feet in a dry spring bares the grass, leaving summer winds to blow the topsoil away across the Plain, and so exposing the henge's layer of earth that the archaeologists most want for themselves – one bluestone chip, one shard of pottery or one fragment of an antler pick *in situ* can change a story.

Stonehenge was once called, in an *Illustrated London News* headline, 'The Frontispiece of English History': it has in fact been treated like a footnote. The hideous car park and entrance area with all the appearance of a motorway pull-in (which Alexander Keiller offered to hide underground fifty years ago), do no justice at all to this wonder of our concern. So what can be done to improve relations between Stonehenge and its caring public?

PLATE 137   Mr Loraine conducting ground-to-air wireless experiments from his aeroplane in 1910.

PLATE 137

There are two obvious alternative sites for the car park. One is in Stonehenge Bottom, just to the east of The Cursus, which I would never recommend. The other is somewhere in the area of the Fargo Plantation very near the western end of The Cursus. There also should be a Stonehenge Museum (which Keiller had envisaged), shops, visitors facilities, etc. – and as many of them *underground* as possible; the development should be self-financing, with the car park let out to a commercial concern (why should it be free at present? It isn't anywhere else nowadays). Before construction begins, there would of course be complete excavation of all the barrows in the Plantation area: their destruction would be the stated price of allowing Stonehenge to breathe again, and would be as a 10p piece compared with the value of what has been allowed to happen to the monument and barrows during the past thirty years. The A303 road, which forks south just before Stonehenge on its way to the south-west, with some 5,000 cars an hour in the summer (and which destroyed barrows and post holes), should stay – but carry *all* traffic coming to Stonehenge from the east, which is the most popular approach. These cars would have to continue 3 km (1¾ miles) before turning north up the A306, and then first right along the present A344 to the proposed new car park on the left beneath the Plantation. Visitors *should have* to walk about 183 m (200 yards): how much nicer than popping out of the present tunnel! The A344 would become one way eastwards, *after* the new car park, on its way past Stonehenge (within 27 m, or 30 yards) to the present junction with the A303. A later phase in this plan to 'save Stonehenge' would involve closing the Stonehenge section of the A344 from the Plantation onwards, and the sinking of new dual carriageway A303 and A360 sections into noiseless grassy cuttings.

Of the Army housing ·8 km (half a mile) to the north, looking over The Cursus, a lady visiting from Idaho told a custodian in 1977: 'The people living over there sure had a good view of this thing being built.' The Army, authorised destroyer of countless barrows on their nearby firing ranges, should be firmly 'invited to volunteer', in its own tradition, to plant dense fast growing ash screening in front of the strip of Larkhill housing.

Agreement from all the relevant authorities to these improvements would surely lead the National Trust to ask for Stonehenge itself to be handed over into their care by the Department of the Environment. The Trust already owns about 1,438 acres of surrounding land – and the way would be clear for the declaration of a fully protected Stonehenge Park, a nice fresh innovation for the National Trust. Will we yet see a Stonehenge Planetarium – a laser-assisted demonstration of 'how it worked'?

The fault for the popularity of Stonehenge can fairly be traced to James I who, as we have seen in Part 1, asked Inigo Jones to examine Stonehenge for him. There and then, he and his host, the Earl of Pembroke, should have cooked up a scheme to get Stonehenge into Royal hands: as a Crown property from that time onwards, the stones might have had a chance to speak their secrets more directly to Professor Hawkins's computer.

The names connected with the 'monument at the perennial popularity of Stonehenge . . . it was once one of the places upon which travelling gentlemen called; it was the thing to do, it was 'taken up' by society: from James I's momentous visit onwards Stonehenge has been a conversation piece. And John Aubrey was a very good gossip indeed, as well as being the founder of British archaeology.

In Part 1 I examined the phenomenon of the attempts to connect Celtic Druidic traditions with Stonehenge, which really began when Stukeley was approaching full spate. He was a Chosen Chief of his Order, of which vaguely related branches are still extant today. The neo-Druidic 'rites' enacted in our time at the midsummer solstice sunrise at Stonehenge have nothing to do with what is known of Celtic Druidism. We should note that before 1906 no 'ceremonies' had been recorded there – but unfortunately Lockyer's published work at the beginning of the century has had its effect. A pop festival now joins the annual neo-Druidic celebrations – illegally on private land, over several days, with very loud music and all that goes with such events. It is a very popular one, and Members of Parliament and the Director-General of The National Trust have urged that some provision is officially made by the Department of the Environment for such midsummer celebrations near Stonehenge. Mr Sid Rawle, ex-squatters' leader and much else, wrote a moving letter to *The Times* on 28 June 1978 which set forth views which should be noted:

'. . . We come to Stonehenge because in an unstable world it is proper that the people should look for stability to the past in order to learn for the future. . . . The evidence is indisputable that Stonehenge and the surrounding area is one of the most powerful spiritual centres in Europe. It is right that we should meekly stand in the presence of God, but it is proper that we should sing and dance and shout for joy for the love and mercy that He shows us. . . . We would not run a road through Stonehenge and given our way it would soon be removed. A very important part of the monument is now a tarmac car park, ugly to behold. We would not surround it with barbed wire and arc lamps . . .. The Director-General well knows that he and he alone is all that stands between the festival as it is at present and what he would call a legal festival. . . . Holy land is holy land and our right to be upon it cannot be denied. . . .'

PLATE 138　Members of the Devizes Cycling Club at Stonehenge at 5 a.m. on 21 June 1895.

PLATE 139 (*next page*)　On 18 June 1976 hundreds of hippies moved into the Stonehenge area just prior to a pop festival. Two years later *The New Musical Express,* London, covered the midsummer solstice in 1978 . . . 'NME's fluid druid, Brian Case, gets unhinged at Stonehenge, meets strange young people with long hair, observes weird rites and inexplicable occurrences and stands in the presence of forces more ancient than man,' – ran the headline on page 30 in the 29 June issue. 'Stonehenge today,' wrote Brian Case, 'is a Tower of Babel, with UFOlogists, pyramidologists, Atlanteans, elf-dabblers, Sacred Mushroom munchers, Third Eye cosmonauts, Rupert Bear fanatics . . .'

PLATE 140 (*next page inset*)　Mr Punch gets to the point of Sir Edmund Antrobus's offer in 1899 to sell Stonehenge and about 1,300 acres of farmland to the nation, for £125,000.

PLATE 138

HOW STONEHENGE MIGHT BE POPULARISED IF THE GOVERNMENT BOUGHT IT. SUGGESTION GRATIS.

STONEHENGE—AND WHAT IT MAY BECOME!

(A Peep into a not very remote Futurity.)

Mr. Punch, understanding from the daily papers that the present owner of Stonehenge proposes—should the War Office decline his terms of £125,000 for the freehold—to put this ancient British monument up for auction to the highest bidder, has been greatly exercised in mind as to the probable fate of the Stones. Wishing to know the worst, he has consulted his own private Clairvoyant, who has been favoured with a second sight of the (as yet unpublished) newspaper files referring to the subject,—with the following interesting, if somewhat conflicting, results :—

Extract No. I. (*From Advertisement Columns, Morning Paper, 1900.*)

"Messrs. Hoarding and Poster, having recently acquired that central and eligible property known as Stonehenge, are thereby enabled to offer a unique opportunity to enterprising British advertisers. Terms :—Single column (per square foot), £6 per annum. Double column, £5. Architrave, £8. Double column (with architrave), £4 10s. Other spaces at rates varying according to position, &c. All advertisements on imperishable galvanised iron plates, enamelled in best Art colours. Selected by a Committee of Taste, comprising several eminent artists and decorators.

"Only one architrave and the top of the Stone of Sacrifice vacant at present. Hurry up !"

Extract No. II. (*From another Advertisement Column.*)

"Messrs. McCrackit and Rollestone, having purchased the ruins of Stonehenge at a remarkably low figure, are prepared to entertain proposals for road-metal from District Councils, contractors, and others.

"In deference to lovers of antiquities, dealers, and others, who may care to preserve some memento of this interesting Link with the Past, Messrs. McC. and R. beg to announce that they have set aside one of the smaller monoliths, and can supply blocks of various sizes, which may be worked up into chimney ornaments, timepieces, paper-weights, &c., according to taste. These blocks will take a fine polish, and are practically indestructible.

"Terms on application to the Head Sawyer, Stonehenge."

Extract No. III. (*Paragraph in Evening Paper, 1900.*)

Reuter's New York correspondent cables to-day :

"Mr. Ezra P. Smart, who became the purchaser of Stonehenge last year, has now succeeded in transporting this highly interesting souvenir in vessels specially constructed for the purpose, and on its arrival in sections yesterday, is understood to have disposed of it to the United States Government for a sum representing a handsome profit. The quaint and unique Prehistoric survival will be carefully re-erected in the Yellowstone Park, where it will, doubtless, form an object of great attraction to British tourists."

Extract No. IV. (*Another paragraph from Evening Paper of later date.*)

"The War Office has now almost completed its great work at Stonehenge, which will henceforth rank as an Ordnance and Ammunition Storehouse of the first importance, while, from its isolated situation, it is unlikely to constitute any danger to the safety of the public. Already, with its frowning battlements and solid gloomy walls, in which portions of the original structure may still be identified in spite of the lead colour that coats them, it forms a striking and impressive landmark, and will doubtless prove of the greatest utility should the country ever unhappily be invaded by a foreign foe. Handsome and spacious barracks are in course of erection in its immediate vicinity, and in a few years Stonehenge Fort will be but the central point of a military *dépôt* rivalling Portsmouth and Woolwich in extent and activity."

Extract No. V. (*Paragraph as before. 1901.*)

"The Salvation Army has now quite settled into its new headquarters at Stonehenge, which, as some readers may remember, they acquired in the autumn of the year before last by public auction. The building has been put into a condition of thorough repair ; all the missing stones being supplemented by blocks of Portland cement, and the interstices neatly filled in with brick. Painted in the Army colours of crimson and dark blue, and adorned with texts and emblems of huge proportions, it is quite a prominent feature in the landscape. It is curious to reflect that after the lapse of so many centuries, this historic edifice should once more be employed for purposes of a devotional character."

Extract No. VI. (*Paragraph from the Era, 1900.*)

"Messrs. Mastodon and Mammoth, the world-renowned Menagerie and Circus proprietors, opened yesterday at the new 'Cirque Stonehenge,' where they will be 'at home' for the future in the intervals of touring. The work of reconstruction has been admirably carried out, and those who knew the forlorn and dilapidated old building in days of yore would find it hard to recognise it in its spruce and transformed condition. With great taste and judgment, the architect, Mr. Girdershell (who has had considerable experience in this class of work) has not attempted to interfere with such portions of the original structure as remained intact, but has used them as a basis for his own design, which is a happy mixture of the Romanesque and Renaissance styles, executed in moulded brick and terra cotta. The scheme of exterior decoration is a warm chocolate picked out with a dainty cream, and harmonises delightfully with the dull greys and greens of the surrounding plain. Inside, there is seating accommodation for over three thousand persons, and it is needless to add that the acoustic and sanitary arrangements, both in the vast stables and the *auditorium*, are absolutely perfect. Lines of electric tramcars and light railways connect this truly Megatherian Hippodrome with Salisbury, Winchester, Dorchester, and other cities and towns in the vicinity.

1901.

The Stonehenge Committee before the Raising of the Leaning Stone.
From Left to Right.

1, 2, 3, Rev E H Goddard. 4, E Doran Webb, C E Ponting, Col Antrobus?
Lord Dillon, Bishop of J F Browne of Bristol, Sir Hercules Read, Dr Gowland?
Sir Will H St John, Lady Antrobus, R N Stay Maskelyne, ?,

Emily Walker

(Hope)

PLATE 141

This expresses one of the nubs of the whole problem of Stonehenge and its popularity with the general public: there should be open discussion forthwith. It is not enough merely to stop at the point Emerson made, after he visited the area with Thomas Carlyle in 1888: 'The chief mystery is, that any mystery should have been allowed to settle on so remarkable a monument, in a country on which all the muses have kept their eyes now for eighteen hundred years.'

Stonehenge was up to its lintels in controversy once again in 1899. Sir Edmund Antrobus had just succeeded to the Amesbury estate, and he offered to sell Stonehenge and about 1,300 acres (417 hectares) of farmland around it to the nation for £125,000. This (then) enormous asking price fuelled many of the current arguments – from those about access, admission times, charges, scaffolding, restoration, etc to those about its value, which its owner seemed to place on a par with the world's most expensive (and moveable) paintings.

And then something happened. 'I very much regret to report,' wrote Mr Arthur Newall, of Salisbury, to *The Times*, 'that two of the stones of the outer circle of Stonehenge fell on the last evening of the nineteenth century. One of them is a large upright sarsen-stone and the other is the lintel, also of sarsen, with yellow garrel and flint embedded in it [Stones 22 and 122]. These are the only stones which have fallen since Charles II made excavations [incorrect: 1797, etc] at the base of one to ascertain on what foundation the stones are placed, whilst staying at Hele House after the Battle of Worcester. It is sad that the acts both of man and of the gods should destroy this fine old sun temple.'

The next day *The Times* urged that there should be no restoration. The Rev. Arthur Phelps, of Amesbury Vicarage (and 'vicar of Stonehenge for 26 years' as he put it), hurried to see the damage; he reported to *The Times*, and expressed the hope that analysis of the fallen lintel 'will result in a scientific investigation as to the composition of the stones – whether natural stones or concrete, as some have maintained.' He thought that to set a leaning sarsen upright would be 'spoiling Stonehenge' – thus quaintly highlighting another mysterious dichotomy about the monument. Lord Nelson wrote urging that Stonehenge should be protected from tourists, and the tenor of subsequent letters and articles urged preservation, and purchase by the nation.

William Flinders Petrie had been in Egypt on pyramid business, and he didn't get his letter to *The Times* until 18 February (1901 – then considered the first year of the new century). He was very clear: 'the sight is the most impressive in England, and on no account should it be destroyed by a hideous iron railing, such as now defaces Kits Coty house. If a fence is necessary, a sunk ha-ha would be the only form permissible.' He goes on to urge very careful excavation: 'Not a handful of soil must be moved except under the instant inspection of a good archaeologist, who must live in a shed at the site. There must be no fooling about driving up each day from an hotel at Salisbury, to find that the workmen have wiped out historical evidences before breakfast.'

In April, Sir Edmund Antrobus gained approval from an authoritative committee (drawn from The Society of Antiquaries, The Society for the Protection of Ancient Build-

PLATE 142

ings and The Wiltshire Archaeological Society) to divert a very old 'trackway or ridgeway' (*The Times* called it a 'grass driving road') through the earthwork, so that he could erect a fence at a distance. The fence went up in May 1901 ('not only unnecessary but highly mischievous, 'said *The Times*). From then until the beginning of October that year some 3,000 people paid their shilling to go through it, while the legality of what is now the A344, running past the Heel Stone, was being questioned. 1901 appropriately concluded with the start of Professor Gowland's restoration work; it had Lockyer and Penrose's survey to result in the publication of Sir Norman Lockyer's important though not

PLATE 141   This photograph, from the archives of Devizes Museum, shows (according to the caption, by an unknown hand) 'The Stonehenge Committee before the raising of the Leaning Stone; From left to right: ? —, ? —, ? —, Rev. E. H. Goddard, Emly (?) Walker, E. Doran Webb, C. E. Ponting, Col. Sir Edmund Antrobus [the owner of the monument, in a cloth cap], Lord Dillon, Bishop G. F. Browne of Bristol [in top hat and cape], Sir Hevenley Read, Dr Gowland [the archaeologist], Sir William H. St. John Hope, Lady Antrobus, N. Story Maskelyne [archaeologist and petrologist], ?

PLATE 142   Stonehenge on 29 September 1904. One of a series of photographs taken for use as evidence in a law suit against the Antrobus family.

always correct book *Stonehenge and Other British Stone Monuments*, which caused a great stir and further increased the general public's awareness of the problems *The Times* was going on about.

Sir Cosmo Antrobus's son and heir was killed in the War early in 1915; and he decided that the family's connection with Stonehenge must end. On Tuesday, 21 September in that year, Messrs Knight, Frank and Rutley (then, as now, of London), held one of their auctions at The New Theatre, Salisbury. Lot 15 was one of the greatest prehistoric wonders of the world: it fetched £6,600.

It was bought by Mr (later Sir) Cecil Chubb, who presented Stonehenge and the immediate land around it to the nation in 1918 with a Deed of Gift specifying 'free access', not long after the Bomb Squadron, who had their new runways and building just to the south-west,

had twice demanded the destruction of the stones because they were a potential air hazard. So the Antrobus family finally got something for their property; it would be interesting to know if the story is true of the American millionaire who offered five million dollars before the War for the stones (he wanted to re-erect them back home) so the neighbouring Army could extend their artillery grounds.

On 21 July 1927, O. G. S. Crawford lunched at Jules, with two good friends, Alexander Keiller and Sir John Squire. The founder of *Antiquity* proposed to the owner and excavator of Avebury and to the founder of the *London Mercury* that a committee be formed to raise funds to purchase the land which had become available to the east, south and west of Stonehenge. A most eminent committee was formed, a lunch was held at the Lord Mayor's Mansion House, daily and weekly journals trumpeted the cause, Crawford broadcast on the radio on 8 August – and £32,000 (which Keiller had in fact already guaranteed) was quickly raised. The land was duly presented to the National Trust. William Long had been granted his wish; in 1876 he had written: 'It is to be hoped that our grand-children will not have to look for Stonehenge in a field of turnips. The cultivation of the down adjoining Stonehenge is gradually closing in on it . . .'

Lot 15.

(Coloured Green on Plan No. 1.)

"STONEHENGE,"

together with about

30 a. 2 r. 37 p. of the adjoining Downland.

A charge is made for seeing Stonehenge and the net receipts average about £360 per annum.

Stonehenge has been scheduled under the Ancient Monuments Consolidation and Amendment Act, 1913.

NOTE.—The Purchaser of this Lot will be required to erect to the satisfaction of the Vendor's Surveyors and maintain a fence on the western boundary of this Lot so far as no fence exists at present.

LANDLORD'S OUTGOINGS.

	£	s.	d.
Tithe Commutation Rent Charge—			
Dean and Chapter of Salisbury Cathedral, £4 16s. 3d.			
Value 1915...	3	14	2
Land Tax	0	3	0
	£3	17	2

SCHEDULE.

No. on 1/2500 Ordnance Map.	Description.	Acreage.
Pt. 22	Stonehenge and Down	30·730

PLATE 144

PLATE 143 (*left*) Lady Antrobus takes shelter with a companion. She was the wife of Sir Edmond Antrobus Bart.

PLATE 144 Lot 15 in the catalogue produced by Knight, Frank & Rutley, London, in association with Eden Baines and Kennaway, Heytesbury, for the action of Sir Cosmo Antrobus's Amesbury Abbey Estate on 21 September 1915. It was held in the New Theatre, Salisbury, and Lot 15 fetched £6,600.

PLATE 145 (*left*) Sir Cecil Chubb (right) about to present Stonehenge to the nation in 1918; Lord Melchett stands beside him.

STONEHENGE SECURED

How the trilithons have been rendered safe from the fiercest storms.

Stone Tenon (pictured for the first time)   *The Slaughtering Stone: the ground below was excavated*

The Method of Arriving at the Age of Stonehenge by Astronomical Means

Showing sunrise on the longest day (June 21)

The above diagram shows the method employed in arriving at the date 1680 B.C. by astronomical means. Acting on the theory that Stonehenge is a solar temple, measurements have been taken of the actual rising of the sun on June 21, the longest day, and compared with the rising point of the sun at the end of the axis which bisects Stonehenge and the avenue leading to the north-east. The present rising point is two sun's diameters to the south of the original point, and calculating by means of precessional tables the amount of time which has elapsed for the sun to recede to the new position the date of 1680 B.C. has been arrived at

Stonehenge is itself again and open to all the winds of heaven; all the tackle, cranes, and impedimenta of the Office of Works have disappeared, and the concrete foundations which now hold the threatened stones securely have vanished beneath a covering of grass.

One sees nothing but the ancient circle as we have long known it, but for certain changes recorded on the preceding pages.

The stones which threatened to collapse have now been rendered secure by concrete bases. This necessitated the removal of the chalk around the bottom of the stones. All excavation was done with the greatest care, every portion being numbered and sifted, so that the position of every object found could be accurately recorded. As in 1901, no metal tools or objects were discovered within the circle, only the stone implements of these pre-metal builders. Each of the uprights was found to have been placed in a rough circular hole without the sloping way which characterised the foundations of the famous leaning stone made erect in 1901. In order to secure the exact replacing of the uprights disturbed, flat wooden moulds or keyboards were cut and fitted round the bases. It is hoped to proceed with the work of securing the foundations of some further stones during the course of next year.

The Meaning of the Aubrey Holes

A very interesting discovery was made during the recent work of a series of holes which had gradually filled up and become covered with the grass of the plain. These holes have been named after Aubrey, the antiquary, who marked their position on his plan of Stonehenge. They lie along the inside of the earthen mound. Some have been found to contain evidences of interment of cremated human remains, and in one case it appears that the cremation took place in the hole itself. Whether these holes contained the bases of upright stones, at the foot of which these burials took place, remains to be further examined.

The Round Barrows Surrounding Stonehenge, which also Help to Fix its Date

Archæology also comes to our aid in fixing an approximate date for Stonehenge. Chips from the sacred blue stones, probably the oldest part of the sun temple, are found buried in the round barrows on the adjacent slopes of Salisbury Plain. The age of these barrows has been ascertained from a great number of inter-relations to be approximately 1800 B.C. to 2,000 B.C. There is a large group of barrows on Normanton Down, and others lie scattered to the south west of the circle. Another group lies to the north west, all evidences of human activity in the neighbourhood of the circle and at a time probably coincident with its period of greatest splendour

Photographed by the Office of Works

Two Little Birds' Nests Tucked Away Under the Hoary Lintels of Stonehenge

When some of the lintel stones were raised for temporary removal two little birds' nests were discovered lying in cavities beneath the great "sarsens." The eggs lay in the nests, but the mother birds had flown. Little did they think that workmen and savants would one day come and disturb their rock-bound shelters

PLATE 146

Two years later 'The Stonehenge Protection Committee' reconvened because The National Trust realized they were facing (as the *Illustrated London News* put it on 23 March 1929) the possibility of seeing 'villadom, and vandalism, teashops, charabancs and petrol pumps on a desirable building plot' of 650 acres immediately to north and north-east of the monument, which included The Cursus and the beginning of The Avenue. A further £16,000 was raised, and so now The National Trust holds much of the surrounding farmland. Thus it is that its management has to decide about the pop festivals and not a government department.

In the same year the gypsy encampments in their derelict aerodrome buildings were all removed; Stonehenge reached a better state than it had been in for a very long time – and visitor figures were still mounting annually.

The household gods of The Giants' Dance have encountered many opponents: politicians, priests, archaeologists, mystics, astronomers, water diviners, lawyers, millionaires, the army and air forces – and the public, which comes in tides and means no harm but does it, more violently than that last enemy, time, with the natural elements in attendance.

Perhaps the lasting and universal appeal of Stonehenge has something to do with the fact that we cannot be told much of its meaning by

PLATE 146 *The Sphere* recorded the end of excavations and restoration work on 2 April 1921; it claimed to be publishing a picture of a tenon for the first time (top left). The opening paragraph is reassuring indeed: 'Stonehenge is itself again and open to all the winds of heaven; all the tackle, cranes, and impedimenta of the Office of Works have disappeared, and the concrete foundations which now hold the threatened stones securely have vanished beneath a covering of grass.'

PLATE 147 Low, the famous *Evening Standard,* cartoonist, gives a characteristic interpretation of the 1929 Stonehenge fund appeal.

DESECRATION OF THE POLITICAL STONEHENGE.

PLATE 147

THE APPEAL FOR STONEHENGE: A NATIONAL MONUMENT.

others. It is there and very big and very old and doesn't move, and yet still no one in the family, school or pub can readily explain it, can they? The strange and challenging story of its construction and purpose, the origins and placing of the stone, the ages of the phases, all necessitate, well, this book probably. There is no one sentence that wraps it all up (and we have after all grown used to that). Stonehenge is one of the few beautiful 'things' in the world that delights without striving to inform; it is utterly defiant and we respect it for that; both the whole and its parts adapt to the prejudices we bring to the place. It is in fact a sort of religious experience.

PLATE 148   This photograph appeared in *The Times* on 11 March 1929, supporting the activities of the Stonehenge Protection Committee; 'Beyond the road which runs diagonally across the picture', the caption stated, 'is the land already acquired for the nation in order to preserve the amenities of Stonehenge, and in the distance are the sheds of the aerodrome which is being demolished. The land in the right foreground is part of the plot for which an appeal was made in *The Times* on Saturday in a letter signed, among others, by the Prime Minister and Mr MacDonald.'

PLATE 149 (*right*)   William Burroughs Hill's photograph of Sir Oliver Lodge at Stonehenge on 28 February 1927.

PLATE 147

A Stonehenge Chronology, A.D.

c.**1130** First mentioned in manuscript, by Henry of Huntingdon

c.**1136** Geoffrey of Monmouth's history completed

1482 William Caxton first to print account of S. in book (Higden's *Polychronicon*)

1571 First recognizable view of S. engraved by 'R. F.'

1620 James I visited

1648 John Aubrey 'discovered' Avebury while fox-hunting

1651 Charles II visited

1654 John Evelyn visited, after a good lunch at his uncle's farm nearby

1655 *Stone-heng Restored* by Inigo Jones published

1663 *Chorea Gigantum* by Walter Charleton published

1665 *A Vindication of Stone-Heng Restored* by John Webb published

c.**1666** John Aubrey wrote manuscript *Monumenta Britannica*: 'X' (later Aubrey) Holes first mentioned, as 'cavities'

1668 Samuel Pepys visited; gave shepherd-women 4d for leading horses

1718 Society of Antiquaries re-founded; William Stukeley first Secretary

1719 William Stukeley first visited S.

1721 Stukeley depicted Avebury inner circles as Lunar and Solar

1723 William Stukeley discovered The Cursus and Stonehenge Avenue

1740 *Stonehenge: A Temple Restor'd to the British Druids* by William Stukeley published

1743 *Abury, A Temple of the British Druids* by William Stukeley published

1747 *Choir Gaure* by John Wood the Elder published

1771 *Choir Gaur* by Dr John Smith small-pox inoculator, published

1776–77 Duke of Northumberland and Colonel Drax excavated at Silbury Hill

1797 Fall of stones

1802 Stonehenge Urn discovered by William Cunnington

1812 Sir Richard Colt-Hoare's volume on South Wiltshire published

1820 First sketched by John Constable

1846 *The Druidical Temples of the County of Wilts* by Edward Duke published

1847 Carlyle and Emerson visited together

1849 John Merewether, Dean of Hereford, and Henry Blandford excavated at Silbury Hill

1860 First known photograph taken

1867 Wiltshire Archaeological Society discovered that there was no Roman road under Silbury Hill

1880 *Stonehenge: Plans, Description and Theories* by Sir William Flinders Petrie published, after most accurate surveys ever conducted (still)

1899 Sir Edmund Antrobus offers S. and 1300 acres farmland to nation for £125,000

1900 Fall of stones

1901 Professor William Gowland's excavations started

1901   Old trackway through S. diverted, and first fence erected; admission by payment

1901   Some stones restored to their positions

1905   First modern Druidic summer solstice ceremony

1906   *Stonehenge and Other British Stone Monuments* by Sir Norman Lockyer published

1907   First photographed from air, by Lieut. P. A. Sharpe, in a balloon

1915   Stonehenge (Lot 15) fetched £6,600 at auction

1918   Stonehenge presented to nation by Cecil Chubb

1919–26   William Hawley's excavations; X Holes re-discovered and named 'Aubrey Holes'

1920   Some stones restored to their positions

1922   Sir William Flinders Petrie excavated at Silbury Hill

1923   Aerial photography revealed again part of lost course of Stonehenge Avenue

1923   Dr Herbert Thomas announces discovery of source of bluestones, in Prescelly Mountains

1924   *The Stones of Stonehenge* by E. H. Stone published

1925   Woodhenge's existence revealed by Sq. Ldr. Insall's aerial photography

1925–9   Excavations at Windmill Hill by Alexander Keiller

1927   Stonehenge Protection Committee raises funds to buy surrounding land, presented to National Trust

1929   Stonehenge Protection Committee raises funds for more surrounding land, presented to National Trust

1929   Aerodrome very near S. demolished

1934–9   Excavations at Avebury by Alexander Keiller

1950   *William Stukeley* by Stuart Piggott published

1953   Professor R. J. C. Atkinson first noticed carvings

1955–6   Professors Atkinson and Piggott excavate West Kennett Long Barrow

1956   *Stonehenge* by Professor R. J. C. Atkinson published; the classic modern account

1958   Some stones restored to their positions

1963   C. A. Newham's theories in *Yorkshire Post* published, about S. and moon

1963   Fall of stones

1964   Some stones restored to their positions

1966   *Stonehenge Decoded* by Professor Gerald S. Hawkins published

1967   *Megalithic Sites In Britain* by Professor Alexander Thom published

1967–70   Professor R. J. C. Atkinson excavated at Silbury Hill, with B.B.C. TV

1971   *Megalithic Lunar Observatories* by Professor Alexander Thom published

1973   *Beyond Stonehenge* by Professor Gerald S. Hawkins published

1977   815,473 people paid for admission

1978   Fence erected around stone circles

Bibliography and References

Anderson, J. R. L. and Godwin, Fay, THE OLDEST ROAD: AN EXPLORATION OF THE RIDGEWAY, Wildwood House, London 1975

Antrobus, Lady Florence, A SENTIMENTAL AND PRACTICAL GUIDE TO AMESBURY AND STONEHENGE, Amesbury 1904

Atkinson, R. J. C., Piggott, Stuart, and Stone, J. F. S., *Antiquaries Journal* 32 (1952), 14–20, 'The Excavation of Two Additional Holes at Stonehenge'

> *Nature* 176 (1954), 474–5, 'Stonehenge in the Light of Recent Research'

> STONEHENGE, Hamish Hamilton, London 1956

> *Antiquity* 35 (1961), 292–9, 'Neolithic Engineering'

> *Nature* 210 (1966), 1302, 'Decoder Misled'

> *Antiquity* 40 (1966), 215, 'Moonshine On Stonehenge'

> *Antiquity* 41 (1967), 92–9, 'Hoyle On Stonehenge: Some Comments'

> *Antiquity* 44 (1970), 313–14, 'Silbury Hill 1969–1970'

> *Philosophical Transactions of the Royal Society* A 276 (1974), 123–131, 'Neolithic Science and Technology'

> *Journal for the History of Astronomy* 6 (1975), 42–52, 'Megalithic Astronomy: A Prehistorian's Comments'

> STONEHENGE AND AVEBURY, H.M.S.O., London 1976 (11th imp.)

> *Journal for the History of Astronomy* 7 (1976), 142–4, 'The Stonehenge Stations'

> *Nature* 275 (1978), 50–52 'Some New Measurements on Stonehenge'

> STONEHENGE AND NEIGHBOURING MONUMENTS, H.M.S.O., London 1978

Aubrey, John, MONUMENTA BRITANNICA: Part One, 'Templa Druidum', Bodl. MSS, Top. Gen. c. 24–45, Oxford c.1666

Barclay, Edgar, STONEHENGE AND ITS EARTH-WORKS, D. Nutt, London 1895

> THE RUINED TEMPLE STONEHENGE, St Catherine Press, London 1911

Beach, A. D., *Nature* 265 (1977), 17–21, 'Stonehenge I and Lunar Dynamics'

Bergström, Theo and Vatcher, Lance, STONEHENGE, Bergström & Boyle Books, London 1974

(Bolton, Edmund), NERO CAESAR OR MONARCHIE DEPRAVED, pub. anon., 1624

Boothby, Capt R., *The Journal of the British Society of Dowsers* 2 (1935)

Bord, Janet and Colin, MYSTERIOUS BRITAIN, Garnstone Press, London 1972

> THE SECRET COUNTRY, Paladin, London 1978

Borlase, William, ANTIQUITIES HISTORICAL AND MONUMENTAL OF THE COUNTY OF CORNWALL, London 1769

Bowles, Rev. W. L. and Nichols, J. G., ANNALS AND ANTIQUITIES OF LACOCK ABBEY, 1835

Bochart, Samuel, GEOGRAPHIA SACRA, France 1646–7

> HIEROZOICON, France 1663

Brinckerhoff, R. F., *Nature* 263 (1976), 456–9, 'Astronomically Orientated Markings on Stonehenge'

Britton, John, THE BEAUTIES OF WILTSHIRE, London 1801 and 1825

> THE NATURAL HISTORY OF WILTSHIRE, Wiltshire Topographical Society, Salisbury 1847

Brome, Rev. James, TRAVELS OVER ENGLAND, SCOTLAND AND WALES, London 1700

Brooks, C. E. P., *Antiquity* I (1927), 412, 'The Climate of Prehistoric Britain'

Browne, Henry, AN ILLUSTRATION OF STONEHENGE AND ABURY, J. Browne, Salisbury 1854

Bryant, Jacob, AN ANALYSIS OF ANTIENT MYTHOLOGY, London 1774–6

Burl, Aubrey, THE STONE CIRCLES OF THE BRITISH ISLES, Yale University Press, New Haven and London 1976

Burton, Richard (pseud. of N. Crouch), WONDERFUL CURIOSITIES RARITIES AND WONDERS IN ENGLAND, SCOTLAND AND IRELAND, London 1682–4

Caesar, Julius, DE BELLO GALLICO, VI

Camden, William, BRITANNIA DESCRIPTIO, London 1586 (1695; trans., ed. and enlarged by Edmund Gibson)

Charleton, Walter, CHOREA GIGANTUM, London 1663

Childe, V. Gordon, THE DAWN OF EUROPEAN CIVILISATION, Routledge and Kegan Paul, London 1925

Clapperton, Walter, STONEHENGE HAND-BOOK, Salisbury c. 1850

Clark, Grahame, WORLD HISTORY – A NEW OUTLINE, Cambridge University Press, 1969

Clayton, Peter, ARCHAEOLOGICAL SITES OF BRITAIN, Weidenfeld and Nicolson, London 1976

Coles, J. ARCHAEOLOGY BY EXPERIMENT, Hutchinson, London 1973

Colt-Hoare, Sir Richard, HISTORY OF ANCIENT WILTSHIRE, 2 vols; South 1812

Colton, R. and Martin, R. L., *Nature* 221 (1969) 1011

Cooke, William, AN ENQUIRY INTO THE PATRIARCHAL AND DRUIDICAL RELIGION, TEMPLES, ETC., London 1754

Cotsworth, Moses B., *The Rational Almanac,* York 1903–4

Crampton, Patrick, STONEHENGE OF THE KINGS, London 1967

Crawford, O. G. S., *Illustrated London News* (18 August 1923), 302–3

   Antiquaries Journal 4 (1924), 57–8, 'The Stonehenge Avenue'

   Antiquity 28 (1954), 25–31, 'The Symbols Carved at Stonehenge'

   SAID AND DONE, London 1955

Cunnington, M. E., WOODHENGE, George Simpson, Devizes 1929

   Wiltshire Archaeological Magazine 45 (1931), 300–35, 'The "Sanctuary" on Overton Hill, near Avebury'

Cunnington, R. H., STONEHENGE AND ITS DATE, Methuen, London 1935

Dalton, G. I., *Folklore* 82 (1971), 'The Loathly Lady'

Dames, Michael, THE SILBURY TREASURE, Thames and Hudson, London 1976

   THE AVEBURY CYCLE, Thames and Hudson, 1977

Daniel, Glyn, THE MEGALITH BUILDERS OF WESTERN EUROPE, Hutchinson, London 1958

   Antiquity 33 (1959), 80 and 238

   Antiquity 34 (1960), 161

   MEGALITHS IN HISTORY, Thames and Hudson, London 1972

Defoe, Daniel, TOUR THROUGH ENGLAND AND WALES, London 1724

Dibble, W. E., *Journal for the History of Astronomy* 7 (1976), 141–2, 'A Possible Pythagorean Triangle at Stonehenge'

Downman, Edward A., EARTHWORKS IN WILTSHIRE, MSS. ADD 37724, 1908

Duke, Rev. Edward, THE DRUIDICAL TEMPLES OF THE COUNTY OF WILTSHIRE, London 1846

Dyer, James, SOUTHERN ENGLAND: AN ARCHAEOLOGICAL GUIDE, Faber and Faber, 1973

Ekwall, Eilert, THE CONCISE OXFORD DICTIONARY OF ENGLISH PLACE-NAMES (4th ed.), Oxford University Press, 1960

Fergusson, James, RUDE STONE MONUMENTS, John Murray, London 1872

Forde-Johnston, J., PREHISTORIC BRITAIN AND IRELAND, J. M. Dent, London 1976

Fowler, P. J., REGIONAL ARCHAEOLOGIES: WESSEX, Heinemann Educational, London 1967

Freeman, P. R., *Journal for the History of Astronomy* 8 (1977), 134–6, 'Thom's Survey of the Avebury Ring'

Fuller, Thomas, THE CHURCH HISTORY OF BRITAIN, 1655

Geoffrey of Monmouth, THE HISTORY OF THE KINGS OF BRITAIN (trans. Lewis Thorpe), Penguin Books, Harmondsworth 1966

(Gibbons, John), A FOOL'S BOLT SOON SHOTT AT STONAGE, c. 1666 printed in T. Hearne's 'Langtoft's Chronicle', Vol ii, 1725

Gidley, Rev. Lewis, STONEHENGE VIEWED BY THE LIGHT OF ANCIENT HISTORY, Salisbury, 1873

Gilpin, Rev. William, OBSERVATIONS ON THE WESTERN PARTS OF ENGLAND, RELATIVE CHIEFLY TO PICTURESQUE BEAUTY, London 1798

Gimbutas, M., THE GODS AND GODDESSES OF OLD EUROPE, Thames and Hudson, London 1974

Gingerich, Owen, *Technology Review* (USA), (Dec. 1977), 64–73, 'The Basic Astronomy of Stonehenge'

Giraldus Cambrensis, TOPOGRAPHIA HIBERNICA, MS., 1185

Gowland, William, *Archaeologia* 58 (1902), 38–119, 'Recent Excavations at Stonehenge'

Gray, St G. H., *Archaeologia* 84 (1935), 99–162, 'The Avebury Excavations, 1908–22'

Grinsell, L. V. THE ARCHAEOLOGY OF WESSEX, London 1958

Grinsell, L. V. and Dyer, James, WESSEX, Shire Publications, Herts 1971

THE ANCIENT BURIAL MOUNDS OF ENGLAND, London 1936

LEGENDARY HISTORY AND FOLKLORE OF STONEHENGE, Toucan Press, Guernsey 1975

THE DRUIDS AND STONEHENGE, Toucan Press, Guernsey 1978

THE STONEHENGE BARROW GROUPS, Salisbury and South Wiltshire Museum, 1978

Grover, Henry M., A VOICE FROM STONEHENGE, W. J. Cleaver, London 1847

Hadingham, Evan, ANCIENT CARVINGS IN BRITAIN, Garnstone Press, London 1974

CIRCLES AND STANDING STONES, Heinemann, London 1975

Halley, Dr Edmund, AN ACCOUNT OF STONEHENGE, 1720

Hardyng, John, THE CHRONICLE OF ENGLAND, MS., 1464

Harris, J. Rendel, THE BUILDERS OF STONEHENGE, W. Heffer, Cambridge 1932

Harrison, W. Jerome, *The Wiltshire Archaeological and Natural History Magazine* 32 (1901) 1–169, 'A Bibliography of the Great Stone Monuments of Wiltshire – Stonehenge and Avebury: with other references' (947 entries and 732 authors)

Harvey, Fleet-Surgeon Christopher, THE ANCIENT TEMPLE OF AVEBURY AND ITS GODS, Watts, London 1923

Hawes, Louis, CONSTABLE'S STONEHENGE, H.M.S.O., London 1975

Hawkes, Jacquetta, A GUIDE TO THE PREHISTORIC AND ROMAN MONUMENTS IN ENGLAND AND WALES, Sphere Books. London 1973

THE ATLAS OF EARLY MAN, Macmillan, London 1977

Hawkins, Gerald S., *Nature* 200 (1963), 306–8, 'Stonehenge Decoded'

Nature 202 (1964), 1258–61, 'Stonehenge: A Neolithic Computer'

American Scientist 53 (1965), 391–408, 'Sun, Moon, Men and Stones'

Science 147 (1965), 127–30, 'Callanish: A Scottish Stonehenge'

STONEHENGE DECODED, Collins/Fontana, London 1970

BEYOND STONEHENGE, Arrow Books, London 1977

Hawley, William, *Antiquaries Journal*, 'Excavations at Stonehenge': 1 (1920), 19–41; 2 (1921), 36–52; 3 (1923), 13–20; 4 (1924) 30–39; 5 (1925), 21–50; 6 (1926), 1–16; 8 (1928), 146–176

Hecataeus of Abdera, HISTORY OF THE HYPERBOREANS, c. 300 BC (MS quoted by Diodorus Siculus)

Heggie, D. C., *Antiquity* 46 (1972), 43–8, 'Megalithic Lunar Observatories: An Astronomer's View'

Heizer, R. F., *Science* 153 (1966), 821–30, 'Ancient Heavy Transport, Methods and Achievements'

Henry of Huntingdon, HISTORIA ANGLORUM, c. 1130

Herbert, Hon. Algernon, CYCLOPS CHRISTIANUS; OR AN ARGUMENT TO DISPROVE THE SUPPOSED ANTIQUITY OF THE STONEHENGE AND OTHER MEGALITHIC ERECTIONS IN ENGLAND AND BRITTANY, London 1849

Heywood, Thomas, THE LIFE OF MERLIN, SIRNAMED AMBROSIUS, HIS PROPHECIES AND PREDICTIONS INTERPRETED, 1641

Higden, Ranulf, POLYCHRONICON, MS, 1327 (first printed by Caxton, 1482)

Higgins, Godfrey, THE CELTIC DRUIDS, London 1829

Hodson, F. R. (ed.), THE PLACE OF ASTRONOMY IN THE ANCIENT WORLD, Oxford University Press, 1974

Hoskins, W. G., THE MAKING OF THE ENGLISH LANDSCAPE, Hodder and Stoughton, London 1955

Hoyle, Fred, *Antiquity* 40 (1966), 272–6, 'Speculations On Stonehenge'

Nature 211 (1966), 454–6, 'Stonehenge: An Eclipse Predictor'

FROM STONEHENGE TO MODERN COSMOLOGY, W. H. Freeman, San Francisco 1972

ON STONEHENGE, Heinemann Educational, London 1977

Hutton, J. H., *Antiquity* 3 (1929), 324–338, 'Assam Megaliths'

Ingram, Rev. James, INAUGURAL LECTURE ON THE UTILITY OF THE SAXON LITERATURE, Oxford 1807

Ivimy, John, THE SPHINX AND THE MEGALITHS, Abacus, London 1976

James, Col. Sir Henry, PLANS AND PHOTOGRAPHS OF STONEHENGE, AND OF TURUSACHAN IN THE ISLAND OF LEWIS, Ordnance Survey, Southampton 1867

Jones, Inigo, THE MOST NOTABLE ANTIQUITY OF GREAT BRITAIN VULGARLY CALLED STONE-HENG ON SALISBURY PLAIN, London 1655

Keiller, Alexander and Piggott, Stuart, *Antiquity* 10 (1936), 417–27, 'The West Kennet Avenue, Avebury; Excavations, 1934–5'

Kellaway, G. A., *Nature* 232 (1971), 30–35, 'Glaciation and the Stones of Stonehenge'

Kendrick, T. D., THE DRUIDS: A STUDY IN KELTIC PREHISTORY, London 1927

Keysler, Johann G., ANTIQUITATES SELECTAE SEPTENTRIONALES ET CELTICAE, Hanover 1720

Layamon, ROMAN DE BRUT or CHRONICLE OF ENGLAND, 1205

Leland, John, COMMENTARI DE SCRIPTORIBUS BRITANNICIS, (ed. Anthony Hall), 1707

THE ITINERARY OF JOHN LELAND THE ANTIQUARY (ed. by Thomas Hearne), Oxford 1710–12

Lockyer, Sir Norman and Penrose, F. C. *Proceedings of the Royal Society of London* 69 (1901), 137–47, 'An Attempt to Ascertain the Date of the Original Construction of Stonehenge from Its Construction'

Lockyer, Sir Norman, STONEHENGE AND OTHER BRITISH STONE MONUMENTS, Macmillan, London 1906

Long, William, 'Stonehenge and Its Barrows', *Wiltshire Archaeological and Natural History Magazine,* Devizes 1876

MacKie, Euan, THE MEGALITH BUILDERS, Phaidon Press, London 1977

Martin, Martin, DESCRIPTION OF THE WESTERN ISLANDS OF SCOTLAND, 1703

Maskelyne, Nevil S., *Wiltshire Archaeological Magazine* 17 (1878), 147–160, 'Stonehenge – The Petrology of Its Stones'

Mela, Pomponius, DE SITU ORBIS III. c. 50 AD

Merewether, J., DIARY OF A DEAN, London 1851

Michell, John, THE VIEW OVER ATLANTIS, Garnstone Press, London 1972

CITY OF REVELATION, Garnstone Press, London 1972

THE OLD STONES OF LAND'S END, Garnstone Press, London 1974

A LITTLE HISTORY OF ASTRO-ARCHAEOLOGY, Thames and Hudson, London 1977

Morgan, M. O., THE ROYAL WINGED SON OF STONEHENGE AND AVEBURY, London 1900

Neckham, Alexander, DE LAUDIBUS DIVINAE SAPIENTIAE, MS., 1215

Nennius, HISTORIA BRITONUM, MS., 796 AD

Newall, R. S., *Antiquity* 3 (1929), 75–88, 'Stonehenge'

STONEHENGE, H.M.S.O., London 1977 (10th imp.)

Newham, C. A., *Yorkshire Post,* 16 March 1963

Nature 211 (1966), 456–68, 'Stonehenge – A Neolithic Observatory'

THE ENIGMA OF STONEHENGE, 1964

THE ASTRONOMICAL SIGNIFICANCE OF STONEHENGE, John Blackburn, Leeds 1972

Paris, Matthew, CHRONICA MAJORA, after 1259

Peach, Wystan A., STONEHENGE: A NEW THEORY, privately published, Cardiff 1961

Petrie, W. M. Flinders, STONEHENGE: PLANS, DESCRIPTION, AND THEORIES, Edward Stanford 1880

Piggott, Stuart, *Proceedings of the Prehistoric Society* 4 (1939), 53–106, 'The Early Bronze Age in Wessex'

Antiquity, XV (1941), 269–86, 305–19

WILLIAM STUKELEY, Clarendon Press, Oxford 1950

NEOLITHIC CULTURES OF THE BRITISH ISLES, Cambridge University Press 1954

Antiquity 28 (1954), 221–4, 'Recent Work at Stonehenge'

Journal of the Royal Institute of British Architects, Series 3, 63 (1956), 175, 'Architecture and Ritual in Megalithic Monuments'

Antiquity 33 (December 1959), 'The Radiocarbon Date from Durrington Walls'

THE DRUIDS, Penguin, Harmondsworth 1974

WEST KENNET LONG BARROW, Dept. of the Environment, London 1975 (2nd imp.)

Piozzi, Hester Lynch, LETTERS TO AND FROM THE LATE SAMUEL JOHNSON, London 1788

Pliny the Elder, NATURAL HISTORY XVI (d. 79 AD)

Probert, William (Trans. from c. 1200? Welsh), THE ANCIENT LAWS OF CAMBRIA: CONTAINING THE INSTITUTIONAL TRIADS OF DYVNWAL MOELMUD 1823

Ray, John, SELECTED REMAINS OF THE LEARNED JOHN RAY, 1662

Renfrew, Colin, *Scientific American* 225 (1971), 63–72, 'Carbon 14 and the Prehistory of Europe'

(ed.), THE EXPLANATION OF CULTURE CHANGE: MODELS IN PREHISTORY, Duckworth, London 1972

BEFORE CIVILIZATION, Jonathan Cape, London 1973

Antiquity 47 (1973), 221–5, 'Wessex as a Social Question'

Roger of Wendover, FLORES HISTORIARUM, MS., 1235

Rowlands, Rev. Henry, MONA ANTIQUA RESTAURATA, Dublin 1723

Sale, J. L., THE SECRETS OF STONEHENGE, privately published 1965

Sammes, Aylett, BRITANNIA ANTIQUA ILLUSTRATA, Vol I, 1676

Saunders, Eleanor, THE PREHISTORIC MONUMENT OF DURRINGTON WALLS, Salisbury and South Wiltshire Museum 1973

Shakley, Myra, *Country Life,* 26 October 1978, 1305, 'How the Megaliths Were Moved'

Shortt, Hugh de S., OLD SARUM, H.M.S.O., London 1976 (6th imp.)

Smith, A. C. A GUIDE TO THE BRITISH AND ROMAN ANTIQUITIES OF THE NORTH WILTSHIRE DOWNS IN A HUNDRED SQUARE MILES AROUND ABURY, Marlborough 1884

Smith, I. F., WINDMILL HILL AND AVEBURY: Excavations by A. Keiller; 1925–39, Clarendon Press, Oxford 1965

Palaeohistoria 12 (1967), 469–81, 'Windmill Hill and Its Implications'

Smith, Dr John, CHOIR GAUR; THE GRAND ORRERY OF THE ANCIENT DRUIDS, COMMONLY CALLED STONEHENGE, Salisbury 1771

Somerville, Rear-Adml. Boyle, *Journal of the British Astronomical Association,* 23 (1912), 83–96, 'Astronomical Indications in the Megalithic Monument at Callanish'

Archaeologia 73 (1923) 'Orientation in Prehistoric Monuments of the British Isles'

Speed, John, THE THEATRE OF THE EMPIRE OF GREAT BRITAIN, London 1627 (many subseq. ed.)

Sprules, John, VISITOR'S ILLUSTRATED POCKET-GUIDE TO STONEHENGE, Oxford, 1884

Stackhouse, T., TWO LECTURES ON THE REMAINS OF ANCIENT PAGAN BRITAIN, privately published,? 1806

Stevens, Edward T., JOTTINGS ON SOME OF THE OBJECTS OF INTEREST IN THE STONEHENGE EXCURSIONS, Simpkin Marshall, London 1882

Stevens, Frank, STONEHENGE TODAY AND YESTERDAY, H.M.S.O., London 1929

Stone, E. Herbert, THE STONES OF STONEHENGE, Robert Scott, London 1924

Stone, J. F. S., *Archaeological Journal* 104 (1948), 7–19, 'The Stonehenge Cursus and Its Affinities'

WESSEX BEFORE THE CELTS, Thames and Hudson, London 1958

Stow, John, THE CHRONICLES OF ENGLAND or ANNALS, London 1580–92

Stukeley, William, STONEHENGE, A TEMPLE RESTOR'D TO THE BRITISH DRUIDS, London 1740

ABURY, A TEMPLE OF THE BRITISH DRUIDS, London 1743

Switsur, V. R., *Antiquity* 47 (1973), 131–7, 'The Radio-carbon Calendar Recalibrated'

Symonds, Col. Richard, DIARY OF THE MARCHES OF THE ROYAL ARMY, MS. Brit. Mus., 1644; pub. Camden Soc. 1859

Tacitus, ANNALS XIV, (d. 120 AD)

Thatcher, A. R., *Antiquity* 49 (1975), 144–6, 'The Station Stones of Stonehenge'

Thorpe, Lewis – *see* Geoffrey of Monmouth

Thom, Alexander, *Mathematics Gazette,* 45 (1961), 83–92, 'The Geometry of Megalithic Man'

Vistas in Astronomy 7 (1965), 1, 'Megalithic Astronomy: Indications in Standing Stones'

Antiquity 40 (1966), 121–8, 'Megaliths and Mathematics'

MEGALITHIC SITES IN BRITAIN, Clarendon Press, Oxford 1967

Vistas in Astronomy 11 (1969), 1, 'The Lunar Observations of Megalithic Man'

MEGALITHIC LUNAR OBSERVATORIES, Clarendon Press, Oxford 1971

Thom, Alexander and Thom, A. S., *Journal for the History of Astronomy,* 7 (1976), 193–7, 'Avebury (2): The West Kennet Avenue'

Thom, Alexander, Thom, A. S., and Foord, T. R., *Journal for the History of Astronomy,* 7 (1976), 183–92, 'Avebury (1): A New Assessment of the Geometry and Metrology of the Ring'

Thom, Alexander, Thom, A. S. and Thom, A. S., *Journal for the History of Astronomy* 5 (1974), 71–90, 'Stonehenge'

Journal for the History of Astronomy 6 (1975), 19–30, 'Stonehenge as a Possible Lunar Observatory'

MEGALITHIC REMAINS IN BRITAIN AND BRITTANY, Clarendon Press, Oxford 1979

Thomas, Herbert H., *Antiquaries Journal* 3 (1923), 239–60

Toland, John, CHRISTIANITY NOT MYSTERIOUS (pamphlet), 1696

HISTORY OF THE DRUIDS, London 1726, 1814 ed.

Tyler, Major F. C., THE GEOMETRICAL ARRANGEMENT OF ANCIENT SITES, Simpkin Marshall, London 1939

Underwood, Guy, THE PATTERN OF THE PAST, Museum Press 1968

Vatcher, Faith de M., *Antiquity* 43 (1969), 310–11, 'Two Incised Chalk Plaques near Stonehenge Bottom'

Vatcher, Faith de M. and Vatcher, Lance, *Wiltshire Archaeological Magazine* 68 (1975), 57–63

THE AVEBURY MONUMENTS, H.M.S.O. 1976

Velikovsky, Immanuel, *Yale Scientific Magazine* (April 1967), 'Stonehenge Decoded' – a review of all Gerald Hawkins's research to 1967; reprinted *Pensée,* May 1972

Victoria History of the Counties of England, A HISTORY OF WILTSHIRE: Volume I, Part 2, Oxford University Press for Institute of Historical Research, 1973

von Daniken, CHARIOTS OF THE GODS?, Corgi, London 1971

Wace, Robert, ROMAN DE BRUT or GESTE DES BRETONS, MS., 1155

Wainright, G. J. with Longworth, I. H., *Reports Of the Research Committee of the Society of Antiquaries,* No. 29 (1971), London, 'Durrington Walls: Excavations, 1966–68'

Watkins, Alfred, THE OLD STRAIGHT TRACK, Garnstone Press, London 1972 (5th ed.)

Webb, John, A VINDICATION OF 'STONE-HENG RESTORED', London 1665

Wheeler, Fred, *New Scientist* (August 1966), 251–3, 'Stonehenge: Further Software'

Williams, Mary (ed.), BRITAIN: A STUDY IN PATTERNS, R.I.L.K.O., London 1971

Wood, Eric S., COLLINS FIELD GUIDE TO ARCHAEOLOGY IN BRITAIN, London 1968

Wood, John, DESCRIPTIONS OF STANTON DREW AND STONEHENGE, 1740, BM, Harleian MS., 7354/5

CHOIR GAURE, Oxford 1747

PARTICULAR DESCRIPTION OF BATH, 1750

Wood, John Edwin, SUN, MOON AND STANDING STONES, Oxford University Press 1978

Worm, Ole, DANICORUM MONUMENTORUM LIBRI SEX, Copenhagen 1643

DANICA LITERATURA ANTIQUISSIMA, Copenhagen 1651

Index